The Complete List of American Jobs

A Total of 820 Occupations Ranked by Salary, With Projected Growth Till 2026 and Education Requirement for Entry Level Positions

JON MACON, Ph.D.

Copyright © 2018 Jon Macon

All rights reserved.

ISBN: 1983537640
ISBN-13: 978-1983537646

DEDICATION

This book is dedicated to every job seeker. May you harness the power of smart strategies formed based on reliable data.

CONTENTS

1 Who Needs This Book   1

2 Salaries in Two Flavors   6

3 Jobs Ranked by Median Salary   12

4 Jobs Ranked Alphabetically   168

1 WHO NEEDS THIS BOOK

This book, *The Complete List of American Jobs*, is a companion book to *America's Best Jobs: Ranked Out of 156 Million Jobs Across 820 Occupations*. Both books are written for the readership who wants to find out about the best jobs in the United States.

Both books are based on data that is of unmatched breadth and quality. The data was collected on 156 million jobs across 820 occupations by the U.S. government, newly released in May and October 2017.

This is doubtlessly the most comprehensive, most authoritative, and most up to date source of employment information. No other source, in public or private domains, could come anywhere close.

Both books are written for anyone who is interested in finding out about the best jobs to help make the best career decisions. For those who are new to the labor market, including college seniors, graduate school students, and high school students, this book provide you with vital information to help you make the right career choices.

For those who are needed to provide career counseling, for instance college and high school career counselors, and student parents and guardians, this book provides you with the most up to date occupational information to help you form your advices and guidance.

For those who already have a job, there is invaluable information contained in this book for you to chew on, and can help you evaluate your current job against what else is out there, within your reach.

Key differences, however, exist between the two books. The *America's Best Jobs* book examines multiple facets of job quality, including salary, job growth outlook, geographical distribution, and impact of education.

If you are a fan of empirical data and insights derived from actual data, *America's Best Jobs* contains a lot for you to feast on. If you are new to data driven insights, *America's Best Jobs* serves as a great opportunity for you to open eyes to the vast amount of occupational insights revealed in this massive data from the most authoritative source.

With a focus on salary and job growth outlook, *America's Best Jobs* also analyzes the reasons behind astonishing disparities in salary and growth outlook across occupations that must be incorporated into one's career decisions.

1 WHO NEEDS THIS BOOK

To facilitate sound career choices, *America's Best Jobs* further teaches a ranking method for the reader to evaluate and compare available occupation options in a consistent and systematic way, toward the end of the book.

This method is straightforward and simple to implement; you can easily incorporate your own preferences and priorities to produce personalized job rankings. In other words, after reading *America's Best Jobs*, you will be able to compare and contrast your occupation choices through the ranking made by yourself.

This stands in sharp contrast to job rankings that are found in the media; there, the rankings are produced by some opaque algorithms that typically do not reflect your priorities in making occupation choices. The reason is simple: The journalists making the rankings in those newspaper or magazine articles do not know you, let alone your preferences or priorities.

America's Best Jobs focuses squarely on presenting and analyzing top occupations, without distracting the reader with the full list of all the 820 occupations covered in the dataset released by the U.S. Department of Labor.

This book, *The Complete List of American Jobs*, has a much narrower focus and complements *America's Best Jobs*. Instead of summarizing observations and deriving insights from employment data, this book presents the data itself, that is, the complete list of the 820 American occupations.

A side note. Similar to *America's Best Jobs,* the focus of this book is not on individual employment opportunities or positions, but rather on occupations. When we say jobs in this book, we mean occupations or professions. The reader should treat jobs, occupations and professions interchangeably in this book.

The only exception is when we say that the data on which this book is based on covers 156 million jobs, we mean 156 million employment positions. Obviously, there are not 156 million different occupations in this world. Not even close. The data covers 156 million positions across 820 occupations.

With this book, you can simply go through the occupation list and form a complete picture of the American occupational landscape.

You can also use this book as a reference book. When you have an occupation in mind, whether it is something you just heard from a friend or it is the job you currently have, pick up this book and look it up, and see where it sits on the list and how it stacks up against other occupations that might interest you.

Between this introductory chapter and Chapter 3 where the full list is presented, Chapter 2 is dedicated to the introduction of two statistics concepts that are needed in this book: the median salary and the 90th percentile salary. The median salary is a measure of the salary paid to an average worker in an occupation, enabling us to compare the job quality in terms of how much an average worker can earn.

The 90th percentile salary measures how much we can earn if we excel at our jobs. It is another measure of an occupation's earning potential. Typically, the median salary and the 90th percentile salary are very different.

Chapter 3 is one of the two main chapters of the book where the reader can find the complete list of all the 820 detailed occupations. This list is **ranked by the median salary** of an occupation, from high to low. Since the level of salary paid in an occupation is often times one of the most important considerations when we make career decisions, this chapter provides a quick way of telling which occupations pay well and which do not.

Chapter 4 is the other main chapter of the book. This chapter contains the same list as the one in Chapter 3. However, the list here is **ranked alphabetically**. Therefore, if the reader has a particular job in mind, these jobs can be looked up quickly in this chapter for relevant information such as its median salary, ranking of the median salary, number of existing positions, job growth outlook, among others.

2 SALARIES IN TWO FLAVORS

When we hear about jobs, a lot of times one of the first things comes to our mind is: How much does it pay? (Other than of course what the job is about.) The truth is that within an occupation, each worker is paid a different amount. If we are deciding what occupation to take, what is a good salary criterion for us to use in comparing different choices now that salaries are different not only across occupations but also within a given occupation?

This chapter introduces two salary measures to enable such comparison: The median salary and the 90th percentile salary.

Clearly both are statistical terms, but the reader is assured that no statistical concepts beyond these two are needed at all in the book.

The median salary concept is described first below,

followed by the explanation of the 90th percentile salary.

What Is the Median Salary

In everyday language, when we say the *median salary* of an occupation, the occupation of secretaries for instance, we mean the *typical* salary paid to secretaries. Or equivalently, by the *median salary*, we mean the *salary paid to an average worker* (secretary in this example).

Therefore, for all purposes in this book, median salary = typical salary = salary paid to an average worker.

If you do not feel like going through the remaining of this brief section below for a more precise definition of the median salary, you can skip it but just remember whenever you see "the median salary" in this book, you can substitute it with either "the typical salary" or "the salary paid to an average worker".

That will do the trick and would not cause any loss in understanding the messages in the book. Take the "Get Out of Jail Free" card now, and skip to the next section if you like.

If you decided to stick around and learn more about the definition of the median salary, here is a more precise definition. The median is the midpoint (a number, or salary in our case here, in the middle) of a bunch of numbers such that among the remaining numbers, half are smaller than the midpoint, while the other half numbers are greater than this midpoint.

The concept of the median can be better grasped with the assistance of an example. Suppose we have 5 workers: Alice, Bob, Charlie, Dylan, and Ethan, making $10, $20, $30, $40, and $900 per hour, respectively.

Now that we have these 5 numbers, applying the median definition above, we know that the wage of $30 that Charlie makes is the median among the 5 numbers. This is because 2 numbers ($10 and $20) are less than $30, while 2 other numbers ($40, $900) are greater than it.

Because Charlie is in the middle of the five people in this example, it is easy to see why loosely we think the median salary is the typical salary, as all other salaries are split into two groups around this number: One group below it and the other above it.

It also makes sense to think that the median salary is the salary paid to an average worker, again because the earner of the median salary, Charlie, lies right in the middle of the 5 workers here in this example who are ranked by salary they make. Supposedly, Charlies is more valuable a worker than Alice and Bob, but less so than Dylan and Ethan, and thus is an average worker.

However, one subtlety is that the median salary is *not* the average salary, and they can be very different. Using this example again, the average salary between the 5 workers here is actually $200, calculated by summing the 5 numbers of $10, $20, 30, $40, and $900 first, and then divide the sum ($1,000) by 5 workers.

Thus, the *average* salary is $200, much more than the median salary of $30. The average salary is dragged off by the top earner in this example, Ethan, who makes $900 per hour, a much higher salary than those of the other four people.

We prefer to use the median salary instead of the average salary to compare different occupations, as we would like to avoid the undue bias introduced by a few top earners.

For example, a salary of $1 million earned by a CEO will drag off the average salary considerably, but it has nothing to anybody other than the CEO herself.

On the contrary, the median salary is much more indicative of the salaries that ordinary workers expect to take home.

The astute reader might already have a question forming in the head: What if, in the above example, there are only four workers? What would be the median?

Good question.

Suppose now we have only four workers: Alice, Bob, Charlie and Dylan (but no more Ethan), making $10, $20, $30, and $40 per hour, respectively.

In this case, no wage out of the above four wages can separate the four wages into two equal groups. So, we take the middle two: $20 and $30, calculate the average ($25) of the two, and then declare $25 to be the median.

Thus, this artificial wage of $25 becomes the midpoint that separates $10, $20, $30 and $40 into two equal halves, one half less than $25 and the other half greater than $25.

OK, this is it. This is all we need to know about what the median salary is.

What Is the 90th Percentile Salary

As described above, the median wage is a good yardstick to compare how well an occupation pays the worker. The median wage is the *wage received by an average person* in an occupation, or the *typical wage* paid in an occupation, to intuit another way.

In addition to the median, here we introduce another statistical concept of the 90th percentile wage. The 90th percentile wage is the wage that is better than 90% of the salaries paid to workers in an occupation. Thus, it measures how well we can do beyond being an average worker.

It might not be realistic to expect ourselves to be **the very top** performer, but it is entirely achievable to work hard enough and smart enough to get ahead of 90% of our colleagues.

If we are paid better than 90% of the people out there, we are by definition **rich** because rich or not is a relative concept by comparison with our fellow citizens. If we take home a wage more than 90% of what other people are paid, we are rich.

Therefore, in this book, we measure the wage paid to an average person using the median wage, and we measure how rich a job can make us using the 90th percentile wage.

One more note. Even though the data released by the Department of Labor is comprehensive, the 90th percentile wage is not available for a small number of detailed occupations. In those case, estimates of the 90th percentile wages are formed in this book using other data available in the database, using a proprietary method developed by the author of this book.

Okay, if you are scratching your head and are getting intimidated by the jargons in statistics, be assured that no more statistics junky terms will be introduced in the book beyond these two, as promised.

3 JOBS RANKED BY MEDIAN SALARY

One of the two main chapters of the book, this chapter presents the complete list of all the 820 detailed occupations. The data of the 820 occupations was collected by the U.S. government, recently released in May and October 2017.

This is doubtlessly the most comprehensive, most authoritative, and most up to date source of employment information. No other source, in public or private domains, could come anywhere close.

The 820 occupations presented below are **ranked by the median salary** of an occupation, from high to low. Since the level of salary paid in an occupation is often times one of the most important considerations when we make career decisions, this chapter provides a quick way of telling which occupations pay well and which do not.

In the complete list of all the 820 occupations presented

below, for each occupation, the following information is provided.

- Median Wage
- Ninetieth Percentile Wage
- Number of Existing Positions
- Projected Growth Between 2016 and 2026
- Typical Education Requirement for Entry Into the Occupation

Brief descriptions of these metrics are as follows.

Median Wage. At the risk of excessive repetition, we point out here once again that by the *median salary*, we mean the *salary paid to an average worker* in an occupation, or equivalently the *typical salary* paid in an occupation.

Therefore, for all purposes in this book, median salary = typical salary = salary paid to an average worker.

Ninetieth Percentile Wage. As explained in the previous chapter, the 90th percentile wage is the wage that is better than 90% of the salaries paid to workers in an occupation. Thus, it measures how well we can do beyond being an average worker.

Number of Existing Positions. This metric is pretty self-explanatory. This is the number of existing positions of an occupation in the American job market, indicating the size of an occupation and thus the demand for the occupation.

Projected Growth Between 2016 and 2026. This is the 10-year percentage growth of a given occupation between 2016 and 2026, forecasted by the U.S. Department of Labor. The data was released only in November 2017, fresh out of the oven.

For instance, the occupation of accountants and auditors had one million and four hundred thousand positions in 2016 across America, and this occupation is projected to grow to one million five hundred and forty thousand in 2026, a 10% increase over the 10-year period.

Typical Education Needed for Entry Into the Occupation. This is the education attainment level typically required for entry positions in an occupation. Here is a list of education levels we can achieve in the U.S. These are the official categorization of education attainment levels in the employment data released by the U.S. Department of Labor:

- No formal educational credential
- High school diploma or equivalent
- Some college, no degree
- Postsecondary nondegree award
- Associate's degree

- Bachelor's degree
- Master's degree
- Doctoral or professional degree.

Now we are all set to present the full list of 820 occupations in the U.S., ranked by median salary.

Occupations Ranked by Median Wage

1. **Anesthesiologists**: $247,339 (median wage), $413,057 (90th percentile wage), 30,190 (number of positions), 17.8% (2016--2026 growth), Doctoral or professional degree (typical education requirement)

2. **Surgeons**: $232,028 (median wage), $387,486 (90th percentile wage), 41,190 (number of positions), 16.8% (2016--2026 growth), Doctoral or professional degree (typical education requirement)

3. **Obstetricians and Gynecologists**: $214,963 (median wage), $358,989 (90th percentile wage), 19,800 (number of positions), 17.9% (2016--2026 growth), Doctoral or professional degree (typical education requirement)

4. **Oral and Maxillofacial Surgeons**: $213,642 (median wage), $356,782 (90th percentile wage), 5,380 (number of positions), 17.2% (2016--2026 growth), Doctoral or professional degree (typical education

requirement)

5. **Orthodontists**: $209,890 (median wage), $350,516 (90th percentile wage), 5,200 (number of positions), 17.3% (2016--2026 growth), Doctoral or professional degree (typical education requirement)

6. **Physicians and Surgeons**, All Other: $206,920 (median wage), $345,556 (90th percentile wage), 338,620 (number of positions), 13.3% (2016--2026 growth), Doctoral or professional degree (typical education requirement)

7. **Internists**, General: $196,380 (median wage), $327,955 (90th percentile wage), 45,290 (number of positions), 16.9% (2016--2026 growth), Doctoral or professional degree (typical education requirement)

8. **Psychiatrists**: $194,740 (median wage), $325,216 (90th percentile wage), 24,820 (number of positions), 13.1% (2016--2026 growth), Doctoral or professional degree (typical education requirement)

9. **Family and General Practitioners**: $190,490 (median wage), $318,118 (90th percentile wage), 122,970 (number of positions), 16.5% (2016--2026 growth), Doctoral or professional degree (typical education requirement)

10. **Chief Executives**: $181,210 (median wage), $302,621 (90th percentile wage), 223,260 (number of

positions), -3.5% (2016--2026 growth), Bachelor's degree (typical education requirement)

11. **Dentists**, All Other Specialists: $173,000 (median wage), $288,910 (90th percentile wage), 5,380 (number of positions), 12% (2016--2026 growth), Doctoral or professional degree (typical education requirement)

12. **Pediatricians**, General: $168,990 (median wage), $282,213 (90th percentile wage), 26,960 (number of positions), 17.8% (2016--2026 growth), Doctoral or professional degree (typical education requirement)

13. **Nurse Anesthetists**: $160,270 (median wage), $267,651 (90th percentile wage), 39,860 (number of positions), 16% (2016--2026 growth), Master's degree (typical education requirement)

14. **Dentists**, General: $153,900 (median wage), $257,013 (90th percentile wage), 105,620 (number of positions), 17.5% (2016--2026 growth), Doctoral or professional degree (typical education requirement)

15. **Computer and Information Systems Managers**: $135,800 (median wage), $226,786 (90th percentile wage), 352,510 (number of positions), 11.9% (2016--2026 growth), Bachelor's degree (typical education requirement)

16. **Architectural and Engineering Managers**: $134,730

(median wage), $207,400 (90th percentile wage), 178,390 (number of positions), 5.5% (2016--2026 growth), Bachelor's degree (typical education requirement)

17. **Marketing Managers**: $131,180 (median wage), $219,071 (90th percentile wage), 205,900 (number of positions), 10% (2016--2026 growth), Bachelor's degree (typical education requirement)

18. **Petroleum Engineers**: $128,230 (median wage), $214,144 (90th percentile wage), 32,780 (number of positions), 14.5% (2016--2026 growth), Bachelor's degree (typical education requirement)

19. **Airline Pilots, Copilots, and Flight Engineers**: $127,820 (median wage), $213,459 (90th percentile wage), 81,520 (number of positions), 3.4% (2016--2026 growth), Bachelor's degree (typical education requirement)

20. **Prosthodontists**: $126,050 (median wage), $210,504 (90th percentile wage), 750 (number of positions), 17.2% (2016--2026 growth), Doctoral or professional degree (typical education requirement)

21. **Judges, Magistrate Judges, and Magistrates**: $125,880 (median wage), $183,570 (90th percentile wage), 27,210 (number of positions), 5.6% (2016--2026 growth), Doctoral or professional degree (typical education requirement)

22. **Podiatrists**: $124,830 (median wage), $208,466 (90th percentile wage), 9,800 (number of positions), 9.7% (2016--2026 growth), Doctoral or professional degree (typical education requirement)

23. **Air Traffic Controllers**: $122,410 (median wage), $172,680 (90th percentile wage), 23,240 (number of positions), 3.5% (2016--2026 growth), Associate's degree (typical education requirement)

24. **Pharmacists**: $122,230 (median wage), $157,950 (90th percentile wage), 305,510 (number of positions), 5.6% (2016--2026 growth), Doctoral or professional degree (typical education requirement)

25. **Financial Managers**: $121,750 (median wage), $203,323 (90th percentile wage), 543,300 (number of positions), 18.7% (2016--2026 growth), Bachelor's degree (typical education requirement)

26. **Natural Sciences Managers**: $119,850 (median wage), $200,150 (90th percentile wage), 54,780 (number of positions), 9.9% (2016--2026 growth), Bachelor's degree (typical education requirement)

27. **Lawyers**: $118,160 (median wage), $197,327 (90th percentile wage), 619,530 (number of positions), 9.4% (2016--2026 growth), Doctoral or professional degree (typical education requirement)

28. **Sales Managers**: $117,960 (median wage), $196,993

(90th percentile wage), 365,230 (number of positions), 7.4% (2016--2026 growth), Bachelor's degree (typical education requirement)

29. **Compensation and Benefits Managers**: $116,240 (median wage), $199,950 (90th percentile wage), 15,230 (number of positions), 5% (2016--2026 growth), Bachelor's degree (typical education requirement)

30. **Physicists**: $115,870 (median wage), $189,560 (90th percentile wage), 16,680 (number of positions), 14.5% (2016--2026 growth), Doctoral or professional degree (typical education requirement)

31. **Computer Hardware Engineers**: $115,080 (median wage), $172,010 (90th percentile wage), 72,950 (number of positions), 5.5% (2016--2026 growth), Bachelor's degree (typical education requirement)

32. **Political Scientists**: $114,290 (median wage), $160,290 (90th percentile wage), 6,350 (number of positions), 2.1% (2016--2026 growth), Master's degree (typical education requirement)

33. **Computer and Information Research Scientists**: $111,840 (median wage), $169,680 (90th percentile wage), 26,580 (number of positions), 19.2% (2016--2026 growth), Master's degree (typical education requirement)

34. **Purchasing Managers**: $111,590 (median wage), $177,560 (90th percentile wage), 71,750 (number of positions), 5.6% (2016--2026 growth), Bachelor's degree (typical education requirement)

35. **Law Teachers, Postsecondary**: $111,210 (median wage), $185,721 (90th percentile wage), 16,010 (number of positions), 12.2% (2016--2026 growth), Doctoral or professional degree (typical education requirement)

36. **Aerospace Engineers**: $109,650 (median wage), $160,290 (90th percentile wage), 68,510 (number of positions), 6.1% (2016--2026 growth), Bachelor's degree (typical education requirement)

37. **Public Relations and Fundraising Managers**: $107,320 (median wage), $205,110 (90th percentile wage), 63,970 (number of positions), 10.4% (2016--2026 growth), Bachelor's degree (typical education requirement)

38. **Human Resources Managers**: $106,910 (median wage), $193,550 (90th percentile wage), 129,810 (number of positions), 8.9% (2016--2026 growth), Bachelor's degree (typical education requirement)

39. **Software Developers**, Systems Software: $106,860 (median wage), $163,220 (90th percentile wage), 409,820 (number of positions), 10.8% (2016--2026 growth), Bachelor's degree (typical education

requirement)

40. **Optometrists**: $106,140 (median wage), $192,050 (90th percentile wage), 36,430 (number of positions), 17.3% (2016--2026 growth), Doctoral or professional degree (typical education requirement)

41. **Training and Development Managers**: $105,830 (median wage), $184,990 (90th percentile wage), 32,880 (number of positions), 10.3% (2016--2026 growth), Bachelor's degree (typical education requirement)

42. **Mathematicians**: $105,810 (median wage), $160,310 (90th percentile wage), 2,730 (number of positions), 29.4% (2016--2026 growth), Master's degree (typical education requirement)

43. **Managers, All Other**: $104,970 (median wage), $172,570 (90th percentile wage), 403,670 (number of positions), 7.6% (2016--2026 growth), Bachelor's degree (typical education requirement)

44. **Astronomers**: $104,740 (median wage), $165,140 (90th percentile wage), 1,830 (number of positions), 10% (2016--2026 growth), Doctoral or professional degree (typical education requirement)

45. **Nuclear Engineers**: $102,220 (median wage), $152,420 (90th percentile wage), 17,680 (number of positions), 3.8% (2016--2026 growth), Bachelor's

degree (typical education requirement)

46. **Physician Assistants**: $101,480 (median wage), $142,210 (90th percentile wage), 104,050 (number of positions), 37.4% (2016--2026 growth), Master's degree (typical education requirement)

47. **Computer Network Architects**: $101,210 (median wage), $158,590 (90th percentile wage), 157,070 (number of positions), 6.4% (2016--2026 growth), Bachelor's degree (typical education requirement)

48. **Economists**: $101,050 (median wage), $181,060 (90th percentile wage), 19,380 (number of positions), 6% (2016--2026 growth), Master's degree (typical education requirement)

49. **Nurse Practitioners**: $100,910 (median wage), $140,930 (90th percentile wage), 150,230 (number of positions), 36% (2016--2026 growth), Master's degree (typical education requirement)

50. **Advertising and Promotions Managers**: $100,810 (median wage), $168,353 (90th percentile wage), 28,860 (number of positions), 5.8% (2016--2026 growth), Bachelor's degree (typical education requirement)

51. **Actuaries**: $100,610 (median wage), $186,250 (90th percentile wage), 19,940 (number of positions), 22.5% (2016--2026 growth), Bachelor's degree (typical

education requirement)

52. **Software Developers**, Applications: $100,080 (median wage), $157,590 (90th percentile wage), 794,000 (number of positions), 30.5% (2016--2026 growth), Bachelor's degree (typical education requirement)

53. **Sales Engineers**: $100,000 (median wage), $166,500 (90th percentile wage), 74,330 (number of positions), 6.9% (2016--2026 growth), Bachelor's degree (typical education requirement)

54. **Nurse Midwives**: $99,770 (median wage), $142,510 (90th percentile wage), 6,270 (number of positions), 20.6% (2016--2026 growth), Master's degree (typical education requirement)

55. **Materials Scientists**: $99,430 (median wage), $157,750 (90th percentile wage), 7,750 (number of positions), 7.1% (2016--2026 growth), Bachelor's degree (typical education requirement)

56. **Health Specialties Teachers**, Postsecondary: $99,360 (median wage), $165,931 (90th percentile wage), 186,740 (number of positions), 25.9% (2016--2026 growth), Doctoral or professional degree (typical education requirement)

57. **General and Operations Managers**: $99,310 (median wage), $165,848 (90th percentile wage), 2,188,870

(number of positions), 9.1% (2016--2026 growth), Bachelor's degree (typical education requirement)

58. **Electronics Engineers**, Except Computer: $99,210 (median wage), $155,330 (90th percentile wage), 132,100 (number of positions), 3.7% (2016--2026 growth), Bachelor's degree (typical education requirement)

59. **Chemical Engineers**: $98,340 (median wage), $158,800 (90th percentile wage), 31,990 (number of positions), 7.6% (2016--2026 growth), Bachelor's degree (typical education requirement)

60. **Engineering Teachers**, Postsecondary: $97,530 (median wage), $176,560 (90th percentile wage), 38,000 (number of positions), 14.5% (2016--2026 growth), Doctoral or professional degree (typical education requirement)

61. **Engineers**, All Other: $97,300 (median wage), $152,970 (90th percentile wage), 123,390 (number of positions), 6.2% (2016--2026 growth), Bachelor's degree (typical education requirement)

62. **Industrial Production Managers**: $97,140 (median wage), $165,450 (90th percentile wage), 168,400 (number of positions), -0.2% (2016--2026 growth), Bachelor's degree (typical education requirement)

63. **Medical and Health Services Managers**: $96,540

(median wage), $172,240 (90th percentile wage), 332,150 (number of positions), 19.8% (2016--2026 growth), Bachelor's degree (typical education requirement)

64. **Physical Scientists**, All Other: $96,070 (median wage), $155,000 (90th percentile wage), 18,960 (number of positions), 6.4% (2016--2026 growth), Bachelor's degree (typical education requirement)

65. **Economics Teachers**, Postsecondary: $95,770 (median wage), $195,730 (90th percentile wage), 13,060 (number of positions), 10.6% (2016--2026 growth), Doctoral or professional degree (typical education requirement)

66. **Psychologists**, All Other: $95,710 (median wage), $127,710 (90th percentile wage), 13,310 (number of positions), 9.1% (2016--2026 growth), Master's degree (typical education requirement)

67. **Electrical Engineers**: $94,210 (median wage), $149,040 (90th percentile wage), 183,770 (number of positions), 8.6% (2016--2026 growth), Bachelor's degree (typical education requirement)

68. **Mining and Geological Engineers**, Including Mining Safety Engineers: $93,720 (median wage), $160,510 (90th percentile wage), 6,940 (number of positions), 7.2% (2016--2026 growth), Bachelor's degree (typical education requirement)

69. **Marine Engineers and Naval Architects**: $93,350 (median wage), $152,450 (90th percentile wage), 8,120 (number of positions), 11.5% (2016--2026 growth), Bachelor's degree (typical education requirement)

70. **Materials Engineers**: $93,310 (median wage), $148,840 (90th percentile wage), 26,800 (number of positions), 1.6% (2016--2026 growth), Bachelor's degree (typical education requirement)

71. **Information Security Analysts**: $92,600 (median wage), $147,290 (90th percentile wage), 96,870 (number of positions), 28.4% (2016--2026 growth), Bachelor's degree (typical education requirement)

72. **Education Administrators, Elementary and Secondary School**: $92,510 (median wage), $135,770 (90th percentile wage), 242,970 (number of positions), 7.8% (2016--2026 growth), Master's degree (typical education requirement)

73. **Atmospheric and Space Scientists**: $92,460 (median wage), $140,830 (90th percentile wage), 9,800 (number of positions), 12% (2016--2026 growth), Bachelor's degree (typical education requirement)

74. **Administrative Law Judges, Adjudicators, and Hearing Officers**: $92,110 (median wage), 162,400 (90th percentile wage), 14,540 (number of positions), 4% (2016--2026 growth), Doctoral or professional

degree (typical education requirement)

75. **Agricultural Sciences Teachers**, Postsecondary: $91,580 (median wage), $153,250 (90th percentile wage), 10,340 (number of positions), 7.5% (2016--2026 growth), Doctoral or professional degree (typical education requirement)

76. **Nuclear Power Reactor Operators**: $91,170 (median wage), $121,570 (90th percentile wage), 7,170 (number of positions), -10.2% (2016--2026 growth), High school diploma or equivalent (typical education requirement)

77. **Education Administrators**, Postsecondary: $90,760 (median wage), $179,250 (90th percentile wage), 138,430 (number of positions), 10% (2016--2026 growth), Master's degree (typical education requirement)

78. **Personal Financial Advisors**: $90,530 (median wage), $151,185 (90th percentile wage), 201,850 (number of positions), 14.4% (2016--2026 growth), Bachelor's degree (typical education requirement)

79. **Administrative Services Managers**: $90,050 (median wage), $159,330 (90th percentile wage), 266,280 (number of positions), 10.1% (2016--2026 growth), Bachelor's degree (typical education requirement)

80. **Art Directors**: $89,820 (median wage), $166,400 (90th

percentile wage), 36,210 (number of positions), 7.4% (2016--2026 growth), Bachelor's degree (typical education requirement)

81. **Geoscientists, Except Hydrologists and Geographers**: $89,780 (median wage), $189,020 (90th percentile wage), 30,420 (number of positions), 13.9% (2016--2026 growth), Bachelor's degree (typical education requirement)

82. **Construction Managers**: $89,300 (median wage), $158,330 (90th percentile wage), 249,650 (number of positions), 11.4% (2016--2026 growth), Bachelor's degree (typical education requirement)

83. **Transportation, Storage, and Distribution Managers**: $89,190 (median wage), $152,730 (90th percentile wage), 113,270 (number of positions), 6.7% (2016--2026 growth), High school diploma or equivalent (typical education requirement)

84. **Veterinarians**: $88,770 (median wage), $161,070 (90th percentile wage), 67,650 (number of positions), 18.1% (2016--2026 growth), Doctoral or professional degree (typical education requirement)

85. **Computer Systems Analysts**: $87,220 (median wage), $137,690 (90th percentile wage), 568,960 (number of positions), 8.8% (2016--2026 growth), Bachelor's degree (typical education requirement)

86. **Health and Safety Engineers**, Except Mining Safety Engineers and Inspectors: $86,720 (median wage), $134,110 (90th percentile wage), 25,410 (number of positions), 8.6% (2016--2026 growth), Bachelor's degree (typical education requirement)

87. **Computer Occupations**, All Other: $86,510 (median wage), $133,890 (90th percentile wage), 261,210 (number of positions), 9% (2016--2026 growth), Bachelor's degree (typical education requirement)

88. **Forestry and Conservation Science Teachers**, Postsecondary: $85,880 (median wage), $144,820 (90th percentile wage), 1,750 (number of positions), 7.7% (2016--2026 growth), Doctoral or professional degree (typical education requirement)

89. **Biomedical Engineers**: $85,620 (median wage), $134,620 (90th percentile wage), 20,590 (number of positions), 7.2% (2016--2026 growth), Bachelor's degree (typical education requirement)

90. **Atmospheric, Earth, Marine, and Space Sciences Teachers**, Postsecondary: $85,410 (median wage), $161,220 (90th percentile wage), 10,850 (number of positions), 9.5% (2016--2026 growth), Doctoral or professional degree (typical education requirement)

91. **Physical Therapists**: $85,400 (median wage), $122,130 (90th percentile wage), 216,920 (number of positions), 25% (2016--2026 growth), Doctoral or

professional degree (typical education requirement)

92. **Database Administrators**: $84,950 (median wage), $129,930 (90th percentile wage), 113,730 (number of positions), 11.5% (2016--2026 growth), Bachelor's degree (typical education requirement)

93. **Environmental Engineers**: $84,890 (median wage), $130,120 (90th percentile wage), 52,280 (number of positions), 8.3% (2016--2026 growth), Bachelor's degree (typical education requirement)

94. **First-Line Supervisors of Police and Detectives**: $84,840 (median wage), $134,810 (90th percentile wage), 100,200 (number of positions), 6.6% (2016--2026 growth), High school diploma or equivalent (typical education requirement)

95. **Physics Teachers**, Postsecondary: $84,570 (median wage), $164,130 (90th percentile wage), 14,160 (number of positions), 10% (2016--2026 growth), Doctoral or professional degree (typical education requirement)

96. **Industrial Engineers**: $84,310 (median wage), $129,390 (90th percentile wage), 256,550 (number of positions), 9.7% (2016--2026 growth), Bachelor's degree (typical education requirement)

97. **Mechanical Engineers**: $84,190 (median wage), $131,350 (90th percentile wage), 285,790 (number of

positions), 8.8% (2016--2026 growth), Bachelor's degree (typical education requirement)

98. **Civil Engineers**: $83,540 (median wage), $132,880 (90th percentile wage), 287,800 (number of positions), 10.6% (2016--2026 growth), Bachelor's degree (typical education requirement)

99. **Industrial-Organizational Psychologists**: $82,760 (median wage), $184,380 (90th percentile wage), 1,020 (number of positions), 5.6% (2016--2026 growth), Master's degree (typical education requirement)

100. **Biochemists and Biophysicists**: $82,180 (median wage), $158,410 (90th percentile wage), 29,200 (number of positions), 11.3% (2016--2026 growth), Doctoral or professional degree (typical education requirement)

101. **Occupational Therapists**: $81,910 (median wage), $119,720 (90th percentile wage), 118,070 (number of positions), 21.2% (2016--2026 growth), Master's degree (typical education requirement)

102. **Power Distributors and Dispatchers**: $81,900 (median wage), $110,340 (90th percentile wage), 11,380 (number of positions), -2.5% (2016--2026 growth), High school diploma or equivalent (typical education requirement)

103. **Financial Analysts**: $81,760 (median wage), $165,100 (90th percentile wage), 281,610 (number of positions), 10.8% (2016--2026 growth), Bachelor's degree (typical education requirement)

104. **Anthropology and Archeology Teachers**, Postsecondary: $81,350 (median wage), $155,500 (90th percentile wage), 5,700 (number of positions), 10% (2016--2026 growth), Doctoral or professional degree (typical education requirement)

105. **Management Analysts**: $81,330 (median wage), $149,720 (90th percentile wage), 637,690 (number of positions), 12% (2016--2026 growth), Bachelor's degree (typical education requirement)

106. **Medical Scientists**, Except Epidemiologists: $80,530 (median wage), $159,570 (90th percentile wage), 108,870 (number of positions), 13.2% (2016--2026 growth), Doctoral or professional degree (typical education requirement)

107. **Statisticians**: $80,500 (median wage), $130,090 (90th percentile wage), 33,440 (number of positions), 33.4% (2016--2026 growth), Master's degree (typical education requirement)

108. **Hydrologists**: $80,480 (median wage), $120,100 (90th percentile wage), 6,300 (number of positions), 9.9% (2016--2026 growth), Bachelor's degree (typical education requirement)

109. **Radiation Therapists**: $80,160 (median wage), $123,710 (90th percentile wage), 17,450 (number of positions), 11.9% (2016--2026 growth), Associate's degree (typical education requirement)

110. **Computer Programmers**: $79,840 (median wage), $130,360 (90th percentile wage), 271,200 (number of positions), -7.6% (2016--2026 growth), Bachelor's degree (typical education requirement)

111. **Sociologists**: $79,750 (median wage), $146,860 (90th percentile wage), 2,870 (number of positions), 0.1% (2016--2026 growth), Master's degree (typical education requirement)

112. **Network and Computer Systems Administrators**: $79,700 (median wage), $127,610 (90th percentile wage), 376,820 (number of positions), 6.1% (2016--2026 growth), Bachelor's degree (typical education requirement)

113. **Financial Examiners**: $79,280 (median wage), $148,390 (90th percentile wage), 49,750 (number of positions), 9.8% (2016--2026 growth), Bachelor's degree (typical education requirement)

114. **Architecture Teachers**, Postsecondary: $79,250 (median wage), $160,220 (90th percentile wage), 7,370 (number of positions), 10.6% (2016--2026 growth), Doctoral or professional degree (typical education requirement)

115. **Political Science Teachers**, Postsecondary: $79,210 (median wage), $164,830 (90th percentile wage), 16,720 (number of positions), 10.5% (2016--2026 growth), Doctoral or professional degree (typical education requirement)

116. **Operations Research Analysts**: $79,200 (median wage), $132,660 (90th percentile wage), 109,150 (number of positions), 27.4% (2016--2026 growth), Bachelor's degree (typical education requirement)

117. **Nuclear Technicians**: $79,140 (median wage), $106,950 (90th percentile wage), 6,840 (number of positions), 0.6% (2016--2026 growth), Associate's degree (typical education requirement)

118. **Sales Representatives, Wholesale and Manufacturing, Technical and Scientific Products**: $78,980 (median wage), $160,940 (90th percentile wage), 328,370 (number of positions), 5.5% (2016--2026 growth), Bachelor's degree (typical education requirement)

119. **Elevator Installers and Repairers**: $78,890 (median wage), $114,980 (90th percentile wage), 22,240 (number of positions), 12.1% (2016--2026 growth), High school diploma or equivalent (typical education requirement)

120. **Environmental Science Teachers**, Postsecondary: $78,340 (median wage), $150,890 (90th percentile

wage), 5,520 (number of positions), 9.6% (2016--2026 growth), Doctoral or professional degree (typical education requirement)

121. **Education Administrators**, All Other: $78,210 (median wage), $131,410 (90th percentile wage), 34,140 (number of positions), 10.4% (2016--2026 growth), Bachelor's degree (typical education requirement)

122. **Detectives and Criminal Investigators**: $78,120 (median wage), $131,200 (90th percentile wage), 104,980 (number of positions), 4.5% (2016--2026 growth), High school diploma or equivalent (typical education requirement)

123. **Computer Science Teachers, Postsecondary**: $77,570 (median wage), $155,580 (90th percentile wage), 32,540 (number of positions), 8% (2016--2026 growth), Doctoral or professional degree (typical education requirement)

124. **Business Teachers**, Postsecondary: $77,490 (median wage), $185,410 (90th percentile wage), 83,030 (number of positions), 18.1% (2016--2026 growth), Doctoral or professional degree (typical education requirement)

125. **Commercial Pilots**: $77,200 (median wage), $147,240 (90th percentile wage), 38,980 (number of positions), 3.8% (2016--2026 growth), High school

diploma or equivalent (typical education requirement)

126. **Social Scientists and Related Workers**, All Other: $77,020 (median wage), $119,800 (90th percentile wage), 36,380 (number of positions), 5.9% (2016--2026 growth), Bachelor's degree (typical education requirement)

127. **Architects, Except Landscape and Naval**: $76,930 (median wage), $129,810 (90th percentile wage), 99,860 (number of positions), 4% (2016--2026 growth), Bachelor's degree (typical education requirement)

128. **Geography Teachers**, Postsecondary: $76,810 (median wage), $134,010 (90th percentile wage), 4,140 (number of positions), 8.4% (2016--2026 growth), Doctoral or professional degree (typical education requirement)

129. **Chemistry Teachers**, Postsecondary: $76,750 (median wage), $153,570 (90th percentile wage), 21,250 (number of positions), 9.9% (2016--2026 growth), Doctoral or professional degree (typical education requirement)

130. **Biological Science Teachers**, Postsecondary: $76,650 (median wage), $157,630 (90th percentile wage), 50,820 (number of positions), 15.1% (2016--2026 growth), Doctoral or professional degree

(typical education requirement)

131. **Audiologists**: $75,980 (median wage), $113,540 (90th percentile wage), 12,310 (number of positions), 20.4% (2016--2026 growth), Doctoral or professional degree (typical education requirement)

132. **Media and Communication Equipment Workers**, All Other: $75,700 (median wage), $118,840 (90th percentile wage), 18,620 (number of positions), 7.9% (2016--2026 growth), High school diploma or equivalent (typical education requirement)

133. **Electrical and Electronics Repairers**, Powerhouse, Substation, and Relay: $75,670 (median wage), $98,890 (90th percentile wage), 23,060 (number of positions), 3.7% (2016--2026 growth), Postsecondary nondegree award (typical education requirement)

134. **Biological Scientists**, All Other: $74,790 (median wage), $116,680 (90th percentile wage), 35,110 (number of positions), 7.9% (2016--2026 growth), Bachelor's degree (typical education requirement)

135. **Power Plant Operators**: $74,690 (median wage), $101,590 (90th percentile wage), 35,010 (number of positions), 1.3% (2016--2026 growth), High school diploma or equivalent (typical education requirement)

136. **Speech-Language Pathologists**: $74,680 (median

wage), $116,810 (90th percentile wage), (number of positions), 17.5% (2016--2026 growth), Master's degree (typical education requirement)

137. **First-Line Supervisors of Fire Fighting and Prevention Workers**: $74,540 (median wage), $117,800 (90th percentile wage), 57,170 (number of positions), 7.2% (2016--2026 growth), Postsecondary nondegree award (typical education requirement)

138. **Health Diagnosing and Treating Practitioners**, All Other: $74,530 (median wage), $135,650 (90th percentile wage), 36,280 (number of positions), 11.4% (2016--2026 growth), Master's degree (typical education requirement)

139. **Nuclear Medicine Technologists**: $74,350 (median wage), $101,850 (90th percentile wage), 19,650 (number of positions), 9.8% (2016--2026 growth), Associate's degree (typical education requirement)

140. **Geographers**: $74,260 (median wage), $101,370 (90th percentile wage), 1,370 (number of positions), 6.2% (2016--2026 growth), Bachelor's degree (typical education requirement)

141. **Logisticians**: $74,170 (median wage), $117,310 (90th percentile wage), 146,060 (number of positions), 6.9% (2016--2026 growth), Bachelor's degree (typical education requirement)

142. **Genetic Counselors**: $74,120 (median wage), $104,770 (90th percentile wage), 2,720 (number of positions), 28.3% (2016--2026 growth), Master's degree (typical education requirement)

143. **Life Scientists**, All Other: $73,860 (median wage), $136,370 (90th percentile wage), 7,890 (number of positions), 9% (2016--2026 growth), Bachelor's degree (typical education requirement)

144. **Budget Analysts**: $73,840 (median wage), $111,460 (90th percentile wage), 54,700 (number of positions), 6.5% (2016--2026 growth), Bachelor's degree (typical education requirement)

145. **Funeral Service Managers**: $73,830 (median wage), $147,990 (90th percentile wage), 8,370 (number of positions), 6.4% (2016--2026 growth), Associate's degree (typical education requirement)

146. **Chemists**: $73,740 (median wage), $129,670 (90th percentile wage), 86,660 (number of positions), 6.5% (2016--2026 growth), Bachelor's degree (typical education requirement)

147. **Agricultural Engineers**: $73,640 (median wage), $117,130 (90th percentile wage), 1,980 (number of positions), 8.1% (2016--2026 growth), Bachelor's degree (typical education requirement)

148. **Clinical, Counseling, and School Psychologists**:

$73,270 (median wage), $120,320 (90th percentile wage), 107,980 (number of positions), 14.2% (2016--2026 growth), Doctoral or professional degree (typical education requirement)

149. **First-Line Supervisors of Non-Retail Sales Workers**: $73,150 (median wage), $150,400 (90th percentile wage), 252,670 (number of positions), 6.4% (2016--2026 growth), High school diploma or equivalent (typical education requirement)

150. **Psychology Teachers**, Postsecondary: $73,140 (median wage), $148,470 (90th percentile wage), 37,640 (number of positions), 15.1% (2016--2026 growth), Doctoral or professional degree (typical education requirement)

151. **Area, Ethnic, and Cultural Studies Teachers**, Postsecondary: $73,020 (median wage), $148,640 (90th percentile wage), 9,060 (number of positions), 10.5% (2016--2026 growth), Doctoral or professional degree (typical education requirement)

152. **Dental Hygienists**: $72,910 (median wage), $100,170 (90th percentile wage), 204,990 (number of positions), 19.6% (2016--2026 growth), Associate's degree (typical education requirement)

153. **Captains, Mates, and Pilots of Water Vessels**: $72,680 (median wage), $134,390 (90th percentile wage), 36,720 (number of positions), 8.8% (2016--

2026 growth), Postsecondary nondegree award (typical education requirement)

154. **Transportation Inspectors**: $72,220 (median wage), $116,990 (90th percentile wage), 27,430 (number of positions), 5.9% (2016--2026 growth), High school diploma or equivalent (typical education requirement)

155. **Sociology Teachers**, Postsecondary: $71,840 (median wage), $133,740 (90th percentile wage), 14,580 (number of positions), 9.8% (2016--2026 growth), Doctoral or professional degree (typical education requirement)

156. **History Teachers**, Postsecondary: $71,820 (median wage), $130,530 (90th percentile wage), 21,800 (number of positions), 10.3% (2016--2026 growth), Doctoral or professional degree (typical education requirement)

157. **Postmasters and Mail Superintendents**: $71,670 (median wage), $89,930 (90th percentile wage), 14,720 (number of positions), -20.9% (2016--2026 growth), High school diploma or equivalent (typical education requirement)

158. **Producers and Directors**: $70,950 (median wage), $189,870 (90th percentile wage), 114,510 (number of positions), 12% (2016--2026 growth), Bachelor's degree (typical education requirement)

159. **Occupational Health and Safety Specialists**: $70,920 (median wage), $104,460 (90th percentile wage), 76,630 (number of positions), 7.6% (2016--2026 growth), Bachelor's degree (typical education requirement)

160. **Epidemiologists**: $70,820 (median wage), $114,510 (90th percentile wage), 5,690 (number of positions), 8.7% (2016--2026 growth), Master's degree (typical education requirement)

161. **Social Sciences Teachers**, Postsecondary, All Other: $70,740 (median wage), $166,830 (90th percentile wage), 13,320 (number of positions), 10% (2016--2026 growth), Doctoral or professional degree (typical education requirement)

162. **Ship Engineers**: $70,570 (median wage), $119,690 (90th percentile wage), 9,750 (number of positions), 6.5% (2016--2026 growth), Postsecondary nondegree award (typical education requirement)

163. **Emergency Management Directors**: $70,500 (median wage), $133,880 (90th percentile wage), 9,570 (number of positions), 7.7% (2016--2026 growth), Bachelor's degree (typical education requirement)

164. **Urban and Regional Planners**: $70,020 (median wage), $105,310 (90th percentile wage), 34,810 (number of positions), 12.8% (2016--2026 growth),

Master's degree (typical education requirement)

165. **Credit Analysts**: $69,930 (median wage), $137,730 (90th percentile wage), 72,930 (number of positions), 8.4% (2016--2026 growth), Bachelor's degree (typical education requirement)

166. **Technical Writers**: $69,850 (median wage), $111,260 (90th percentile wage), 49,780 (number of positions), 10.9% (2016--2026 growth), Bachelor's degree (typical education requirement)

167. **Diagnostic Medical Sonographers**: $69,650 (median wage), $99,100 (90th percentile wage), 65,790 (number of positions), 23.2% (2016--2026 growth), Associate's degree (typical education requirement)

168. **Mathematical Science Teachers**, Postsecondary: $69,520 (median wage), $147,700 (90th percentile wage), 52,020 (number of positions), 9.2% (2016--2026 growth), Doctoral or professional degree (typical education requirement)

169. **Financial Specialists**, All Other: $69,470 (median wage), $118,780 (90th percentile wage), 123,270 (number of positions), 8.7% (2016--2026 growth), Bachelor's degree (typical education requirement)

170. **Home Economics Teachers**, Postsecondary: $69,190 (median wage), $115,910 (90th percentile

wage), 2,970 (number of positions), 7.8% (2016--2026 growth), Master's degree (typical education requirement)

171. **Gaming Managers**: $69,180 (median wage), $124,400 (90th percentile wage), 4,280 (number of positions), 2.5% (2016--2026 growth), High school diploma or equivalent (typical education requirement)

172. **Nursing Instructors and Teachers**, Postsecondary: $69,130 (median wage), $117,540 (90th percentile wage), 56,210 (number of positions), 24% (2016--2026 growth), Doctoral or professional degree (typical education requirement)

173. **Business Operations Specialists**, All Other: $69,040 (median wage), $118,500 (90th percentile wage), 958,670 (number of positions), 8.8% (2016--2026 growth), Bachelor's degree (typical education requirement)

174. **Environmental Scientists and Specialists**, Including Health: $68,910 (median wage), $120,320 (90th percentile wage), 84,250 (number of positions), 11.1% (2016--2026 growth), Bachelor's degree (typical education requirement)

175. **Art, Drama, and Music Teachers**, Postsecondary: $68,650 (median wage), $140,070 (90th percentile wage), 99,020 (number of positions), 12% (2016--2026

growth), Master's degree (typical education requirement)

176. **Registered Nurses**: $68,450 (median wage), $102,990 (90th percentile wage), 2,857,180 (number of positions), 14.8% (2016--2026 growth), Bachelor's degree (typical education requirement)

177. **Magnetic Resonance Imaging Technologists**: $68,420 (median wage), $95,890 (90th percentile wage), 35,850 (number of positions), 13.6% (2016--2026 growth), Associate's degree (typical education requirement)

178. **Library Science Teachers**, Postsecondary: $68,410 (median wage), $106,960 (90th percentile wage), 4,870 (number of positions), 9% (2016--2026 growth), Doctoral or professional degree (typical education requirement)

179. **Philosophy and Religion Teachers**, Postsecondary: $68,360 (median wage), $127,740 (90th percentile wage), 23,180 (number of positions), 12.3% (2016--2026 growth), Doctoral or professional degree (typical education requirement)

180. **Accountants and Auditors**: $68,150 (median wage), $120,910 (90th percentile wage), 1,246,540 (number of positions), 10% (2016--2026 growth), Bachelor's degree (typical education requirement)

181. **Aerospace Engineering and Operations Technicians**: $68,020 (median wage), $102,000 (90th percentile wage), 11,970 (number of positions), 6.6% (2016--2026 growth), Associate's degree (typical education requirement)

182. **Electrical Power-Line Installers and Repairers**: $68,010 (median wage), $98,190 (90th percentile wage), 117,670 (number of positions), 13.9% (2016--2026 growth), High school diploma or equivalent (typical education requirement)

183. **Commercial and Industrial Designers**: $67,790 (median wage), $105,690 (90th percentile wage), 31,860 (number of positions), 5% (2016--2026 growth), Bachelor's degree (typical education requirement)

184. **Insurance Underwriters**: $67,680 (median wage), $121,430 (90th percentile wage), 91,650 (number of positions), -5.2% (2016--2026 growth), Bachelor's degree (typical education requirement)

185. **Gas Plant Operators**: $67,580 (median wage), $95,030 (90th percentile wage), 17,350 (number of positions), 0% (2016--2026 growth), High school diploma or equivalent (typical education requirement)

186. **Chiropractors**: $67,520 (median wage), $141,030 (90th percentile wage), 32,960 (number of positions),

10.5% (2016--2026 growth), Doctoral or professional degree (typical education requirement)

187. **Petroleum Pump System Operators, Refinery Operators, and Gaugers**: $67,400 (median wage), $96,070 (90th percentile wage), 41,630 (number of positions), 2.8% (2016--2026 growth), High school diploma or equivalent (typical education requirement)

188. **Securities, Commodities, and Financial Services Sales Agents**: $67,310 (median wage), $112,408 (90th percentile wage), 353,780 (number of positions), 6.1% (2016--2026 growth), Bachelor's degree (typical education requirement)

189. **Microbiologists**: $66,850 (median wage), $128,190 (90th percentile wage), 21,670 (number of positions), 8% (2016--2026 growth), Bachelor's degree (typical education requirement)

190. **Transit and Railroad Police**: $66,610 (median wage), $96,670 (90th percentile wage), 4,810 (number of positions), 6.3% (2016--2026 growth), High school diploma or equivalent (typical education requirement)

191. **Compliance Officers**: $66,540 (median wage), $105,260 (90th percentile wage), 273,910 (number of positions), 8.2% (2016--2026 growth), Bachelor's degree (typical education requirement)

192. **Farmers, Ranchers, and Other Agricultural Managers**: $66,360 (median wage), $126,070 (90th percentile wage), 4,560 (number of positions), 6.7% (2016--2026 growth), High school diploma or equivalent (typical education requirement)

193. **Web Developers**: $66,130 (median wage), $119,550 (90th percentile wage), 129,540 (number of positions), 13.1% (2016--2026 growth), Associate's degree (typical education requirement)

194. **Communications Teachers**, Postsecondary: $65,640 (median wage), $125,630 (90th percentile wage), 28,180 (number of positions), 10% (2016--2026 growth), Doctoral or professional degree (typical education requirement)

195. **Orthotists and Prosthetists**: $65,630 (median wage), $104,010 (90th percentile wage), 7,500 (number of positions), 21.9% (2016--2026 growth), Master's degree (typical education requirement)

196. **Signal and Track Switch Repairers**: $65,350 (median wage), $82,800 (90th percentile wage), 8,680 (number of positions), 1.1% (2016--2026 growth), High school diploma or equivalent (typical education requirement)

197. **Multimedia Artists and Animators**: $65,300 (median wage), $115,960 (90th percentile wage), 29,810 (number of positions), 10.4% (2016--2026

growth), Bachelor's degree (typical education requirement)

198. **Fashion Designers**: $65,170 (median wage), $130,050 (90th percentile wage), 19,230 (number of positions), 3.1% (2016--2026 growth), Bachelor's degree (typical education requirement)

199. **Mathematical Science Occupations**, All Other: $65,050 (median wage), $157,600 (90th percentile wage), 2,000 (number of positions), 10.7% (2016--2026 growth), Bachelor's degree (typical education requirement)

200. **Social and Community Service Managers**: $64,680 (median wage), $110,970 (90th percentile wage), 126,230 (number of positions), 15.7% (2016--2026 growth), Bachelor's degree (typical education requirement)

201. **Subway and Streetcar Operators**: $64,680 (median wage), $80,910 (90th percentile wage), 12,350 (number of positions), 4.1% (2016--2026 growth), High school diploma or equivalent (typical education requirement)

202. **Postsecondary Teachers**, All Other: $64,400 (median wage), $130,090 (90th percentile wage), 194,870 (number of positions), 9.4% (2016--2026 growth), Doctoral or professional degree (typical education requirement)

203. **Social Work Teachers**, Postsecondary: $64,030 (median wage), $130,520 (90th percentile wage), 11,860 (number of positions), 9.9% (2016--2026 growth), Doctoral or professional degree (typical education requirement)

204. **Food Scientists and Technologists**: $63,950 (median wage), $117,480 (90th percentile wage), 14,200 (number of positions), 6% (2016--2026 growth), Bachelor's degree (typical education requirement)

205. **English Language and Literature Teachers**, Postsecondary: $63,730 (median wage), $130,890 (90th percentile wage), 71,270 (number of positions), 9.8% (2016--2026 growth), Doctoral or professional degree (typical education requirement)

206. **Claims Adjusters, Examiners, and Investigators**: $63,680 (median wage), $95,760 (90th percentile wage), 274,420 (number of positions), -1.5% (2016--2026 growth), High school diploma or equivalent (typical education requirement)

207. **Loan Officers**: $63,650 (median wage), $132,290 (90th percentile wage), 305,700 (number of positions), 11.5% (2016--2026 growth), Bachelor's degree (typical education requirement)

208. **First-Line Supervisors of Mechanics**, Installers, and Repairers: $63,540 (median wage), $100,480 (90th

percentile wage), 453,330 (number of positions), 7.1% (2016--2026 growth), High school diploma or equivalent (typical education requirement)

209. **Insurance Appraisers**, Auto Damage: $63,510 (median wage), $95,000 (90th percentile wage), 15,130 (number of positions), 4.9% (2016--2026 growth), Postsecondary nondegree award (typical education requirement)

210. **Foreign Language and Literature Teachers**, Postsecondary: $63,500 (median wage), $125,580 (90th percentile wage), 28,720 (number of positions), 11.8% (2016--2026 growth), Doctoral or professional degree (typical education requirement)

211. **Landscape Architects**: $63,480 (median wage), $106,770 (90th percentile wage), 19,420 (number of positions), 6.2% (2016--2026 growth), Bachelor's degree (typical education requirement)

212. **Purchasing Agents**, Except Wholesale, Retail, and Farm Products: $63,300 (median wage), $101,770 (90th percentile wage), 297,600 (number of positions), -5.6% (2016--2026 growth), Bachelor's degree (typical education requirement)

213. **Anthropologists and Archeologists**: $63,190 (median wage), $99,590 (90th percentile wage), 6,470 (number of positions), 3.3% (2016--2026 growth), Master's degree (typical education requirement)

214. **First-Line Supervisors of Construction Trades and Extraction Workers**: $62,980 (median wage), $102,880 (90th percentile wage), 538,220 (number of positions), 12.7% (2016--2026 growth), High school diploma or equivalent (typical education requirement)

215. **Film and Video Editors**: $62,760 (median wage), $162,260 (90th percentile wage), 29,880 (number of positions), 16.3% (2016--2026 growth), Bachelor's degree (typical education requirement)

216. **Cartographers and Photogrammetrists**: $62,750 (median wage), $99,800 (90th percentile wage), 12,100 (number of positions), 19.4% (2016--2026 growth), Bachelor's degree (typical education requirement)

217. **Computer Network Support Specialists**: $62,670 (median wage), $105,910 (90th percentile wage), 188,740 (number of positions), 8.1% (2016--2026 growth), Associate's degree (typical education requirement)

218. **Market Research Analysts and Marketing Specialists**: $62,560 (median wage), $121,720 (90th percentile wage), 558,630 (number of positions), 22.8% (2016--2026 growth), Bachelor's degree (typical education requirement)

219. **Education Teachers**, Postsecondary: $62,520

(median wage), $118,160 (90th percentile wage), 58,850 (number of positions), 10.3% (2016--2026 growth), Doctoral or professional degree (typical education requirement)

220. **Instructional Coordinators**: $62,460 (median wage), $100,320 (90th percentile wage), 147,330 (number of positions), 10.1% (2016--2026 growth), Master's degree (typical education requirement)

221. **Engineering Technicians**, Except Drafters, All Other: $62,330 (median wage), $95,960 (90th percentile wage), 74,290 (number of positions), 5.2% (2016--2026 growth), Associate's degree (typical education requirement)

222. **Labor Relations Specialists**: $62,310 (median wage), $114,340 (90th percentile wage), 79,430 (number of positions), -7.8% (2016--2026 growth), Bachelor's degree (typical education requirement)

223. **Soil and Plant Scientists**: $62,300 (median wage), $114,390 (90th percentile wage), 14,690 (number of positions), 9% (2016--2026 growth), Bachelor's degree (typical education requirement)

224. **Electrical and Electronics Engineering Technicians**: $62,190 (median wage), $91,640 (90th percentile wage), 134,870 (number of positions), 2% (2016--2026 growth), Associate's degree (typical education requirement)

225. **Agents and Business Managers of Artists**, Performers, and Athletes: $62,080 (median wage), $194,810 (90th percentile wage), 13,470 (number of positions), 4.9% (2016--2026 growth), Bachelor's degree (typical education requirement)

226. **Compensation, Benefits, and Job Analysis Specialists**: $62,080 (median wage), $101,020 (90th percentile wage), 79,190 (number of positions), 8.5% (2016--2026 growth), Bachelor's degree (typical education requirement)

227. **Boilermakers**: $62,060 (median wage), $85,800 (90th percentile wage), 16,660 (number of positions), 8.4% (2016--2026 growth), High school diploma or equivalent (typical education requirement)

228. **Conservation Scientists**: $61,810 (median wage), $95,970 (90th percentile wage), 20,470 (number of positions), 6.5% (2016--2026 growth), Bachelor's degree (typical education requirement)

229. **Cost Estimators**: $61,790 (median wage), $103,250 (90th percentile wage), 214,610 (number of positions), 10.6% (2016--2026 growth), Bachelor's degree (typical education requirement)

230. **Artists and Related Workers**, All Other: $61,360 (median wage), $103,860 (90th percentile wage), 7,010 (number of positions), 6.9% (2016--2026 growth), No formal educational credential (typical

education requirement)

231. **Writers and Authors**: $61,240 (median wage), $118,640 (90th percentile wage), 44,690 (number of positions), 8.3% (2016--2026 growth), Bachelor's degree (typical education requirement)

232. **Medical and Clinical Laboratory Technologists**: $61,070 (median wage), $85,160 (90th percentile wage), 166,730 (number of positions), 11.5% (2016--2026 growth), Bachelor's degree (typical education requirement)

233. **Makeup Artists, Theatrical and Performance**: $60,970 (median wage), $124,960 (90th percentile wage), 3,600 (number of positions), 11.2% (2016--2026 growth), Postsecondary nondegree award (typical education requirement)

234. **Avionics Technicians**: $60,760 (median wage), $83,260 (90th percentile wage), 17,330 (number of positions), 6% (2016--2026 growth), Associate's degree (typical education requirement)

235. **First-Line Supervisors of Correctional Officers**: $60,560 (median wage), $98,290 (90th percentile wage), 43,230 (number of positions), -7.8% (2016--2026 growth), High school diploma or equivalent (typical education requirement)

236. **Zoologists and Wildlife Biologists**: $60,520

(median wage), $98,540 (90th percentile wage), 17,720 (number of positions), 7.5% (2016--2026 growth), Bachelor's degree (typical education requirement)

237. **Gas Compressor and Gas Pumping Station Operators**: $60,470 (median wage), $78,920 (90th percentile wage), 3,890 (number of positions), 3.3% (2016--2026 growth), High school diploma or equivalent (typical education requirement)

238. **Rail Transportation Workers**, All Other: $60,420 (median wage), $90,580 (90th percentile wage), 4,470 (number of positions), 3.2% (2016--2026 growth), High school diploma or equivalent (typical education requirement)

239. **Animal Scientists**: $60,330 (median wage), $126,190 (90th percentile wage), 2,470 (number of positions), 6% (2016--2026 growth), Bachelor's degree (typical education requirement)

240. **Social Workers**, All Other: $60,230 (median wage), $85,190 (90th percentile wage), 59,540 (number of positions), 7.9% (2016--2026 growth), Bachelor's degree (typical education requirement)

241. **Aircraft Mechanics and Service Technicians**: $60,170 (median wage), $87,880 (90th percentile wage), 128,570 (number of positions), 4.9% (2016--2026 growth), Postsecondary nondegree award

(typical education requirement)

242. **Electrical and Electronics Drafters**: $59,970 (median wage), $96,820 (90th percentile wage), 26,750 (number of positions), 6.7% (2016--2026 growth), Associate's degree (typical education requirement)

243. **Chemical Plant and System Operators**: $59,920 (median wage), $81,970 (90th percentile wage), 33,300 (number of positions), -9.2% (2016--2026 growth), High school diploma or equivalent (typical education requirement)

244. **Arbitrators, Mediators, and Conciliators**: $59,770 (median wage), $123,930 (90th percentile wage), 6,300 (number of positions), 11.3% (2016--2026 growth), Bachelor's degree (typical education requirement)

245. **Special Education Teachers, Secondary School**: $59,700 (median wage), $96,930 (90th percentile wage), 132,490 (number of positions), 7.4% (2016--2026 growth), Bachelor's degree (typical education requirement)

246. **Police and Sheriff's Patrol Officers**: $59,680 (median wage), $98,510 (90th percentile wage), 657,690 (number of positions), 7% (2016--2026 growth), High school diploma or equivalent (typical education requirement)

3 JOBS RANKED BY MEDIAN SALARY

247. **Criminal Justice and Law Enforcement Teachers**, Postsecondary: $59,590 (median wage), $105,210 (90th percentile wage), 14,620 (number of positions), 12.5% (2016--2026 growth), Doctoral or professional degree (typical education requirement)

248. **Stationary Engineers and Boiler Operators**: $59,400 (median wage), $93,300 (90th percentile wage), 33,720 (number of positions), 4.8% (2016--2026 growth), High school diploma or equivalent (typical education requirement)

249. **Surveyors**: $59,390 (median wage), $98,360 (90th percentile wage), 43,340 (number of positions), 11.2% (2016--2026 growth), Bachelor's degree (typical education requirement)

250. **Electrical and Electronics Installers and Repairers**, Transportation Equipment: $59,280 (median wage), $83,450 (90th percentile wage), 13,960 (number of positions), 2.9% (2016--2026 growth), Postsecondary nondegree award (typical education requirement)

251. **Human Resources Specialists**: $59,180 (median wage), $101,420 (90th percentile wage), 524,800 (number of positions), 7.1% (2016--2026 growth), Bachelor's degree (typical education requirement)

252. **Recreation and Fitness Studies Teachers**, Postsecondary: $59,180 (median wage), $119,830

(90th percentile wage), 17,390 (number of positions), 9.6% (2016--2026 growth), Doctoral or professional degree (typical education requirement)

253. **Training and Development Specialists**: $59,020 (median wage), $101,010 (90th percentile wage), 269,710 (number of positions), 11.5% (2016--2026 growth), Bachelor's degree (typical education requirement)

254. **Occupational Therapy Assistants**: $59,010 (median wage), $80,090 (90th percentile wage), 38,170 (number of positions), 28.9% (2016--2026 growth), Associate's degree (typical education requirement)

255. **Dietitians and Nutritionists**: $58,920 (median wage), $82,410 (90th percentile wage), 61,430 (number of positions), 14.1% (2016--2026 growth), Bachelor's degree (typical education requirement)

256. **Foresters**: $58,700 (median wage), $82,400 (90th percentile wage), 8,420 (number of positions), 5.2% (2016--2026 growth), Bachelor's degree (typical education requirement)

257. **Respiratory Therapists**: $58,670 (median wage), $81,550 (90th percentile wage), 126,770 (number of positions), 23.4% (2016--2026 growth), Associate's degree (typical education requirement)

258. **Special Education Teachers**, Middle School: $58,560 (median wage), $93,260 (90th percentile wage), 90,250 (number of positions), 7.1% (2016--2026 growth), Bachelor's degree (typical education requirement)

259. **Construction and Building Inspectors**: $58,480 (median wage), $94,220 (90th percentile wage), 94,960 (number of positions), 9.9% (2016--2026 growth), High school diploma or equivalent (typical education requirement)

260. **Fire Inspectors and Investigators**: $58,440 (median wage), $95,270 (90th percentile wage), 11,910 (number of positions), 7.3% (2016--2026 growth), Postsecondary nondegree award (typical education requirement)

261. **Buyers and Purchasing Agents**, Farm Products: $58,430 (median wage), $102,410 (90th percentile wage), 11,490 (number of positions), -5.9% (2016--2026 growth), Bachelor's degree (typical education requirement)

262. **Locomotive Firers**: $58,230 (median wage), $97,820 (90th percentile wage), 1,210 (number of positions), -78.6% (2016--2026 growth), High school diploma or equivalent (typical education requirement)

263. **Postal Service Mail Carriers**: $58,110 (median

wage), $61,100 (90th percentile wage), 328,950 (number of positions), -12.1% (2016--2026 growth), High school diploma or equivalent (typical education requirement)

264. **Secondary School Teachers, Except Special and Career/Technical Education**: $58,030 (median wage), $92,920 (90th percentile wage), 1,003,250 (number of positions), 7.5% (2016--2026 growth), Bachelor's degree (typical education requirement)

265. **Public Relations Specialists**: $58,020 (median wage), $110,560 (90th percentile wage), 226,940 (number of positions), 9% (2016--2026 growth), Bachelor's degree (typical education requirement)

266. **First-Line Supervisors of Production and Operating Workers**: $57,780 (median wage), $95,800 (90th percentile wage), 610,480 (number of positions), -0.1% (2016--2026 growth), High school diploma or equivalent (typical education requirement)

267. **Librarians**: $57,680 (median wage), $90,140 (90th percentile wage), 129,350 (number of positions), 8.9% (2016--2026 growth), Master's degree (typical education requirement)

268. **Locomotive Engineers**: $57,670 (median wage), $85,290 (90th percentile wage), 39,900 (number of positions), -2.8% (2016--2026 growth), High school

diploma or equivalent (typical educa requirement)

269. **Career/Technical Education Teachers**, Middle School: $57,560 (median wage), $87,980 (90th percentile wage), 12,730 (number of positions), 7.3% (2016--2026 growth), Bachelor's degree (typical education requirement)

270. **Railroad Conductors and Yardmasters**: $57,480 (median wage), $79,620 (90th percentile wage), 42,880 (number of positions), -2.1% (2016--2026 growth), High school diploma or equivalent (typical education requirement)

271. **Radiologic Technologists**: $57,450 (median wage), $82,590 (90th percentile wage), 200,650 (number of positions), 12.3% (2016--2026 growth), Associate's degree (typical education requirement)

272. **Career/Technical Education Teachers**, Secondary School: $57,320 (median wage), $86,570 (90th percentile wage), 80,100 (number of positions), 6.4% (2016--2026 growth), Bachelor's degree (typical education requirement)

273. **First-Line Supervisors of Transportation and Material-Moving Machine and Vehicle Operators**: $57,270 (median wage), $89,670 (90th percentile wage), 202,760 (number of positions), 6.6% (2016--2026 growth), High school diploma or equivalent

(typical education requirement)

274. **Editors**: $57,210 (median wage), $111,610 (90th percentile wage), 97,170 (number of positions), -0.1% (2016--2026 growth), Bachelor's degree (typical education requirement)

275. **Sales Representatives, Wholesale and Manufacturing, Except Technical and Scientific Products**: $57,140 (median wage), $121,080 (90th percentile wage), 1,404,050 (number of positions), 5.5% (2016--2026 growth), High school diploma or equivalent (typical education requirement)

276. **Special Education Teachers, Kindergarten and Elementary School**: $57,040 (median wage), $90,260 (90th percentile wage), 190,530 (number of positions), 7.4% (2016--2026 growth), Bachelor's degree (typical education requirement)

277. **Property, Real Estate, and Community Association Managers**: $57,040 (median wage), $126,390 (90th percentile wage), 180,290 (number of positions), 10.7% (2016--2026 growth), High school diploma or equivalent (typical education requirement)

278. **Real Estate Brokers**: $56,790 (median wage), $162,260 (90th percentile wage), 40,850 (number of positions), 5.4% (2016--2026 growth), High school diploma or equivalent (typical education

requirement)

279. **Postal Service Clerks**: $56,790 (median wage), $57,990 (90th percentile wage), 82,030 (number of positions), -12.1% (2016--2026 growth), High school diploma or equivalent (typical education requirement)

280. **Roof Bolters**, Mining: $56,780 (median wage), $76,640 (90th percentile wage), 3,930 (number of positions), -5.2% (2016--2026 growth), High school diploma or equivalent (typical education requirement)

281. **Forensic Science Technicians**: $56,750 (median wage), $97,400 (90th percentile wage), 14,800 (number of positions), 16.8% (2016--2026 growth), Bachelor's degree (typical education requirement)

282. **Middle School Teachers**, Except Special and Career/Technical Education: $56,720 (median wage), $89,120 (90th percentile wage), 626,310 (number of positions), 7.5% (2016--2026 growth), Bachelor's degree (typical education requirement)

283. **Therapists**, All Other: $56,700 (median wage), $95,530 (90th percentile wage), 11,320 (number of positions), 19.7% (2016--2026 growth), Bachelor's degree (typical education requirement)

284. **Broadcast News Analysts**: $56,680 (median wage),

$163,490 (90th percentile wage), 5,070 (number of positions), -1% (2016--2026 growth), Bachelor's degree (typical education requirement)

285. **Physical Therapist Assistants**: $56,610 (median wage), $79,040 (90th percentile wage), 85,580 (number of positions), 30.8% (2016--2026 growth), Associate's degree (typical education requirement)

286. **Railroad Brake, Signal, and Switch Operators**: $56,570 (median wage), $76,110 (90th percentile wage), 19,860 (number of positions), -1.6% (2016--2026 growth), High school diploma or equivalent (typical education requirement)

287. **Geological and Petroleum Technicians**: $56,470 (median wage), $103,080 (90th percentile wage), 15,100 (number of positions), 16.4% (2016--2026 growth), Associate's degree (typical education requirement)

288. **Mine Shuttle Car Operators**: $56,450 (median wage), $68,080 (90th percentile wage), 1,590 (number of positions), -21.9% (2016--2026 growth), No formal educational credential (typical education requirement)

289. **Electrical and Electronics Repairers**, Commercial and Industrial Equipment: $56,250 (median wage), $80,160 (90th percentile wage), 67,390 (number of positions), 2.4% (2016--2026 growth), Postsecondary

nondegree award (typical education requirement)

290. **Precision Instrument and Equipment Repairers**, All Other: $56,230 (median wage), $81,310 (90th percentile wage), 11,640 (number of positions), 2.9% (2016--2026 growth), High school diploma or equivalent (typical education requirement)

291. **Postal Service Mail Sorters**, Processors, and Processing Machine Operators: $56,220 (median wage), $57,300 (90th percentile wage), 110,770 (number of positions), -16.5% (2016--2026 growth), High school diploma or equivalent (typical education requirement)

292. **Executive Secretaries and Executive Administrative Assistants**: $55,860 (median wage), $83,070 (90th percentile wage), 631,610 (number of positions), -17.4% (2016--2026 growth), High school diploma or equivalent (typical education requirement)

293. **Elementary School Teachers**, Except Special Education: $55,800 (median wage), $88,590 (90th percentile wage), 1,392,660 (number of positions), 7.4% (2016--2026 growth), Bachelor's degree (typical education requirement)

294. **Electro-Mechanical Technicians**: $55,610 (median wage), $85,440 (90th percentile wage), 13,710 (number of positions), 3.5% (2016--2026 growth),

Associate's degree (typical education requirement)

295. **Cardiovascular Technologists and Technicians**: $55,570 (median wage), $89,450 (90th percentile wage), 53,760 (number of positions), 9.9% (2016--2026 growth), Associate's degree (typical education requirement)

296. **Historians**: $55,110 (median wage), $102,830 (90th percentile wage), 2,950 (number of positions), 5.4% (2016--2026 growth), Master's degree (typical education requirement)

297. **Camera Operators**, Television, Video, and Motion Picture: $55,080 (median wage), $109,200 (90th percentile wage), 21,710 (number of positions), 6.4% (2016--2026 growth), Bachelor's degree (typical education requirement)

298. **Pile-Driver Operators**: $55,070 (median wage), $98,840 (90th percentile wage), 3,570 (number of positions), 14.7% (2016--2026 growth), High school diploma or equivalent (typical education requirement)

299. **Rail Car Repairers**: $55,000 (median wage), $76,220 (90th percentile wage), 22,090 (number of positions), 5.1% (2016--2026 growth), High school diploma or equivalent (typical education requirement)

300. **Plant and System Operators**, All Other: $54,930 (median wage), $78,630 (90th percentile wage), 11,970 (number of positions), 1.9% (2016--2026 growth), High school diploma or equivalent (typical education requirement)

301. **Legal Support Workers**, All Other: $54,650 (median wage), $127,650 (90th percentile wage), 44,960 (number of positions), 3.6% (2016--2026 growth), Associate's degree (typical education requirement)

302. **Educational, Guidance, School, and Vocational Counselors**: $54,560 (median wage), $90,030 (90th percentile wage), 260,670 (number of positions), 11.3% (2016--2026 growth), Master's degree (typical education requirement)

303. **Control and Valve Installers and Repairers**, Except Mechanical Door: $54,520 (median wage), $86,420 (90th percentile wage), 45,740 (number of positions), 5% (2016--2026 growth), High school diploma or equivalent (typical education requirement)

304. **Mechanical Drafters**: $54,480 (median wage), $85,920 (90th percentile wage), 63,630 (number of positions), 5.1% (2016--2026 growth), Associate's degree (typical education requirement)

305. **Mechanical Engineering Technicians**: $54,480

(median wage), $82,810 (90th percentile wage), 45,510 (number of positions), 5% (2016--2026 growth), Associate's degree (typical education requirement)

306. **Survey Researchers**: $54,470 (median wage), $100,250 (90th percentile wage), 11,930 (number of positions), 0.9% (2016--2026 growth), Master's degree (typical education requirement)

307. **Rotary Drill Operators**, Oil and Gas: $54,430 (median wage), $87,170 (90th percentile wage), 17,400 (number of positions), 24.2% (2016--2026 growth), No formal educational credential (typical education requirement)

308. **First-Line Supervisors of Office and Administrative Support Workers**: $54,340 (median wage), $87,690 (90th percentile wage), 1,443,150 (number of positions), 3.4% (2016--2026 growth), High school diploma or equivalent (typical education requirement)

309. **Fundraisers**: $54,130 (median wage), $91,530 (90th percentile wage), 68,910 (number of positions), 14.6% (2016--2026 growth), Bachelor's degree (typical education requirement)

310. **Rail-Track Laying and Maintenance Equipment Operators**: $53,970 (median wage), $72,810 (90th percentile wage), 14,250 (number of positions), 8.6%

(2016--2026 growth), High school diploma or equivalent (typical education requirement)

311. **Special Education Teachers**, All Other: $53,860 (median wage), $93,620 (90th percentile wage), 40,190 (number of positions), 9.8% (2016--2026 growth), Bachelor's degree (typical education requirement)

312. **Healthcare Social Workers**: $53,760 (median wage), $80,020 (90th percentile wage), 159,310 (number of positions), 18.5% (2016--2026 growth), Master's degree (typical education requirement)

313. **Sound Engineering Technicians**: $53,680 (median wage), $121,630 (90th percentile wage), 15,210 (number of positions), 6.3% (2016--2026 growth), Postsecondary nondegree award (typical education requirement)

314. **Telecommunications Equipment Installers and Repairers**, Except Line Installers: $53,640 (median wage), $79,500 (90th percentile wage), 228,430 (number of positions), -7.6% (2016--2026 growth), Postsecondary nondegree award (typical education requirement)

315. **Loading Machine Operators**, Underground Mining: $53,420 (median wage), $67,100 (90th percentile wage), 2,550 (number of positions), -3.2% (2016--2026 growth), No formal educational

credential (typical education requirement)

316. **Designers**, All Other: $53,380 (median wage), $116,250 (90th percentile wage), 7,230 (number of positions), 6.4% (2016--2026 growth), Bachelor's degree (typical education requirement)

317. **Curators**: $53,360 (median wage), $94,430 (90th percentile wage), 11,170 (number of positions), 14% (2016--2026 growth), Master's degree (typical education requirement)

318. **Wholesale and Retail Buyers**, Except Farm Products: $53,340 (median wage), $97,830 (90th percentile wage), 109,440 (number of positions), -1.9% (2016--2026 growth), Bachelor's degree (typical education requirement)

319. **Industrial Engineering Technicians**: $53,330 (median wage), $86,430 (90th percentile wage), 63,220 (number of positions), 0.6% (2016--2026 growth), Associate's degree (typical education requirement)

320. **Health Educators**: $53,070 (median wage), $95,730 (90th percentile wage), 57,570 (number of positions), 14.5% (2016--2026 growth), Bachelor's degree (typical education requirement)

321. **Electricians**: $52,720 (median wage), $90,420 (90th percentile wage), 607,120 (number of positions), 9%

(2016--2026 growth), High school diploma or equivalent (typical education requirement)

322. **Kindergarten Teachers**, Except Special Education: $52,620 (median wage), $81,210 (90th percentile wage), 151,290 (number of positions), 7.9% (2016--2026 growth), Bachelor's degree (typical education requirement)

323. **Telecommunications Line Installers and Repairers**: $52,590 (median wage), $83,260 (90th percentile wage), 100,080 (number of positions), 1.6% (2016--2026 growth), High school diploma or equivalent (typical education requirement)

324. **Sales Representatives, Services**, All Other: $52,490 (median wage), $113,950 (90th percentile wage), 953,870 (number of positions), 9.6% (2016--2026 growth), High school diploma or equivalent (typical education requirement)

325. **Radio, Cellular, and Tower Equipment Installers and Repairers**: $52,480 (median wage), $78,930 (90th percentile wage), 14,120 (number of positions), 5.5% (2016--2026 growth), Associate's degree (typical education requirement)

326. **Special Education Teachers**, Preschool: $52,460 (median wage), $89,290 (90th percentile wage), 28,140 (number of positions), 11.2% (2016--2026 growth), Bachelor's degree (typical education

requirement)

327. **Millwrights**: $52,440 (median wage), $78,390 (90th percentile wage), 39,670 (number of positions), 9.8% (2016--2026 growth), High school diploma or equivalent (typical education requirement)

328. **Musicians and Singers**: $52,291 (median wage), $141,710 (90th percentile wage), 40,110 (number of positions), 6.6% (2016--2026 growth), No formal educational credential (typical education requirement)

329. **Wind Turbine Service Technicians**: $52,260 (median wage), $76,250 (90th percentile wage), 4,580 (number of positions), 96.1% (2016--2026 growth), Postsecondary nondegree award (typical education requirement)

330. **Explosives Workers**, Ordnance Handling Experts, and Blasters: $52,170 (median wage), $78,660 (90th percentile wage), 6,310 (number of positions), 7.1% (2016--2026 growth), High school diploma or equivalent (typical education requirement)

331. **Crane and Tower Operators**: $52,170 (median wage), $82,600 (90th percentile wage), 45,020 (number of positions), 8.6% (2016--2026 growth), High school diploma or equivalent (typical education requirement)

332. **Tax Examiners and Collectors**, and Revenue Agents: $52,060 (median wage), $97,440 (90th percentile wage), 58,450 (number of positions), -0.6% (2016--2026 growth), Bachelor's degree (typical education requirement)

333. **Mine Cutting and Channeling Machine Operators**: $51,900 (median wage), $73,280 (90th percentile wage), 5,930 (number of positions), -4.7% (2016--2026 growth), High school diploma or equivalent (typical education requirement)

334. **Appraisers and Assessors of Real Estate**: $51,850 (median wage), $97,120 (90th percentile wage), 60,770 (number of positions), 14.4% (2016--2026 growth), Bachelor's degree (typical education requirement)

335. **Lodging Managers**: $51,840 (median wage), $96,570 (90th percentile wage), 35,410 (number of positions), 5.9% (2016--2026 growth), High school diploma or equivalent (typical education requirement)

336. **Continuous Mining Machine Operators**: $51,840 (median wage), $74,240 (90th percentile wage), 12,030 (number of positions), -3.9% (2016--2026 growth), No formal educational credential (typical education requirement)

337. **Structural Iron and Steel Workers**: $51,800

(median wage), $91,830 (90th percentile wage), 69,440 (number of positions), 12.8% (2016--2026 growth), High school diploma or equivalent (typical education requirement)

338. **Judicial Law Clerks**: $51,760 (median wage), $106,640 (90th percentile wage), 13,410 (number of positions), 5.5% (2016--2026 growth), Doctoral or professional degree (typical education requirement)

339. **Fish and Game Wardens**: $51,730 (median wage), $77,440 (90th percentile wage), 6,610 (number of positions), 4.3% (2016--2026 growth), Bachelor's degree (typical education requirement)

340. **Architectural and Civil Drafters**: $51,640 (median wage), $78,770 (90th percentile wage), 96,810 (number of positions), 8.1% (2016--2026 growth), Associate's degree (typical education requirement)

341. **Plumbers, Pipefitters, and Steamfitters**: $51,450 (median wage), $90,530 (90th percentile wage), 411,870 (number of positions), 15.8% (2016--2026 growth), High school diploma or equivalent (typical education requirement)

342. **Court Reporters**: $51,320 (median wage), $95,990 (90th percentile wage), 17,700 (number of positions), 3.3% (2016--2026 growth), Postsecondary nondegree award (typical education requirement)

3 JOBS RANKED BY MEDIAN SALARY

343. **Tool and Die Makers**: $51,060 (median wage), $74,230 (90th percentile wage), 72,210 (number of positions), -7.3% (2016--2026 growth), Postsecondary nondegree award (typical education requirement)

344. **Set and Exhibit Designers**: $50,990 (median wage), $97,320 (90th percentile wage), 12,060 (number of positions), 10.9% (2016--2026 growth), Bachelor's degree (typical education requirement)

345. **Food Service Managers**: $50,820 (median wage), $87,120 (90th percentile wage), 201,470 (number of positions), 8.8% (2016--2026 growth), High school diploma or equivalent (typical education requirement)

346. **Fine Artists**, Including Painters, Sculptors, and Illustrators: $50,790 (median wage), $103,680 (90th percentile wage), 11,520 (number of positions), 8.6% (2016--2026 growth), Bachelor's degree (typical education requirement)

347. **Vocational Education Teachers**, Postsecondary: $50,660 (median wage), $90,320 (90th percentile wage), 116,430 (number of positions), 1.3% (2016--2026 growth), Bachelor's degree (typical education requirement)

348. **Adult Basic and Secondary Education and Literacy Teachers and Instructors**: $50,650 (median wage), $84,740 (90th percentile wage), 58,810

(number of positions), -5.6% (2016--2026 growth), Bachelor's degree (typical education requirement)

349. **Computer Numerically Controlled Machine Tool Programmers**, Metal and Plastic: $50,580 (median wage), $78,760 (90th percentile wage), 25,180 (number of positions), 16.3% (2016--2026 growth), Postsecondary nondegree award (typical education requirement)

350. **Gaming Supervisors**: $50,520 (median wage), $74,660 (90th percentile wage), 22,130 (number of positions), 3.5% (2016--2026 growth), High school diploma or equivalent (typical education requirement)

351. **Archivists**: $50,500 (median wage), $88,160 (90th percentile wage), 5,760 (number of positions), 14.3% (2016--2026 growth), Master's degree (typical education requirement)

352. **Rail Yard Engineers, Dinkey Operators, and Hostlers**: $50,470 (median wage), $87,770 (90th percentile wage), 4,530 (number of positions), 3.7% (2016--2026 growth), High school diploma or equivalent (typical education requirement)

353. **Drafters**, All Other: $50,470 (median wage), $82,680 (90th percentile wage), 15,530 (number of positions), 7.9% (2016--2026 growth), Associate's degree (typical education requirement)

354. **Advertising Sales Agents**: $50,380 (median wage), $115,430 (90th percentile wage), 141,100 (number of positions), -2.9% (2016--2026 growth), High school diploma or equivalent (typical education requirement)

355. **Hearing Aid Specialists**: $50,250 (median wage), $80,940 (90th percentile wage), 6,740 (number of positions), 19.2% (2016--2026 growth), High school diploma or equivalent (typical education requirement)

356. **Probation Officers and Correctional Treatment Specialists**: $50,160 (median wage), $88,930 (90th percentile wage), 87,500 (number of positions), 5.7% (2016--2026 growth), Bachelor's degree (typical education requirement)

357. **Music Directors and Composers**: $50,110 (median wage), $106,700 (90th percentile wage), 18,380 (number of positions), 6.1% (2016--2026 growth), Bachelor's degree (typical education requirement)

358. **Morticians, Undertakers, and Funeral Directors**: $50,090 (median wage), $83,980 (90th percentile wage), 25,850 (number of positions), 4.6% (2016--2026 growth), Associate's degree (typical education requirement)

359. **Aircraft Structure, Surfaces, Rigging, and Systems Assemblers**: $50,050 (median wage),

$78,150 (90th percentile wage), 42,010 (number of positions), -17.4% (2016--2026 growth), High school diploma or equivalent (typical education requirement)

360. **Industrial Machinery Mechanics**: $50,040 (median wage), $76,110 (90th percentile wage), 334,490 (number of positions), 6.8% (2016--2026 growth), High school diploma or equivalent (typical education requirement)

361. **Insurance Sales Agents**: $49,990 (median wage), $128,070 (90th percentile wage), 385,700 (number of positions), 9.7% (2016--2026 growth), High school diploma or equivalent (typical education requirement)

362. **Civil Engineering Technicians**: $49,980 (median wage), $77,500 (90th percentile wage), 72,150 (number of positions), 8.8% (2016--2026 growth), Associate's degree (typical education requirement)

363. **Interior Designers**: $49,810 (median wage), $91,230 (90th percentile wage), 53,160 (number of positions), 4.9% (2016--2026 growth), Bachelor's degree (typical education requirement)

364. **Respiratory Therapy Technicians**: $49,780 (median wage), $72,970 (90th percentile wage), 10,600 (number of positions), -56.3% (2016--2026 growth), Associate's degree (typical education

requirement)

365. **Mathematical Technicians**: $49,660 (median wage), $100,730 (90th percentile wage), 510 (number of positions), 7.5% (2016--2026 growth), Bachelor's degree (typical education requirement)

366. **Wellhead Pumpers**: $49,610 (median wage), $75,610 (90th percentile wage), 11,610 (number of positions), 21.7% (2016--2026 growth), High school diploma or equivalent (typical education requirement)

367. **Paralegals and Legal Assistants**: $49,500 (median wage), $80,260 (90th percentile wage), 277,310 (number of positions), 14.6% (2016--2026 growth), Associate's degree (typical education requirement)

368. **Farm and Home Management Advisors**: $49,490 (median wage), $80,900 (90th percentile wage), 8,620 (number of positions), 7.3% (2016--2026 growth), Master's degree (typical education requirement)

369. **Computer User Support Specialists**: $49,390 (median wage), $82,160 (90th percentile wage), 602,840 (number of positions), 11.2% (2016--2026 growth), Some college, no degree (typical education requirement)

370. **Mobile Heavy Equipment Mechanics**, Except Engines: $49,370 (median wage), $72,740 (90th

percentile wage), 123,570 (number of positions), 8.2% (2016--2026 growth), High school diploma or equivalent (typical education requirement)

371. **Brickmasons and Blockmasons**: $49,250 (median wage), $84,100 (90th percentile wage), 64,370 (number of positions), 10.6% (2016--2026 growth), High school diploma or equivalent (typical education requirement)

372. **Brokerage Clerks**: $49,200 (median wage), $76,390 (90th percentile wage), 59,820 (number of positions), 5% (2016--2026 growth), High school diploma or equivalent (typical education requirement)

373. **Environmental Engineering Technicians**: $49,170 (median wage), $80,780 (90th percentile wage), 16,550 (number of positions), 12.9% (2016--2026 growth), Associate's degree (typical education requirement)

374. **Marriage and Family Therapists**: $49,170 (median wage), $81,960 (90th percentile wage), 36,960 (number of positions), 20.2% (2016--2026 growth), Master's degree (typical education requirement)

375. **Commercial Divers**: $49,090 (median wage), $83,730 (90th percentile wage), 3,370 (number of positions), 10.6% (2016--2026 growth), Postsecondary nondegree award (typical education requirement)

3 JOBS RANKED BY MEDIAN SALARY

376. **Bridge and Lock Tenders**: $49,090 (median wage), $61,740 (90th percentile wage), 3,510 (number of positions), 4.9% (2016--2026 growth), High school diploma or equivalent (typical education requirement)

377. **Tapers**: $48,990 (median wage), $90,260 (90th percentile wage), 18,480 (number of positions), 0.6% (2016--2026 growth), No formal educational credential (typical education requirement)

378. **Airfield Operations Specialists**: $48,910 (median wage), $90,350 (90th percentile wage), 8,760 (number of positions), 8.8% (2016--2026 growth), High school diploma or equivalent (typical education requirement)

379. **Healthcare Practitioners and Technical Workers**, All Other: $48,820 (median wage), $104,050 (90th percentile wage), 36,000 (number of positions), 12.1% (2016--2026 growth), Postsecondary nondegree award (typical education requirement)

380. **Occupational Health and Safety Technicians**: $48,820 (median wage), $79,990 (90th percentile wage), 16,560 (number of positions), 9.5% (2016--2026 growth), High school diploma or equivalent (typical education requirement)

381. **Extraction Workers**, All Other: $48,750 (median wage), $74,700 (90th percentile wage), 4,320 (number

of positions), 15.9% (2016--2026 growth), High school diploma or equivalent (typical education requirement)

382. **Service Unit Operators**, Oil, Gas, and Mining: $48,610 (median wage), $79,770 (90th percentile wage), 42,890 (number of positions), 23.4% (2016--2026 growth), No formal educational credential (typical education requirement)

383. **Model Makers**, Metal and Plastic: $48,550 (median wage), $78,010 (90th percentile wage), 6,250 (number of positions), -12.2% (2016--2026 growth), High school diploma or equivalent (typical education requirement)

384. **Flight Attendants**: $48,500 (median wage), $78,650 (90th percentile wage), 113,390 (number of positions), 10.2% (2016--2026 growth), High school diploma or equivalent (typical education requirement)

385. **Choreographers**: $48,240 (median wage), $94,400 (90th percentile wage), 5,160 (number of positions), 3.2% (2016--2026 growth), High school diploma or equivalent (typical education requirement)

386. **Private Detectives and Investigators**: $48,190 (median wage), $87,070 (90th percentile wage), 28,490 (number of positions), 10.5% (2016--2026 growth), High school diploma or equivalent (typical

education requirement)

387. **Derrick Operators**, Oil and Gas: $48,130 (median wage), $75,520 (90th percentile wage), 11,580 (number of positions), 25.7% (2016--2026 growth), No formal educational credential (typical education requirement)

388. **Medical Equipment Repairers**: $48,070 (median wage), $78,520 (90th percentile wage), 43,370 (number of positions), 5.3% (2016--2026 growth), Associate's degree (typical education requirement)

389. **Firefighters**: $48,030 (median wage), $81,110 (90th percentile wage), 315,910 (number of positions), 7.2% (2016--2026 growth), Postsecondary nondegree award (typical education requirement)

390. **Mining Machine Operators**, All Other: $48,010 (median wage), $73,920 (90th percentile wage), 2,160 (number of positions), 0.1% (2016--2026 growth), High school diploma or equivalent (typical education requirement)

391. **Audio-Visual and Multimedia Collections Specialists**: $47,840 (median wage), $78,090 (90th percentile wage), 10,300 (number of positions), 8.7% (2016--2026 growth), Bachelor's degree (typical education requirement)

392. **First-Line Supervisors of Protective Service**

Workers, All Other: $47,820 (median wage), $78,740 (90th percentile wage), 72,880 (number of positions), 4.6% (2016--2026 growth), High school diploma or equivalent (typical education requirement)

393. **Chemical Equipment Operators and Tenders**: $47,780 (median wage), $77,640 (90th percentile wage), 73,840 (number of positions), -4.9% (2016--2026 growth), High school diploma or equivalent (typical education requirement)

394. **Athletes and Sports Competitors**: $47,710 (median wage), $79,676 (90th percentile wage), 10,260 (number of positions), 7.2% (2016--2026 growth), No formal educational credential (typical education requirement)

395. **Graphic Designers**: $47,640 (median wage), $82,020 (90th percentile wage), 210,710 (number of positions), 4.7% (2016--2026 growth), Bachelor's degree (typical education requirement)

396. **Reinforcing Iron and Rebar Workers**: $47,600 (median wage), $89,980 (90th percentile wage), 20,020 (number of positions), 12.1% (2016--2026 growth), High school diploma or equivalent (typical education requirement)

397. **Aircraft Cargo Handling Supervisors**: $47,360 (median wage), $81,620 (90th percentile wage), 7,460 (number of positions), 5.9% (2016--2026 growth),

High school diploma or equivalent (typical education requirement)

398. **Meeting, Convention, and Event Planners**: $47,350 (median wage), $83,030 (90th percentile wage), 95,850 (number of positions), 10.2% (2016--2026 growth), Bachelor's degree (typical education requirement)

399. **Exercise Physiologists**: $47,340 (median wage), $74,330 (90th percentile wage), 6,880 (number of positions), 12.9% (2016--2026 growth), Bachelor's degree (typical education requirement)

400. **First-Line Supervisors of Helpers**, Laborers, and Material Movers, Hand: $47,230 (median wage), $77,060 (90th percentile wage), 183,620 (number of positions), 8.5% (2016--2026 growth), High school diploma or equivalent (typical education requirement)

401. **Sheet Metal Workers**: $46,940 (median wage), $85,340 (90th percentile wage), 134,450 (number of positions), 8.7% (2016--2026 growth), High school diploma or equivalent (typical education requirement)

402. **Statistical Assistants**: $46,850 (median wage), $69,480 (90th percentile wage), 10,900 (number of positions), 9.2% (2016--2026 growth), Bachelor's degree (typical education requirement)

403. **Production, Planning, and Expediting Clerks**: $46,760 (median wage), $74,340 (90th percentile wage), 321,780 (number of positions), 5.4% (2016--2026 growth), High school diploma or equivalent (typical education requirement)

404. **Patternmakers, Wood**: $46,510 (median wage), $72,950 (90th percentile wage), 970 (number of positions), 3.9% (2016--2026 growth), High school diploma or equivalent (typical education requirement)

405. **Recreational Therapists**: $46,410 (median wage), $72,340 (90th percentile wage), 18,100 (number of positions), 6.5% (2016--2026 growth), Bachelor's degree (typical education requirement)

406. **Radio Operators**: $46,250 (median wage), $73,930 (90th percentile wage), 870 (number of positions), -1% (2016--2026 growth), High school diploma or equivalent (typical education requirement)

407. **Interpreters and Translators**: $46,120 (median wage), $83,010 (90th percentile wage), 51,350 (number of positions), 16.7% (2016--2026 growth), Bachelor's degree (typical education requirement)

408. **Life, Physical, and Social Science Technicians**, All Other: $46,040 (median wage), $77,010 (90th percentile wage), 68,540 (number of positions), 9.6% (2016--2026 growth), Associate's degree (typical

education requirement)

409. **Heating, Air Conditioning, and Refrigeration Mechanics and Installers**: $45,910 (median wage), $73,350 (90th percentile wage), 294,730 (number of positions), 14.7% (2016--2026 growth), Postsecondary nondegree award (typical education requirement)

410. **Costume Attendants**: $45,900 (median wage), $87,310 (90th percentile wage), 6,640 (number of positions), 9.7% (2016--2026 growth), High school diploma or equivalent (typical education requirement)

411. **Operating Engineers and Other Construction Equipment Operators**: $45,890 (median wage), $80,200 (90th percentile wage), 356,750 (number of positions), 12.4% (2016--2026 growth), High school diploma or equivalent (typical education requirement)

412. **Chemical Technicians**: $45,840 (median wage), $76,930 (90th percentile wage), 65,510 (number of positions), 3.9% (2016--2026 growth), Associate's degree (typical education requirement)

413. **Layout Workers**, Metal and Plastic: $45,820 (median wage), $66,010 (90th percentile wage), 9,070 (number of positions), -6.8% (2016--2026 growth), High school diploma or equivalent (typical education requirement)

414. **Title Examiners, Abstractors, and Searchers:** $45,800 (median wage), $81,800 (90th percentile wage), 54,560 (number of positions), 4% (2016--2026 growth), High school diploma or equivalent (typical education requirement)

415. **Education Administrators,** Preschool and Childcare Center/Program: $45,790 (median wage), $82,790 (90th percentile wage), 48,530 (number of positions), 10.6% (2016--2026 growth), Bachelor's degree (typical education requirement)

416. **Water and Wastewater Treatment Plant and System Operators:** $45,760 (median wage), $73,120 (90th percentile wage), 115,840 (number of positions), -3.2% (2016--2026 growth), High school diploma or equivalent (typical education requirement)

417. **Clergy:** $45,740 (median wage), $79,110 (90th percentile wage), 49,320 (number of positions), 8% (2016--2026 growth), Bachelor's degree (typical education requirement)

418. **First-Line Supervisors of Landscaping, Lawn Service, and Groundskeeping Workers:** $45,740 (median wage), $75,060 (90th percentile wage), 103,070 (number of positions), 9.6% (2016--2026 growth), High school diploma or equivalent (typical education requirement)

419. **Riggers**: $45,690 (median wage), $74,750 (90th percentile wage), 21,020 (number of positions), 9.8% (2016--2026 growth), High school diploma or equivalent (typical education requirement)

420. **Athletic Trainers**: $45,630 (median wage), $69,140 (90th percentile wage), 24,130 (number of positions), 22.2% (2016--2026 growth), Bachelor's degree (typical education requirement)

421. **Insulation Workers**, Mechanical: $45,430 (median wage), $84,230 (90th percentile wage), 27,270 (number of positions), 9.7% (2016--2026 growth), High school diploma or equivalent (typical education requirement)

422. **First-Line Supervisors of Farming, Fishing, and Forestry Workers**: $45,320 (median wage), $76,270 (90th percentile wage), 19,550 (number of positions), 4.6% (2016--2026 growth), High school diploma or equivalent (typical education requirement)

423. **Refractory Materials Repairers, Except Brickmasons**: $45,230 (median wage), $66,710 (90th percentile wage), 1,540 (number of positions), -3.5% (2016--2026 growth), High school diploma or equivalent (typical education requirement)

424. **Bus and Truck Mechanics and Diesel Engine Specialists**: $45,170 (median wage), $67,550 (90th percentile wage), 254,280 (number of positions), 9.5%

(2016--2026 growth), High school diploma or equivalent (typical education requirement)

425. **Surgical Technologists**: $45,160 (median wage), $64,800 (90th percentile wage), 105,720 (number of positions), 11.7% (2016--2026 growth), Postsecondary nondegree award (typical education requirement)

426. **Traffic Technicians**: $45,150 (median wage), $76,720 (90th percentile wage), 6,410 (number of positions), 9.1% (2016--2026 growth), High school diploma or equivalent (typical education requirement)

427. **Maintenance Workers**, Machinery: $44,550 (median wage), $66,240 (90th percentile wage), 89,630 (number of positions), 5.6% (2016--2026 growth), High school diploma or equivalent (typical education requirement)

428. **Credit Counselors**: $44,380 (median wage), $75,220 (90th percentile wage), 34,110 (number of positions), 13.9% (2016--2026 growth), Bachelor's degree (typical education requirement)

429. **Earth Drillers**, Except Oil and Gas: $44,360 (median wage), $75,880 (90th percentile wage), 18,500 (number of positions), 19.7% (2016--2026 growth), High school diploma or equivalent (typical education requirement)

430. **Counselors**, All Other: $44,350 (median wage), $74,810 (90th percentile wage), 28,380 (number of positions), 14.3% (2016--2026 growth), Master's degree (typical education requirement)

431. **Security and Fire Alarm Systems Installers**: $44,330 (median wage), $65,470 (90th percentile wage), 67,700 (number of positions), 14.4% (2016--2026 growth), High school diploma or equivalent (typical education requirement)

432. **Patternmakers**, Metal and Plastic: $44,210 (median wage), $62,590 (90th percentile wage), 3,420 (number of positions), -15.5% (2016--2026 growth), High school diploma or equivalent (typical education requirement)

433. **Environmental Science and Protection Technicians**, Including Health: $44,190 (median wage), $75,980 (90th percentile wage), 32,950 (number of positions), 11.9% (2016--2026 growth), Associate's degree (typical education requirement)

434. **Legal Secretaries**: $44,180 (median wage), $75,530 (90th percentile wage), 191,200 (number of positions), -19.1% (2016--2026 growth), High school diploma or equivalent (typical education requirement)

435. **Real Estate Sales Agents**: $44,090 (median wage), $112,570 (90th percentile wage), 151,840 (number of

positions), 6.2% (2016--2026 growth), High school diploma or equivalent (typical education requirement)

436. **Licensed Practical and Licensed Vocational Nurses**: $44,090 (median wage), $60,420 (90th percentile wage), 702,400 (number of positions), 12.2% (2016--2026 growth), Postsecondary nondegree award (typical education requirement)

437. **Media and Communication Workers**, All Other: $43,600 (median wage), $91,820 (90th percentile wage), 23,310 (number of positions), 8.7% (2016--2026 growth), High school diploma or equivalent (typical education requirement)

438. **Carpenters**: $43,600 (median wage), $79,480 (90th percentile wage), 676,980 (number of positions), 8.5% (2016--2026 growth), High school diploma or equivalent (typical education requirement)

439. **Eligibility Interviewers**, Government Programs: $43,350 (median wage), $58,810 (90th percentile wage), 135,940 (number of positions), 6% (2016--2026 growth), High school diploma or equivalent (typical education requirement)

440. **Child, Family, and School Social Workers**: $43,250 (median wage), $75,140 (90th percentile wage), 298,840 (number of positions), 13.3% (2016--2026 growth), Bachelor's degree (typical education

requirement)

441. **Social Science Research Assistants**: $43,190 (median wage), $74,900 (90th percentile wage), 30,030 (number of positions), 4.1% (2016--2026 growth), Bachelor's degree (typical education requirement)

442. **Chefs and Head Cooks**: $43,180 (median wage), $76,280 (90th percentile wage), 134,190 (number of positions), 9.6% (2016--2026 growth), High school diploma or equivalent (typical education requirement)

443. **Community and Social Service Specialists**, All Other: $43,120 (median wage), $71,040 (90th percentile wage), 91,860 (number of positions), 13.2% (2016--2026 growth), Bachelor's degree (typical education requirement)

444. **Mental Health Counselors**: $42,840 (median wage), $70,100 (90th percentile wage), 139,820 (number of positions), 19.8% (2016--2026 growth), Master's degree (typical education requirement)

445. **Correctional Officers and Jailers**: $42,820 (median wage), $74,630 (90th percentile wage), 431,600 (number of positions), -7.7% (2016--2026 growth), High school diploma or equivalent (typical education requirement)

446. **Agricultural Inspectors**: $42,800 (median wage), $63,840 (90th percentile wage), 14,710 (number of positions), 4.6% (2016--2026 growth), Bachelor's degree (typical education requirement)

447. **Mental Health and Substance Abuse Social Workers**: $42,700 (median wage), $74,650 (90th percentile wage), 114,040 (number of positions), 17.9% (2016--2026 growth), Master's degree (typical education requirement)

448. **Bailiffs**: $42,670 (median wage), $74,300 (90th percentile wage), 17,880 (number of positions), -2.1% (2016--2026 growth), High school diploma or equivalent (typical education requirement)

449. **Education, Training, and Library Workers, All Other**: $42,600 (median wage), $78,270 (90th percentile wage), 100,640 (number of positions), 10.5% (2016--2026 growth), Bachelor's degree (typical education requirement)

450. **Hoist and Winch Operators**: $42,530 (median wage), $91,330 (90th percentile wage), 2,960 (number of positions), -0.7% (2016--2026 growth), No formal educational credential (typical education requirement)

451. **Biological Technicians**: $42,520 (median wage), $69,590 (90th percentile wage), 74,720 (number of positions), 10.2% (2016--2026 growth), Bachelor's

degree (typical education requirement)

452. **Pump Operators**, Except Wellhead Pumpers: $42,470 (median wage), $73,750 (90th percentile wage), 12,030 (number of positions), 13.8% (2016--2026 growth), High school diploma or equivalent (typical education requirement)

453. **Surveying and Mapping Technicians**: $42,450 (median wage), $70,280 (90th percentile wage), 53,920 (number of positions), 10.6% (2016--2026 growth), High school diploma or equivalent (typical education requirement)

454. **Dredge Operators**: $42,420 (median wage), $70,510 (90th percentile wage), 1,760 (number of positions), 5.3% (2016--2026 growth), High school diploma or equivalent (typical education requirement)

455. **Payroll and Timekeeping Clerks**: $42,390 (median wage), $62,030 (90th percentile wage), 159,650 (number of positions), -0.9% (2016--2026 growth), High school diploma or equivalent (typical education requirement)

456. **Computer Operators**: $42,270 (median wage), $63,430 (90th percentile wage), 46,810 (number of positions), -22.9% (2016--2026 growth), High school diploma or equivalent (typical education requirement)

457. **Audio and Video Equipment Technicians:** $42,230 (median wage), $78,980 (90th percentile wage), 69,670 (number of positions), 12.9% (2016--2026 growth), Postsecondary nondegree award (typical education requirement)

458. **Painters, Transportation Equipment:** $42,150 (median wage), $70,580 (90th percentile wage), 54,860 (number of positions), 6.9% (2016--2026 growth), High school diploma or equivalent (typical education requirement)

459. **Sailors and Marine Oilers:** $42,060 (median wage), $72,100 (90th percentile wage), 32,530 (number of positions), 7.6% (2016--2026 growth), No formal educational credential (typical education requirement)

460. **Glaziers:** $41,920 (median wage), $81,050 (90th percentile wage), 47,140 (number of positions), 10.6% (2016--2026 growth), High school diploma or equivalent (typical education requirement)

461. **Cargo and Freight Agents:** $41,920 (median wage), $64,340 (90th percentile wage), 88,920 (number of positions), 10.4% (2016--2026 growth), High school diploma or equivalent (typical education requirement)

462. **Machinists:** $41,700 (median wage), $62,590 (90th percentile wage), 391,120 (number of positions), 2.1%

(2016--2026 growth), High school diploma or equivalent (typical education requirement)

463. **Tire Builders**: $41,680 (median wage), $60,690 (90th percentile wage), 22,280 (number of positions), -12.1% (2016--2026 growth), High school diploma or equivalent (typical education requirement)

464. **Electric Motor, Power Tool, and Related Repairers**: $41,570 (median wage), $71,260 (90th percentile wage), 17,050 (number of positions), 7% (2016--2026 growth), High school diploma or equivalent (typical education requirement)

465. **Automotive Body and Related Repairers**: $41,540 (median wage), $70,620 (90th percentile wage), 143,940 (number of positions), 8.7% (2016--2026 growth), High school diploma or equivalent (typical education requirement)

466. **Procurement Clerks**: $41,410 (median wage), $58,110 (90th percentile wage), 72,120 (number of positions), -4.2% (2016--2026 growth), High school diploma or equivalent (typical education requirement)

467. **Heavy and Tractor-Trailer Truck Drivers**: $41,340 (median wage), $63,140 (90th percentile wage), 1,704,520 (number of positions), 6.1% (2016--2026 growth), Postsecondary nondegree award (typical education requirement)

468. **Engine and Other Machine Assemblers**: $41,210 (median wage), $61,800 (90th percentile wage), 38,150 (number of positions), -17.2% (2016--2026 growth), High school diploma or equivalent (typical education requirement)

469. **Drywall and Ceiling Tile Installers**: $41,090 (median wage), $79,660 (90th percentile wage), 93,180 (number of positions), 1.2% (2016--2026 growth), No formal educational credential (typical education requirement)

470. **Desktop Publishers**: $41,090 (median wage), $70,290 (90th percentile wage), 13,090 (number of positions), -13.9% (2016--2026 growth), Associate's degree (typical education requirement)

471. **Health Technologists and Technicians**, All Other: $41,070 (median wage), $71,280 (90th percentile wage), 122,170 (number of positions), 19.4% (2016--2026 growth), Postsecondary nondegree award (typical education requirement)

472. **Substance Abuse and Behavioral Disorder Counselors**: $41,070 (median wage), $65,080 (90th percentile wage), 91,040 (number of positions), 19.9% (2016--2026 growth), Bachelor's degree (typical education requirement)

473. **Camera and Photographic Equipment Repairers**: $41,060 (median wage), $66,150 (90th percentile

wage), 3,760 (number of positions), 3.3% (2016--2026 growth), High school diploma or equivalent (typical education requirement)

474. **Metal-Refining Furnace Operators and Tenders**: $41,040 (median wage), $59,980 (90th percentile wage), 17,730 (number of positions), -8.1% (2016--2026 growth), High school diploma or equivalent (typical education requirement)

475. **Excavating and Loading Machine and Dragline Operators**: $41,030 (median wage), $69,280 (90th percentile wage), 48,320 (number of positions), 8.4% (2016--2026 growth), High school diploma or equivalent (typical education requirement)

476. **Terrazzo Workers and Finishers**: $40,930 (median wage), $75,470 (90th percentile wage), 3,420 (number of positions), 12.3% (2016--2026 growth), High school diploma or equivalent (typical education requirement)

477. **Model Makers**, Wood: $40,890 (median wage), $76,480 (90th percentile wage), 1,040 (number of positions), 3.6% (2016--2026 growth), High school diploma or equivalent (typical education requirement)

478. **Rolling Machine Setters**, Operators, and Tenders, Metal and Plastic: $40,680 (median wage), $60,750 (90th percentile wage), 29,060 (number of positions),

-12.9% (2016--2026 growth), High school diploma or equivalent (typical education requirement)

479. **Hazardous Materials Removal Workers**: $40,640 (median wage), $74,160 (90th percentile wage), 44,280 (number of positions), 17.1% (2016--2026 growth), High school diploma or equivalent (typical education requirement)

480. **Tile and Marble Setters**: $40,460 (median wage), $71,260 (90th percentile wage), 36,830 (number of positions), 10% (2016--2026 growth), No formal educational credential (typical education requirement)

481. **Locksmiths and Safe Repairers**: $40,420 (median wage), $62,960 (90th percentile wage), 18,640 (number of positions), -3.2% (2016--2026 growth), High school diploma or equivalent (typical education requirement)

482. **Motorboat Operators**: $40,210 (median wage), $72,820 (90th percentile wage), 3,290 (number of positions), 7.6% (2016--2026 growth), Postsecondary nondegree award (typical education requirement)

483. **Embalmers**: $40,150 (median wage), $63,090 (90th percentile wage), 3,710 (number of positions), -0.8% (2016--2026 growth), Associate's degree (typical education requirement)

484. **Museum Technicians and Conservators**: $40,040 (median wage), $73,080 (90th percentile wage), 10,970 (number of positions), 12.4% (2016--2026 growth), Bachelor's degree (typical education requirement)

485. **Massage Therapists**: $39,860 (median wage), $74,870 (90th percentile wage), 95,830 (number of positions), 23.5% (2016--2026 growth), Postsecondary nondegree award (typical education requirement)

486. **Milling and Planing Machine Setters, Operators**, and Tenders, Metal and Plastic: $39,840 (median wage), $60,930 (90th percentile wage), 17,560 (number of positions), -19.3% (2016--2026 growth), High school diploma or equivalent (typical education requirement)

487. **Bus Drivers**, Transit and Intercity: $39,790 (median wage), $64,290 (90th percentile wage), 169,680 (number of positions), 8.8% (2016--2026 growth), High school diploma or equivalent (typical education requirement)

488. **Stonemasons**: $39,780 (median wage), $65,790 (90th percentile wage), 13,190 (number of positions), 9.8% (2016--2026 growth), High school diploma or equivalent (typical education requirement)

489. **Transportation Security Screeners**: $39,680 (median wage), $47,300 (90th percentile wage),

42,750 (number of positions), 2.6% (2016--2026 growth), High school diploma or equivalent (typical education requirement)

490. **Fabric and Apparel Patternmakers**: $39,650 (median wage), $86,960 (90th percentile wage), 5,310 (number of positions), -15% (2016--2026 growth), High school diploma or equivalent (typical education requirement)

491. **Communications Equipment Operators**, All Other: $39,640 (median wage), $61,720 (90th percentile wage), 2,150 (number of positions), 10.4% (2016--2026 growth), High school diploma or equivalent (typical education requirement)

492. **Teachers and Instructors**, All Other, Except Substitute Teachers: $39,570 (median wage), $82,960 (90th percentile wage), 292,950 (number of positions), 2016--2026 growth project not available, typical education requirement not available

493. **Financial Clerks**, All Other: $39,540 (median wage), $60,950 (90th percentile wage), 34,540 (number of positions), 9.9% (2016--2026 growth), High school diploma or equivalent (typical education requirement)

494. **Welders, Cutters, Solderers, and Brazers**: $39,390 (median wage), $62,100 (90th percentile wage), 382,730 (number of positions), 5.5% (2016--2026

growth), High school diploma or equivalent (typical education requirement)

495. **Information and Record Clerks**, All Other: $39,260 (median wage), $56,650 (90th percentile wage), 166,850 (number of positions), 7.6% (2016--2026 growth), High school diploma or equivalent (typical education requirement)

496. **Solar Photovoltaic Installers**: $39,240 (median wage), $60,570 (90th percentile wage), 8,870 (number of positions), 105.3% (2016--2026 growth), High school diploma or equivalent (typical education requirement)

497. **Cement Masons and Concrete Finishers**: $39,180 (median wage), $68,470 (90th percentile wage), 173,920 (number of positions), 12.6% (2016--2026 growth), No formal educational credential (typical education requirement)

498. **First-Line Supervisors of Retail Sales Workers**: $39,040 (median wage), $66,480 (90th percentile wage), 1,194,220 (number of positions), 5% (2016--2026 growth), High school diploma or equivalent (typical education requirement)

499. **Human Resources Assistants**, Except Payroll and Timekeeping: $39,020 (median wage), $56,440 (90th percentile wage), 137,150 (number of positions), -1.8% (2016--2026 growth), Associate's degree (typical

education requirement)

500. **Paving, Surfacing, and Tamping Equipment Operators**: $38,970 (median wage), $70,270 (90th percentile wage), 51,880 (number of positions), 12.1% (2016--2026 growth), High school diploma or equivalent (typical education requirement)

501. **Medical and Clinical Laboratory Technicians**: $38,950 (median wage), $61,720 (90th percentile wage), 160,190 (number of positions), 14% (2016--2026 growth), Associate's degree (typical education requirement)

502. **Logging Workers**, All Other: $38,950 (median wage), $57,430 (90th percentile wage), 3,010 (number of positions), -9.5% (2016--2026 growth), High school diploma or equivalent (typical education requirement)

503. **Meter Readers**, Utilities: $38,940 (median wage), $65,970 (90th percentile wage), 34,070 (number of positions), -4.4% (2016--2026 growth), High school diploma or equivalent (typical education requirement)

504. **Prepress Technicians and Workers**: $38,930 (median wage), $60,590 (90th percentile wage), 33,340 (number of positions), -19% (2016--2026 growth), Postsecondary nondegree award (typical education requirement)

505. **Actors**: $38,896 (median wage), $64,956 (90th percentile wage), 48,620 (number of positions), 11.7% (2016--2026 growth), Some college, no degree (typical education requirement)

506. **Plasterers and Stucco Masons**: $38,890 (median wage), $71,290 (90th percentile wage), 22,810 (number of positions), 4% (2016--2026 growth), No formal educational credential (typical education requirement)

507. **Police, Fire, and Ambulance Dispatchers**: $38,870 (median wage), $61,270 (90th percentile wage), 95,170 (number of positions), 8.3% (2016--2026 growth), High school diploma or equivalent (typical education requirement)

508. **Motorboat Mechanics and Service Technicians**: $38,780 (median wage), $61,200 (90th percentile wage), 20,260 (number of positions), 0.6% (2016--2026 growth), High school diploma or equivalent (typical education requirement)

509. **Word Processors and Typists**: $38,740 (median wage), $55,810 (90th percentile wage), 67,230 (number of positions), -33.4% (2016--2026 growth), High school diploma or equivalent (typical education requirement)

510. **Loan Interviewers and Clerks**: $38,630 (median wage), $58,630 (90th percentile wage), 224,340

(number of positions), 12.4% (2016--2026 growth), High school diploma or equivalent (typical education requirement)

511. **Directors, Religious Activities and Education**: $38,610 (median wage), $79,380 (90th percentile wage), 20,590 (number of positions), 7.3% (2016--2026 growth), Bachelor's degree (typical education requirement)

512. **Broadcast Technicians**: $38,550 (median wage), $80,280 (90th percentile wage), 30,330 (number of positions), -3.2% (2016--2026 growth), Associate's degree (typical education requirement)

513. **Installation, Maintenance, and Repair Workers, All Other**: $38,480 (median wage), $64,560 (90th percentile wage), 146,460 (number of positions), 8% (2016--2026 growth), High school diploma or equivalent (typical education requirement)

514. **Mechanical Door Repairers**: $38,480 (median wage), $58,000 (90th percentile wage), 19,840 (number of positions), 10.4% (2016--2026 growth), High school diploma or equivalent (typical education requirement)

515. **Lathe and Turning Machine Tool Setters**, Operators, and Tenders, Metal and Plastic: $38,480 (median wage), $56,990 (90th percentile wage), 33,850 (number of positions), -8.4% (2016--2026

growth), High school diploma or equivalent (typical education requirement)

516. **Automotive Service Technicians and Mechanics**: $38,470 (median wage), $64,070 (90th percentile wage), 647,380 (number of positions), 6.3% (2016--2026 growth), Postsecondary nondegree award (typical education requirement)

517. **Insurance Claims and Policy Processing Clerks**: $38,430 (median wage), $59,310 (90th percentile wage), 274,350 (number of positions), 11% (2016--2026 growth), High school diploma or equivalent (typical education requirement)

518. **Pipelayers**: $38,410 (median wage), $67,550 (90th percentile wage), 39,620 (number of positions), 17.3% (2016--2026 growth), No formal educational credential (typical education requirement)

519. **Bookkeeping, Accounting, and Auditing Clerks**: $38,390 (median wage), $59,630 (90th percentile wage), 1,566,960 (number of positions), -1.4% (2016--2026 growth), Some college, no degree (typical education requirement)

520. **Separating, Filtering, Clarifying, Precipitating, and Still Machine Setters**, Operators, and Tenders: $38,360 (median wage), $63,020 (90th percentile wage), 47,160 (number of positions), 0.2% (2016--2026 growth), High school diploma or equivalent

(typical education requirement)

521. **Carpet Installers**: $38,280 (median wage), $80,440 (90th percentile wage), 25,660 (number of positions), 9.8% (2016--2026 growth), No formal educational credential (typical education requirement)

522. **Jewelers and Precious Stone and Metal Workers**: $38,200 (median wage), $66,110 (90th percentile wage), 26,480 (number of positions), -3.1% (2016--2026 growth), High school diploma or equivalent (typical education requirement)

523. **First-Line Supervisors of Housekeeping and Janitorial Workers**: $38,190 (median wage), $63,350 (90th percentile wage), 161,140 (number of positions), 8.6% (2016--2026 growth), High school diploma or equivalent (typical education requirement)

524. **Fitness Trainers and Aerobics Instructors**: $38,160 (median wage), $72,980 (90th percentile wage), 257,410 (number of positions), 9.8% (2016--2026 growth), High school diploma or equivalent (typical education requirement)

525. **Highway Maintenance Workers**: $38,130 (median wage), $56,820 (90th percentile wage), 143,320 (number of positions), 6.9% (2016--2026 growth), High school diploma or equivalent (typical education requirement)

526. **Medical Records and Health Information Technicians**: $38,040 (median wage), $62,840 (90th percentile wage), 200,140 (number of positions), 13.5% (2016--2026 growth), Postsecondary nondegree award (typical education requirement)

527. **Parking Enforcement Workers**: $37,950 (median wage), $60,110 (90th percentile wage), 8,920 (number of positions), -35.3% (2016--2026 growth), High school diploma or equivalent (typical education requirement)

528. **Dispatchers, Except Police, Fire, and Ambulance**: $37,940 (median wage), $63,420 (90th percentile wage), 197,910 (number of positions), 0% (2016--2026 growth), High school diploma or equivalent (typical education requirement)

529. **Computer-Controlled Machine Tool Operators**, Metal and Plastic: $37,880 (median wage), $57,750 (90th percentile wage), 146,190 (number of positions), 1.1% (2016--2026 growth), High school diploma or equivalent (typical education requirement)

530. **Floor Layers**, Except Carpet, Wood, and Hard Tiles: $37,840 (median wage), $68,720 (90th percentile wage), 10,340 (number of positions), 10% (2016--2026 growth), No formal educational credential (typical education requirement)

531. **Reporters and Correspondents**: $37,820 (median wage), $86,610 (90th percentile wage), 40,090 (number of positions), -10.7% (2016--2026 growth), Bachelor's degree (typical education requirement)

532. **Farm Equipment Mechanics and Service Technicians**: $37,820 (median wage), $57,420 (90th percentile wage), 35,110 (number of positions), 7.4% (2016--2026 growth), High school diploma or equivalent (typical education requirement)

533. **Roofers**: $37,760 (median wage), $64,630 (90th percentile wage), 116,410 (number of positions), 11.3% (2016--2026 growth), No formal educational credential (typical education requirement)

534. **Structural Metal Fabricators and Fitters**: $37,730 (median wage), $58,900 (90th percentile wage), 77,270 (number of positions), -15.3% (2016--2026 growth), High school diploma or equivalent (typical education requirement)

535. **Dental Laboratory Technicians**: $37,680 (median wage), $61,970 (90th percentile wage), 37,110 (number of positions), 14.5% (2016--2026 growth), High school diploma or equivalent (typical education requirement)

536. **Painters**, Construction and Maintenance: $37,570 (median wage), $63,670 (90th percentile wage), 217,280 (number of positions), 6.1% (2016--2026

growth), No formal educational credential (typical education requirement)

537. **Home Appliance Repairers**: $37,570 (median wage), $62,600 (90th percentile wage), 33,480 (number of positions), -0.9% (2016--2026 growth), High school diploma or equivalent (typical education requirement)

538. **Agricultural and Food Science Technicians**: $37,550 (median wage), $61,450 (90th percentile wage), 20,420 (number of positions), 6.3% (2016--2026 growth), Associate's degree (typical education requirement)

539. **Logging Equipment Operators**: $37,490 (median wage), $56,110 (90th percentile wage), 27,250 (number of positions), -7% (2016--2026 growth), High school diploma or equivalent (typical education requirement)

540. **Electronic Home Entertainment Equipment Installers and Repairers**: $37,410 (median wage), $59,640 (90th percentile wage), 25,550 (number of positions), 1.2% (2016--2026 growth), Postsecondary nondegree award (typical education requirement)

541. **Fallers**: $37,370 (median wage), $71,590 (90th percentile wage), 5,370 (number of positions), -10.5% (2016--2026 growth), High school diploma or equivalent (typical education requirement)

542. **Roustabouts**, Oil and Gas: $37,340 (median wage), $60,600 (90th percentile wage), 51,290 (number of positions), 24.5% (2016--2026 growth), No formal educational credential (typical education requirement)

543. **Self-Enrichment Education Teachers**: $37,330 (median wage), $74,700 (90th percentile wage), 229,840 (number of positions), 14.9% (2016--2026 growth), High school diploma or equivalent (typical education requirement)

544. **Community Health Workers**: $37,330 (median wage), $63,880 (90th percentile wage), 51,900 (number of positions), 18.1% (2016--2026 growth), High school diploma or equivalent (typical education requirement)

545. **Sales and Related Workers**, All Other: $37,190 (median wage), $73,000 (90th percentile wage), 81,080 (number of positions), 9.8% (2016--2026 growth), High school diploma or equivalent (typical education requirement)

546. **Heat Treating Equipment Setters**, Operators, and Tenders, Metal and Plastic: $37,180 (median wage), $57,290 (90th percentile wage), 19,780 (number of positions), -14.1% (2016--2026 growth), High school diploma or equivalent (typical education requirement)

547. **Computer, Automated Teller**, and Office Machine Repairers: $37,100 (median wage), $60,260 (90th percentile wage), 102,170 (number of positions), -0.7% (2016--2026 growth), Some college, no degree (typical education requirement)

548. **Log Graders and Scalers**: $37,090 (median wage), $53,110 (90th percentile wage), 3,020 (number of positions), 2.7% (2016--2026 growth), High school diploma or equivalent (typical education requirement)

549. **Timing Device Assemblers and Adjusters**: $37,040 (median wage), $74,740 (90th percentile wage), 790 (number of positions), -19.9% (2016--2026 growth), High school diploma or equivalent (typical education requirement)

550. **Telephone Operators**: $37,000 (median wage), $66,230 (90th percentile wage), 8,860 (number of positions), -22.6% (2016--2026 growth), High school diploma or equivalent (typical education requirement)

551. **Paper Goods Machine Setters**, Operators, and Tenders: $36,990 (median wage), $58,720 (90th percentile wage), 93,100 (number of positions), -9% (2016--2026 growth), High school diploma or equivalent (typical education requirement)

552. **Welding, Soldering, and Brazing Machine**

Setters, Operators, and Tenders: $36,980 (median wage), $54,300 (90th percentile wage), 46,920 (number of positions), -10.3% (2016--2026 growth), High school diploma or equivalent (typical education requirement)

553. **Proofreaders and Copy Markers**: $36,960 (median wage), $60,530 (90th percentile wage), 11,430 (number of positions), 2.2% (2016--2026 growth), Bachelor's degree (typical education requirement)

554. **Maintenance and Repair Workers**, General: $36,940 (median wage), $60,660 (90th percentile wage), 1,332,480 (number of positions), 7.9% (2016--2026 growth), High school diploma or equivalent (typical education requirement)

555. **Dental Assistants**: $36,940 (median wage), $52,000 (90th percentile wage), 327,290 (number of positions), 19.5% (2016--2026 growth), Postsecondary nondegree award (typical education requirement)

556. **Credit Authorizers, Checkers, and Clerks**: $36,930 (median wage), $58,800 (90th percentile wage), 37,680 (number of positions), -2.8% (2016--2026 growth), High school diploma or equivalent (typical education requirement)

557. **Forging Machine Setters, Operators, and Tenders**, Metal and Plastic: $36,930 (median wage), $57,860 (90th percentile wage), 19,160 (number of

positions), -19.2% (2016--2026 growth), High school diploma or equivalent (typical education requirement)

558. **Construction and Related Workers**, All Other: $36,890 (median wage), $61,940 (90th percentile wage), 35,340 (number of positions), 9.9% (2016--2026 growth), High school diploma or equivalent (typical education requirement)

559. **Floor Sanders and Finishers**: $36,860 (median wage), $59,660 (90th percentile wage), 4,590 (number of positions), 9.8% (2016--2026 growth), No formal educational credential (typical education requirement)

560. **Inspectors, Testers, Sorters, Samplers, and Weighers**: $36,780 (median wage), $63,590 (90th percentile wage), 518,950 (number of positions), -10.7% (2016--2026 growth), High school diploma or equivalent (typical education requirement)

561. **Watch Repairers**: $36,740 (median wage), $61,880 (90th percentile wage), 1,620 (number of positions), -28.7% (2016--2026 growth), High school diploma or equivalent (typical education requirement)

562. **First-Line Supervisors of Personal Service Workers**: $36,700 (median wage), $61,850 (90th percentile wage), 190,420 (number of positions), 13% (2016--2026 growth), High school diploma or

equivalent (typical education requirement)

563. **Court, Municipal, and License Clerks**: $36,670 (median wage), $57,420 (90th percentile wage), 128,620 (number of positions), 6.6% (2016--2026 growth), High school diploma or equivalent (typical education requirement)

564. **Tool Grinders, Filers, and Sharpeners**: $36,650 (median wage), $57,590 (90th percentile wage), 9,550 (number of positions), -3.5% (2016--2026 growth), High school diploma or equivalent (typical education requirement)

565. **Tax Preparers**: $36,550 (median wage), $80,250 (90th percentile wage), 70,030 (number of positions), 10.8% (2016--2026 growth), High school diploma or equivalent (typical education requirement)

566. **Travel Agents**: $36,460 (median wage), $61,890 (90th percentile wage), 68,680 (number of positions), -9.1% (2016--2026 growth), High school diploma or equivalent (typical education requirement)

567. **Recreational Vehicle Service Technicians**: $36,430 (median wage), $56,610 (90th percentile wage), 13,520 (number of positions), -1.1% (2016--2026 growth), High school diploma or equivalent (typical education requirement)

568. **Septic Tank Servicers and Sewer Pipe Cleaners**:

$36,430 (median wage), $59,290 (90th percentile wage), 26,320 (number of positions), 16.9% (2016--2026 growth), High school diploma or equivalent (typical education requirement)

569. **Drilling and Boring Machine Tool Setters**, Operators, and Tenders, Metal and Plastic: $36,410 (median wage), $57,660 (90th percentile wage), 12,290 (number of positions), -19.4% (2016--2026 growth), High school diploma or equivalent (typical education requirement)

570. **Correspondence Clerks**: $36,370 (median wage), $53,630 (90th percentile wage), 6,780 (number of positions), 2.1% (2016--2026 growth), High school diploma or equivalent (typical education requirement)

571. **Healthcare Support Workers**, All Other: $36,330 (median wage), $54,240 (90th percentile wage), 93,830 (number of positions), 11.6% (2016--2026 growth), High school diploma or equivalent (typical education requirement)

572. **Forest Fire Inspectors and Prevention Specialists**: $36,230 (median wage), $76,660 (90th percentile wage), 1,650 (number of positions), 26.6% (2016--2026 growth), High school diploma or equivalent (typical education requirement)

573. **Pourers and Casters**, Metal: $36,180 (median

wage), $52,590 (90th percentile wage), 8,560 (number of positions), -23.4% (2016--2026 growth), High school diploma or equivalent (typical education requirement)

574. **Billing and Posting Clerks**: $36,150 (median wage), $52,150 (90th percentile wage), 485,220 (number of positions), 14.2% (2016--2026 growth), High school diploma or equivalent (typical education requirement)

575. **Slot Supervisors**: $36,080 (median wage), $60,630 (90th percentile wage), 7,640 (number of positions), 4.3% (2016--2026 growth), High school diploma or equivalent (typical education requirement)

576. **Entertainers and Performers**, Sports and Related Workers, All Other: $36,067 (median wage), $82,222 (90th percentile wage), 13,150 (number of positions), 8% (2016--2026 growth), No formal educational credential (typical education requirement)

577. **Furnace, Kiln, Oven, Drier, and Kettle Operators and Tenders**: $36,040 (median wage), $56,040 (90th percentile wage), 19,520 (number of positions), -5% (2016--2026 growth), High school diploma or equivalent (typical education requirement)

578. **Medical Appliance Technicians**: $35,980 (median wage), $62,720 (90th percentile wage), 14,570 (number of positions), 13.7% (2016--2026 growth),

High school diploma or equivalent (typical education requirement)

579. **Helpers--Extraction Workers**: $35,790 (median wage), $51,220 (90th percentile wage), 17,660 (number of positions), 19.7% (2016--2026 growth), High school diploma or equivalent (typical education requirement)

580. **Tank Car, Truck, and Ship Loaders**: $35,770 (median wage), $66,190 (90th percentile wage), 10,920 (number of positions), 5.2% (2016--2026 growth), No formal educational credential (typical education requirement)

581. **Medical Transcriptionists**: $35,720 (median wage), $51,640 (90th percentile wage), 54,070 (number of positions), -3.5% (2016--2026 growth), Postsecondary nondegree award (typical education requirement)

582. **Animal Breeders**: $35,690 (median wage), $73,130 (90th percentile wage), 1,270 (number of positions), 2% (2016--2026 growth), High school diploma or equivalent (typical education requirement)

583. **Mixing and Blending Machine Setters, Operators, and Tenders**: $35,680 (median wage), $55,960 (90th percentile wage), 130,480 (number of positions), -3.1% (2016--2026 growth), High school diploma or equivalent (typical education

requirement)

584. **Insulation Workers, Floor, Ceiling, and Wall**: $35,660 (median wage), $61,520 (90th percentile wage), 29,500 (number of positions), 1.3% (2016--2026 growth), No formal educational credential (typical education requirement)

585. **Transportation Workers, All Other**: $35,660 (median wage), $60,640 (90th percentile wage), 37,660 (number of positions), 8.3% (2016--2026 growth), High school diploma or equivalent (typical education requirement)

586. **Semiconductor Processors**: $35,660 (median wage), $53,540 (90th percentile wage), 24,430 (number of positions), -5.1% (2016--2026 growth), High school diploma or equivalent (typical education requirement)

587. **Forest and Conservation Technicians**: $35,560 (median wage), $55,510 (90th percentile wage), 30,090 (number of positions), 3.8% (2016--2026 growth), Associate's degree (typical education requirement)

588. **Printing Press Operators**: $35,530 (median wage), $57,610 (90th percentile wage), 169,910 (number of positions), -9.4% (2016--2026 growth), High school diploma or equivalent (typical education requirement)

589. **Opticians, Dispensing**: $35,530 (median wage), $57,180 (90th percentile wage), 75,270 (number of positions), 14.5% (2016--2026 growth), High school diploma or equivalent (typical education requirement)

590. **Ophthalmic Medical Technicians**: $35,530 (median wage), $51,330 (90th percentile wage), 43,990 (number of positions), 19.4% (2016--2026 growth), Postsecondary nondegree award (typical education requirement)

591. **Bill and Account Collectors**: $35,350 (median wage), $54,970 (90th percentile wage), 298,960 (number of positions), -3% (2016--2026 growth), High school diploma or equivalent (typical education requirement)

592. **Refuse and Recyclable Material Collectors**: $35,270 (median wage), $60,500 (90th percentile wage), 114,680 (number of positions), 13% (2016--2026 growth), No formal educational credential (typical education requirement)

593. **Reservation and Transportation Ticket Agents and Travel Clerks**: $35,230 (median wage), $59,270 (90th percentile wage), 146,350 (number of positions), 3.7% (2016--2026 growth), High school diploma or equivalent (typical education requirement)

594. **Farm Labor Contractors**: $35,160 (median wage), $95,360 (90th percentile wage), 810 (number of positions), 8% (2016--2026 growth), No formal educational credential (typical education requirement)

595. **Tree Trimmers and Pruners**: $35,030 (median wage), $56,970 (90th percentile wage), 40,680 (number of positions), 10.7% (2016--2026 growth), High school diploma or equivalent (typical education requirement)

596. **Musical Instrument Repairers and Tuners**: $35,010 (median wage), $59,350 (90th percentile wage), 7,980 (number of positions), 2.3% (2016--2026 growth), High school diploma or equivalent (typical education requirement)

597. **New Accounts Clerks**: $34,990 (median wage), $50,010 (90th percentile wage), 41,630 (number of positions), -6.2% (2016--2026 growth), High school diploma or equivalent (typical education requirement)

598. **Secretaries and Administrative Assistants**, Except Legal, Medical, and Executive: $34,820 (median wage), $53,060 (90th percentile wage), 2,295,510 (number of positions), -6.5% (2016--2026 growth), High school diploma or equivalent (typical education requirement)

599. **Foundry Mold and Coremakers**: $34,790 (median wage), $49,970 (90th percentile wage), 12,810 (number of positions), -24% (2016--2026 growth), High school diploma or equivalent (typical education requirement)

600. **Motorcycle Mechanics**: $34,720 (median wage), $56,350 (90th percentile wage), 16,000 (number of positions), 1.4% (2016--2026 growth), Postsecondary nondegree award (typical education requirement)

601. **Rehabilitation Counselors**: $34,670 (median wage), $62,010 (90th percentile wage), 103,030 (number of positions), 9.7% (2016--2026 growth), Master's degree (typical education requirement)

602. **Animal Control Workers**: $34,550 (median wage), $55,600 (90th percentile wage), 12,970 (number of positions), 8.4% (2016--2026 growth), High school diploma or equivalent (typical education requirement)

603. **Medical Equipment Preparers**: $34,400 (median wage), $50,620 (90th percentile wage), 52,500 (number of positions), 10.9% (2016--2026 growth), High school diploma or equivalent (typical education requirement)

604. **Crushing, Grinding, and Polishing Machine Setters, Operators, and Tenders**: $34,390 (median wage), $52,060 (90th percentile wage), 29,830

(number of positions), -6.7% (2016--2026 growth), High school diploma or equivalent (typical education requirement)

605. **Multiple Machine Tool Setters, Operators, and Tenders, Metal and Plastic**: $34,340 (median wage), $53,090 (90th percentile wage), 117,300 (number of positions), -2.6% (2016--2026 growth), High school diploma or equivalent (typical education requirement)

606. **Automotive Glass Installers and Repairers**: $34,340 (median wage), $51,540 (90th percentile wage), 18,610 (number of positions), 6.6% (2016--2026 growth), High school diploma or equivalent (typical education requirement)

607. **Graduate Teaching Assistants**: $34,240 (median wage), $55,080 (90th percentile wage), 135,130 (number of positions), 7.7% (2016--2026 growth), Bachelor's degree (typical education requirement)

608. **Extruding and Forming Machine Setters, Operators, and Tenders, Synthetic and Glass Fibers**: $34,240 (median wage), $49,810 (90th percentile wage), 19,340 (number of positions), -8.5% (2016--2026 growth), High school diploma or equivalent (typical education requirement)

609. **Photographers**: $34,070 (median wage), $76,220 (90th percentile wage), 48,660 (number of positions),

3 JOBS RANKED BY MEDIAN SALARY

-8.4% (2016--2026 growth), High school diploma or equivalent (typical education requirement)

610. **Office and Administrative Support Workers, All Other**: $34,020 (median wage), $55,210 (90th percentile wage), 216,650 (number of positions), 9.2% (2016--2026 growth), High school diploma or equivalent (typical education requirement)

611. **Rock Splitters, Quarry**: $34,020 (median wage), $49,370 (90th percentile wage), 3,770 (number of positions), -6.3% (2016--2026 growth), No formal educational credential (typical education requirement)

612. **Coil Winders, Tapers, and Finishers**: $33,940 (median wage), $50,820 (90th percentile wage), 14,090 (number of positions), -20.6% (2016--2026 growth), High school diploma or equivalent (typical education requirement)

613. **Extruding and Drawing Machine Setters, Operators, and Tenders, Metal and Plastic**: $33,870 (median wage), $50,260 (90th percentile wage), 71,960 (number of positions), -15.2% (2016--2026 growth), High school diploma or equivalent (typical education requirement)

614. **Paperhangers**: $33,770 (median wage), $53,560 (90th percentile wage), 3,190 (number of positions), 5% (2016--2026 growth), No formal educational

credential (typical education requirement)

615. **Pesticide Handlers, Sprayers, and Applicators, Vegetation**: $33,740 (median wage), $51,030 (90th percentile wage), 25,230 (number of positions), 7% (2016--2026 growth), High school diploma or equivalent (typical education requirement)

616. **Outdoor Power Equipment and Other Small Engine Mechanics**: $33,730 (median wage), $51,360 (90th percentile wage), 33,020 (number of positions), 11.4% (2016--2026 growth), High school diploma or equivalent (typical education requirement)

617. **Medical Secretaries**: $33,730 (median wage), $49,730 (90th percentile wage), 556,820 (number of positions), 22.5% (2016--2026 growth), High school diploma or equivalent (typical education requirement)

618. **Segmental Pavers**: $33,530 (median wage), $50,900 (90th percentile wage), 1,720 (number of positions), 12.4% (2016--2026 growth), High school diploma or equivalent (typical education requirement)

619. **Craft Artists**: $33,440 (median wage), $65,080 (90th percentile wage), 5,070 (number of positions), 6.3% (2016--2026 growth), No formal educational credential (typical education requirement)

620. **Construction Laborers**: $33,430 (median wage),

3 JOBS RANKED BY MEDIAN SALARY

$62,600 (90th percentile wage), 912,100 (number of positions), 12.6% (2016--2026 growth), No formal educational credential (typical education requirement)

621. **Order Clerks**: $33,370 (median wage), $52,130 (90th percentile wage), 176,850 (number of positions), -2% (2016--2026 growth), High school diploma or equivalent (typical education requirement)

622. **Electromechanical Equipment Assemblers**: $33,350 (median wage), $51,080 (90th percentile wage), 45,540 (number of positions), -21.3% (2016--2026 growth), High school diploma or equivalent (typical education requirement)

623. **Metal Workers and Plastic Workers, All Other**: $33,280 (median wage), $56,490 (90th percentile wage), 22,930 (number of positions), -6.6% (2016--2026 growth), High school diploma or equivalent (typical education requirement)

624. **Fence Erectors**: $33,150 (median wage), $58,080 (90th percentile wage), 21,500 (number of positions), 11.2% (2016--2026 growth), No formal educational credential (typical education requirement)

625. **Coin, Vending, and Amusement Machine Servicers and Repairers**: $33,070 (median wage), $51,540 (90th percentile wage), 33,600 (number of

positions), -12.4% (2016--2026 growth), High school diploma or equivalent (typical education requirement)

626. **Cabinetmakers and Bench Carpenters**: $33,050 (median wage), $51,470 (90th percentile wage), 97,980 (number of positions), 3.4% (2016--2026 growth), High school diploma or equivalent (typical education requirement)

627. **Upholsterers**: $33,050 (median wage), $51,260 (90th percentile wage), 32,520 (number of positions), 2.5% (2016--2026 growth), High school diploma or equivalent (typical education requirement)

628. **Pest Control Workers**: $33,040 (median wage), $50,920 (90th percentile wage), 72,830 (number of positions), 8% (2016--2026 growth), High school diploma or equivalent (typical education requirement)

629. **Library Technicians**: $32,890 (median wage), $52,880 (90th percentile wage), 93,410 (number of positions), 9.1% (2016--2026 growth), Postsecondary nondegree award (typical education requirement)

630. **Grinding, Lapping, Polishing, and Buffing Machine Tool Setters**, Operators, and Tenders, Metal and Plastic: $32,890 (median wage), $50,640 (90th percentile wage), 74,600 (number of positions), -10% (2016--2026 growth), High school diploma or

equivalent (typical education requirement)

631. **Cutting and Slicing Machine Setters, Operators, and Tenders**: $32,870 (median wage), $48,840 (90th percentile wage), 61,330 (number of positions), -3.9% (2016--2026 growth), High school diploma or equivalent (typical education requirement)

632. **Coating, Painting, and Spraying Machine Setters, Operators, and Tenders**: $32,790 (median wage), $49,440 (90th percentile wage), 85,760 (number of positions), 0.2% (2016--2026 growth), High school diploma or equivalent (typical education requirement)

633. **Phlebotomists**: $32,710 (median wage), $46,850 (90th percentile wage), 120,970 (number of positions), 24.4% (2016--2026 growth), Postsecondary nondegree award (typical education requirement)

634. **Emergency Medical Technicians and Paramedics**: $32,670 (median wage), $56,310 (90th percentile wage), 244,960 (number of positions), 15.1% (2016--2026 growth), Postsecondary nondegree award (typical education requirement)

635. **Gaming Surveillance Officers and Gaming Investigators**: $32,630 (median wage), $52,500 (90th percentile wage), 10,460 (number of positions), 3.5% (2016--2026 growth), High school diploma or equivalent (typical education requirement)

636. **Extruding, Forming, Pressing, and Compacting Machine Setters, Operators, and Tenders**: $32,510 (median wage), $50,330 (90th percentile wage), 71,260 (number of positions), -5.4% (2016--2026 growth), High school diploma or equivalent (typical education requirement)

637. **Veterinary Technologists and Technicians**: $32,490 (median wage), $48,330 (90th percentile wage), 99,390 (number of positions), 19.9% (2016--2026 growth), Associate's degree (typical education requirement)

638. **Industrial Truck and Tractor Operators**: $32,460 (median wage), $48,850 (90th percentile wage), 542,750 (number of positions), 6.6% (2016--2026 growth), No formal educational credential (typical education requirement)

639. **Cutting, Punching, and Press Machine Setters, Operators, and Tenders**, Metal and Plastic: $32,370 (median wage), $50,330 (90th percentile wage), 192,800 (number of positions), -8.7% (2016--2026 growth), High school diploma or equivalent (typical education requirement)

640. **Customer Service Representatives**: $32,300 (median wage), $53,730 (90th percentile wage), 2,707,040 (number of positions), 4.9% (2016--2026 growth), High school diploma or equivalent (typical

education requirement)

641. **Adhesive Bonding Machine Operators and Tenders**: $32,290 (median wage), $50,910 (90th percentile wage), 16,940 (number of positions), -2.7% (2016--2026 growth), High school diploma or equivalent (typical education requirement)

642. **Electronic Equipment Installers and Repairers**, Motor Vehicles: $32,220 (median wage), $50,770 (90th percentile wage), 11,750 (number of positions), -25.2% (2016--2026 growth), High school diploma or equivalent (typical education requirement)

643. **Interviewers**, Except Eligibility and Loan: $32,150 (median wage), $48,420 (90th percentile wage), 186,030 (number of positions), 5.7% (2016--2026 growth), High school diploma or equivalent (typical education requirement)

644. **Travel Guides**: $32,100 (median wage), $58,400 (90th percentile wage), 3,030 (number of positions), 5.5% (2016--2026 growth), High school diploma or equivalent (typical education requirement)

645. **Cooks, Private Household**: $32,060 (median wage), $62,730 (90th percentile wage), 370 (number of positions), 5.7% (2016--2026 growth), Postsecondary nondegree award (typical education requirement)

646. **Social and Human Service Assistants**: $31,810 (median wage), $50,640 (90th percentile wage), 360,650 (number of positions), 16.4% (2016--2026 growth), High school diploma or equivalent (typical education requirement)

647. **Medical Assistants**: $31,540 (median wage), $45,310 (90th percentile wage), 623,560 (number of positions), 29.1% (2016--2026 growth), Postsecondary nondegree award (typical education requirement)

648. **First-Line Supervisors of Food Preparation and Serving Workers**: $31,480 (median wage), $54,510 (90th percentile wage), 908,550 (number of positions), 9.3% (2016--2026 growth), High school diploma or equivalent (typical education requirement)

649. **Coaches and Scouts**: $31,460 (median wage), $71,940 (90th percentile wage), 230,930 (number of positions), 12.7% (2016--2026 growth), Bachelor's degree (typical education requirement)

650. **Conveyor Operators and Tenders**: $31,410 (median wage), $49,880 (90th percentile wage), 28,590 (number of positions), -1.2% (2016--2026 growth), No formal educational credential (typical education requirement)

651. **Print Binding and Finishing Workers**: $31,410 (median wage), $49,320 (90th percentile wage),

3 JOBS RANKED BY MEDIAN SALARY

52,730 (number of positions), -11.3% (2016--2026 growth), High school diploma or equivalent (typical education requirement)

652. **Radio and Television Announcers**: $31,400 (median wage), $89,720 (90th percentile wage), 29,210 (number of positions), -10.9% (2016--2026 growth), Bachelor's degree (typical education requirement)

653. **Electrical and Electronic Equipment Assemblers**: $31,310 (median wage), $49,600 (90th percentile wage), 218,530 (number of positions), -20.7% (2016--2026 growth), High school diploma or equivalent (typical education requirement)

654. **Plating and Coating Machine Setters, Operators, and Tenders**, Metal and Plastic: $31,280 (median wage), $50,290 (90th percentile wage), 35,570 (number of positions), -13.8% (2016--2026 growth), High school diploma or equivalent (typical education requirement)

655. **Shipping, Receiving, and Traffic Clerks**: $31,180 (median wage), $48,760 (90th percentile wage), 676,990 (number of positions), 0% (2016--2026 growth), High school diploma or equivalent (typical education requirement)

656. **Agricultural Workers**, All Other: $31,160 (median wage), $54,520 (90th percentile wage), 5,040 (number

of positions), 4.5% (2016--2026 growth), No formal educational credential (typical education requirement)

657. **Etchers and Engravers**: $31,110 (median wage), $51,270 (90th percentile wage), 9,520 (number of positions), 1% (2016--2026 growth), High school diploma or equivalent (typical education requirement)

658. **Psychiatric Technicians**: $30,970 (median wage), $59,960 (90th percentile wage), 61,720 (number of positions), 5.9% (2016--2026 growth), Postsecondary nondegree award (typical education requirement)

659. **Pharmacy Technicians**: $30,920 (median wage), $45,710 (90th percentile wage), 398,390 (number of positions), 11.8% (2016--2026 growth), High school diploma or equivalent (typical education requirement)

660. **Fiberglass Laminators and Fabricators**: $30,870 (median wage), $47,670 (90th percentile wage), 19,400 (number of positions), -1.3% (2016--2026 growth), High school diploma or equivalent (typical education requirement)

661. **Ophthalmic Laboratory Technicians**: $30,640 (median wage), $51,830 (90th percentile wage), 28,570 (number of positions), 11.9% (2016--2026 growth), High school diploma or equivalent (typical

education requirement)

662. **Molders, Shapers, and Casters**, Except Metal and Plastic: $30,610 (median wage), $47,720 (90th percentile wage), 39,450 (number of positions), -1% (2016--2026 growth), High school diploma or equivalent (typical education requirement)

663. **Office Clerks**, General: $30,580 (median wage), $50,410 (90th percentile wage), 2,955,550 (number of positions), -1% (2016--2026 growth), High school diploma or equivalent (typical education requirement)

664. **Light Truck or Delivery Services Drivers**: $30,580 (median wage), $60,630 (90th percentile wage), 858,710 (number of positions), 6.8% (2016--2026 growth), High school diploma or equivalent (typical education requirement)

665. **Helpers--Brickmasons, Blockmasons, Stonemasons, and Tile and Marble Setters**: $30,570 (median wage), $49,990 (90th percentile wage), 23,950 (number of positions), 12.1% (2016--2026 growth), No formal educational credential (typical education requirement)

666. **Furniture Finishers**: $30,550 (median wage), $47,890 (90th percentile wage), 17,370 (number of positions), 2.5% (2016--2026 growth), High school diploma or equivalent (typical education

requirement)

667. **Molding, Coremaking, and Casting Machine Setters, Operators, and Tenders**, Metal and Plastic: $30,480 (median wage), $48,550 (90th percentile wage), 145,560 (number of positions), -15% (2016--2026 growth), High school diploma or equivalent (typical education requirement)

668. **Office Machine Operators**, Except Computer: $30,460 (median wage), $48,240 (90th percentile wage), 58,160 (number of positions), -15.6% (2016--2026 growth), High school diploma or equivalent (typical education requirement)

669. **Skincare Specialists**: $30,270 (median wage), $59,780 (90th percentile wage), 43,980 (number of positions), 12.6% (2016--2026 growth), Postsecondary nondegree award (typical education requirement)

670. **Bus Drivers**, School or Special Client: $30,150 (median wage), $46,390 (90th percentile wage), 515,020 (number of positions), 5.2% (2016--2026 growth), High school diploma or equivalent (typical education requirement)

671. **Data Entry Keyers**: $30,100 (median wage), $45,360 (90th percentile wage), 194,810 (number of positions), -21.1% (2016--2026 growth), High school diploma or equivalent (typical education requirement)

672. **Team Assemblers**: $30,060 (median wage), $50,980 (90th percentile wage), 1,112,780 (number of positions), -12.6% (2016--2026 growth), High school diploma or equivalent (typical education requirement)

673. **Painting, Coating, and Decorating Workers**: $30,030 (median wage), $47,560 (90th percentile wage), 15,450 (number of positions), 1.1% (2016--2026 growth), No formal educational credential (typical education requirement)

674. **Butchers and Meat Cutters**: $29,870 (median wage), $47,960 (90th percentile wage), 133,880 (number of positions), 5.7% (2016--2026 growth), No formal educational credential (typical education requirement)

675. **Manufactured Building and Mobile Home Installers**: $29,810 (median wage), $43,400 (90th percentile wage), 3,200 (number of positions), -8.8% (2016--2026 growth), High school diploma or equivalent (typical education requirement)

676. **Parts Salespersons**: $29,780 (median wage), $52,430 (90th percentile wage), 248,740 (number of positions), 5.1% (2016--2026 growth), No formal educational credential (typical education requirement)

677. **Building Cleaning Workers**, All Other: $29,700

(median wage), $45,140 (90th percentile wage), 15,020 (number of positions), 12.6% (2016--2026 growth), No formal educational credential (typical education requirement)

678. **Helpers--Electricians**: $29,530 (median wage), $44,450 (90th percentile wage), 71,890 (number of positions), 10.6% (2016--2026 growth), High school diploma or equivalent (typical education requirement)

679. **Helpers, Construction Trades**, All Other: $29,270 (median wage), $46,220 (90th percentile wage), 21,820 (number of positions), 12.1% (2016--2026 growth), No formal educational credential (typical education requirement)

680. **Concierges**: $29,250 (median wage), $46,750 (90th percentile wage), 32,020 (number of positions), 11.3% (2016--2026 growth), High school diploma or equivalent (typical education requirement)

681. **Cooling and Freezing Equipment Operators and Tenders**: $29,190 (median wage), $50,210 (90th percentile wage), 8,170 (number of positions), 1.9% (2016--2026 growth), High school diploma or equivalent (typical education requirement)

682. **Mail Clerks and Mail Machine Operators**, Except Postal Service: $29,160 (median wage), $45,220 (90th percentile wage), 91,530 (number of positions), -7.5%

(2016--2026 growth), High school diploma or equivalent (typical education requirement)

683. **File Clerks**: $29,090 (median wage), $47,410 (90th percentile wage), 130,950 (number of positions), -10.3% (2016--2026 growth), High school diploma or equivalent (typical education requirement)

684. **Helpers--Pipelayers, Plumbers, Pipefitters, and Steamfitters**: $29,030 (median wage), $43,470 (90th percentile wage), 54,080 (number of positions), 18.6% (2016--2026 growth), High school diploma or equivalent (typical education requirement)

685. **Public Address System and Other Announcers**: $28,940 (median wage), $77,640 (90th percentile wage), 8,020 (number of positions), 3.2% (2016--2026 growth), High school diploma or equivalent (typical education requirement)

686. **Agricultural Equipment Operators**: $28,850 (median wage), $43,690 (90th percentile wage), 28,700 (number of positions), 5.6% (2016--2026 growth), No formal educational credential (typical education requirement)

687. **Religious Workers**, All Other: $28,820 (median wage), $58,970 (90th percentile wage), 8,250 (number of positions), 7.7% (2016--2026 growth), Bachelor's degree (typical education requirement)

688. **Helpers--Carpenters**: $28,810 (median wage), $43,030 (90th percentile wage), 35,890 (number of positions), 12.8% (2016--2026 growth), No formal educational credential (typical education requirement)

689. **Weighers, Measurers, Checkers, and Samplers, Recordkeeping**: $28,790 (median wage), $47,280 (90th percentile wage), 74,460 (number of positions), 1.9% (2016--2026 growth), High school diploma or equivalent (typical education requirement)

690. **Preschool Teachers**, Except Special Education: $28,790 (median wage), $54,310 (90th percentile wage), 385,550 (number of positions), 10.5% (2016--2026 growth), Associate's degree (typical education requirement)

691. **Production Workers**, All Other: $28,770 (median wage), $51,470 (90th percentile wage), 251,670 (number of positions), 4.9% (2016--2026 growth), High school diploma or equivalent (typical education requirement)

692. **Protective Service Workers**, All Other: $28,720 (median wage), $53,460 (90th percentile wage), 135,120 (number of positions), 8.4% (2016--2026 growth), High school diploma or equivalent (typical education requirement)

693. **Grinding and Polishing Workers**, Hand: $28,720

(median wage), $45,440 (90th percentile wage), 26,670 (number of positions), -20.5% (2016--2026 growth), No formal educational credential (typical education requirement)

694. **Dancers**: $28,579 (median wage), $69,347 (90th percentile wage), 10,060 (number of positions), 5% (2016--2026 growth), No formal educational credential (typical education requirement)

695. **Food and Tobacco Roasting, Baking, and Drying Machine Operators and Tenders**: $28,570 (median wage), $48,550 (90th percentile wage), 20,080 (number of positions), -0.6% (2016--2026 growth), No formal educational credential (typical education requirement)

696. **Cleaning, Washing, and Metal Pickling Equipment Operators and Tenders**: $28,550 (median wage), $45,190 (90th percentile wage), 17,860 (number of positions), 0.4% (2016--2026 growth), High school diploma or equivalent (typical education requirement)

697. **Assemblers and Fabricators**, All Other: $28,550 (median wage), $47,390 (90th percentile wage), 230,310 (number of positions), -13.8% (2016--2026 growth), High school diploma or equivalent (typical education requirement)

698. **Woodworking Machine Setters, Operators, and**

Tenders, Except Sawing: $28,510 (median wage), $42,220 (90th percentile wage), 76,130 (number of positions), 0.7% (2016--2026 growth), High school diploma or equivalent (typical education requirement)

699. **Woodworkers, All Other**: $28,500 (median wage), $50,540 (90th percentile wage), 6,750 (number of positions), 4.1% (2016--2026 growth), High school diploma or equivalent (typical education requirement)

700. **Grounds Maintenance Workers, All Other**: $28,470 (median wage), $56,430 (90th percentile wage), 15,170 (number of positions), 8.5% (2016--2026 growth), No formal educational credential (typical education requirement)

701. **Machine Feeders and Offbearers**: $28,410 (median wage), $46,140 (90th percentile wage), 88,070 (number of positions), 1.8% (2016--2026 growth), No formal educational credential (typical education requirement)

702. **Sawing Machine Setters, Operators, and Tenders, Wood**: $28,380 (median wage), $43,530 (90th percentile wage), 50,640 (number of positions), 0.8% (2016--2026 growth), High school diploma or equivalent (typical education requirement)

703. **Material Moving Workers**, All Other: $28,370

3 JOBS RANKED BY MEDIAN SALARY

(median wage), $58,840 (90th percentile wage), 23,880 (number of positions), 9.3% (2016--2026 growth), No formal educational credential (typical education requirement)

704. **Food Cooking Machine Operators and Tenders**: $28,350 (median wage), $45,830 (90th percentile wage), 36,520 (number of positions), 2.6% (2016--2026 growth), High school diploma or equivalent (typical education requirement)

705. **Occupational Therapy Aides**: $28,330 (median wage), $51,180 (90th percentile wage), 7,210 (number of positions), 24.7% (2016--2026 growth), High school diploma or equivalent (typical education requirement)

706. **Packaging and Filling Machine Operators and Tenders**: $28,290 (median wage), $47,620 (90th percentile wage), 386,520 (number of positions), 1.7% (2016--2026 growth), High school diploma or equivalent (typical education requirement)

707. **Tailors, Dressmakers, and Custom Sewers**: $28,240 (median wage), $46,960 (90th percentile wage), 21,660 (number of positions), -0.3% (2016--2026 growth), No formal educational credential (typical education requirement)

708. **Couriers and Messengers**: $28,170 (median wage), $44,440 (90th percentile wage), 74,120 (number of

positions), 8.4% (2016--2026 growth), High school diploma or equivalent (typical education requirement)

709. **Switchboard Operators**, Including Answering Service: $28,030 (median wage), $42,090 (90th percentile wage), 90,910 (number of positions), -19.9% (2016--2026 growth), High school diploma or equivalent (typical education requirement)

710. **Substitute Teachers**: $28,010 (median wage), $46,140 (90th percentile wage), 609,960 (number of positions), 2016--2026 growth projection not available, typical education requirement not available

711. **Receptionists and Information Clerks**: $27,920 (median wage), $40,380 (90th percentile wage), 997,770 (number of positions), 9.1% (2016--2026 growth), High school diploma or equivalent (typical education requirement)

712. **Food Batchmakers**: $27,810 (median wage), $46,010 (90th percentile wage), 148,540 (number of positions), 1.3% (2016--2026 growth), High school diploma or equivalent (typical education requirement)

713. **Animal Trainers**: $27,690 (median wage), $58,050 (90th percentile wage), 13,590 (number of positions), 10.7% (2016--2026 growth), High school diploma or

equivalent (typical education requirement)

714. **Helpers--Roofers**: $27,670 (median wage), $39,110 (90th percentile wage), 10,190 (number of positions), 12.4% (2016--2026 growth), No formal educational credential (typical education requirement)

715. **Bicycle Repairers**: $27,630 (median wage), $39,150 (90th percentile wage), 12,560 (number of positions), 29.4% (2016--2026 growth), High school diploma or equivalent (typical education requirement)

716. **Cutters and Trimmers**, Hand: $27,600 (median wage), $42,450 (90th percentile wage), 14,250 (number of positions), -10% (2016--2026 growth), No formal educational credential (typical education requirement)

717. **Helpers--Installation, Maintenance, and Repair Workers**: $27,510 (median wage), $43,680 (90th percentile wage), 118,720 (number of positions), 11.1% (2016--2026 growth), High school diploma or equivalent (typical education requirement)

718. **Textile Winding, Twisting, and Drawing Out Machine Setters, Operators, and Tenders**: $27,500 (median wage), $37,880 (90th percentile wage), 30,340 (number of positions), -16.3% (2016--2026 growth), High school diploma or equivalent (typical education requirement)

719. **Textile Knitting and Weaving Machine Setters, Operators, and Tenders**: $27,470 (median wage), $38,750 (90th percentile wage), 21,550 (number of positions), -18.3% (2016--2026 growth), High school diploma or equivalent (typical education requirement)

720. **Helpers--Painters, Paperhangers, Plasterers, and Stucco Masons**: $27,310 (median wage), $39,670 (90th percentile wage), 10,780 (number of positions), 4.1% (2016--2026 growth), No formal educational credential (typical education requirement)

721. **Textile Bleaching and Dyeing Machine Operators and Tenders**: $27,270 (median wage), $38,700 (90th percentile wage), 10,860 (number of positions), -17% (2016--2026 growth), High school diploma or equivalent (typical education requirement)

722. **Tellers**: $27,260 (median wage), $37,760 (90th percentile wage), 496,760 (number of positions), -8.3% (2016--2026 growth), High school diploma or equivalent (typical education requirement)

723. **Motor Vehicle Operators**, All Other: $27,150 (median wage), $53,880 (90th percentile wage), 53,680 (number of positions), 10.3% (2016--2026 growth), No formal educational credential (typical education requirement)

724. **Cooks**, All Other: $27,120 (median wage), $43,580 (90th percentile wage), 15,490 (number of positions), 9% (2016--2026 growth), No formal educational credential (typical education requirement)

725. **Fishers and Related Fishing Workers**: $27,110 (median wage), $48,080 (90th percentile wage), 520 (number of positions), 2016--2026 growth project not available, typical education requirement not available

726. **Forest and Conservation Workers**: $26,940 (median wage), $49,150 (90th percentile wage), 7,170 (number of positions), -1.3% (2016--2026 growth), High school diploma or equivalent (typical education requirement)

727. **Fabric Menders**, Except Garment: $26,920 (median wage), $37,430 (90th percentile wage), 550 (number of positions), -7.6% (2016--2026 growth), High school diploma or equivalent (typical education requirement)

728. **Psychiatric Aides**: $26,720 (median wage), $42,220 (90th percentile wage), 67,410 (number of positions), 5.2% (2016--2026 growth), High school diploma or equivalent (typical education requirement)

729. **Crossing Guards**: $26,700 (median wage), $42,210 (90th percentile wage), 72,900 (number of positions), 8.5% (2016--2026 growth), No formal educational

credential (typical education requirement)

730. **Merchandise Displayers and Window Trimmers**: $26,700 (median wage), $47,150 (90th percentile wage), 114,690 (number of positions), 3.8% (2016--2026 growth), High school diploma or equivalent (typical education requirement)

731. **Orderlies**: $26,690 (median wage), $40,180 (90th percentile wage), 52,940 (number of positions), 8.1% (2016--2026 growth), High school diploma or equivalent (typical education requirement)

732. **Slaughterers and Meat Packers**: $26,590 (median wage), $36,170 (90th percentile wage), 80,780 (number of positions), 0.5% (2016--2026 growth), No formal educational credential (typical education requirement)

733. **Nursing Assistants**: $26,590 (median wage), $37,900 (90th percentile wage), 1,443,150 (number of positions), 10.9% (2016--2026 growth), Postsecondary nondegree award (typical education requirement)

734. **Photographic Process Workers and Processing Machine Operators**: $26,470 (median wage), $48,030 (90th percentile wage), 26,430 (number of positions), -18.4% (2016--2026 growth), High school diploma or equivalent (typical education requirement)

735. **Dietetic Technicians**: $26,350 (median wage),

$45,960 (90th percentile wage), 32,240 (number of positions), 9.3% (2016--2026 growth), Associate's degree (typical education requirement)

736. **Landscaping and Groundskeeping Workers**: $26,320 (median wage), $41,070 (90th percentile wage), 906,570 (number of positions), 10.3% (2016--2026 growth), No formal educational credential (typical education requirement)

737. **Shoe Machine Operators and Tenders**: $26,150 (median wage), $36,400 (90th percentile wage), 3,500 (number of positions), -8.5% (2016--2026 growth), High school diploma or equivalent (typical education requirement)

738. **Textile Cutting Machine Setters, Operators, and Tenders**: $26,090 (median wage), $39,880 (90th percentile wage), 15,040 (number of positions), -15.8% (2016--2026 growth), High school diploma or equivalent (typical education requirement)

739. **Transportation Attendants**, Except Flight Attendants: $26,060 (median wage), $54,450 (90th percentile wage), 18,410 (number of positions), 8.4% (2016--2026 growth), High school diploma or equivalent (typical education requirement)

740. **Gaming Cage Workers**: $25,990 (median wage), $40,640 (90th percentile wage), 18,810 (number of positions), 1.4% (2016--2026 growth), High school

diploma or equivalent (typical education requirement)

741. **Laborers and Freight, Stock, and Material Movers, Hand**: $25,980 (median wage), $42,690 (90th percentile wage), 2,587,900 (number of positions), 7.6% (2016--2026 growth), No formal educational credential (typical education requirement)

742. **Textile, Apparel, and Furnishings Workers, All Other**: $25,890 (median wage), $52,300 (90th percentile wage), 15,650 (number of positions), -3% (2016--2026 growth), High school diploma or equivalent (typical education requirement)

743. **Floral Designers**: $25,850 (median wage), $39,130 (90th percentile wage), 43,990 (number of positions), -5.9% (2016--2026 growth), High school diploma or equivalent (typical education requirement)

744. **Security Guards**: $25,770 (median wage), $47,260 (90th percentile wage), 1,103,120 (number of positions), 6.3% (2016--2026 growth), High school diploma or equivalent (typical education requirement)

745. **Barbers**: $25,760 (median wage), $47,400 (90th percentile wage), 15,900 (number of positions), 9.2% (2016--2026 growth), Postsecondary nondegree award (typical education requirement)

746. **Physical Therapist Aides**: $25,680 (median wage), $38,340 (90th percentile wage), 50,030 (number of positions), 29.1% (2016--2026 growth), High school diploma or equivalent (typical education requirement)

747. **Umpires, Referees, and Other Sports Officials**: $25,660 (median wage), $58,160 (90th percentile wage), 18,660 (number of positions), 7.4% (2016--2026 growth), High school diploma or equivalent (typical education requirement)

748. **Demonstrators and Product Promoters**: $25,610 (median wage), $48,480 (90th percentile wage), 86,500 (number of positions), 7% (2016--2026 growth), No formal educational credential (typical education requirement)

749. **Residential Advisors**: $25,570 (median wage), $39,960 (90th percentile wage), 110,330 (number of positions), 12.9% (2016--2026 growth), High school diploma or equivalent (typical education requirement)

750. **Counter and Rental Clerks**: $25,550 (median wage), $46,740 (90th percentile wage), 450,330 (number of positions), 5.5% (2016--2026 growth), No formal educational credential (typical education requirement)

751. **Personal Care and Service Workers**, All Other:

$25,420 (median wage), $38,460 (90th percentile wage), 54,520 (number of positions), 6.8% (2016--2026 growth), High school diploma or equivalent (typical education requirement)

752. **Teacher Assistants**: $25,410 (median wage), $38,820 (90th percentile wage), 1,263,820 (number of positions), 8.4% (2016--2026 growth), Some college, no degree (typical education requirement)

753. **Veterinary Assistants and Laboratory Animal Caretakers**: $25,250 (median wage), $37,810 (90th percentile wage), 79,990 (number of positions), 19.4% (2016--2026 growth), High school diploma or equivalent (typical education requirement)

754. **Pharmacy Aides**: $25,240 (median wage), $44,380 (90th percentile wage), 36,660 (number of positions), -4.8% (2016--2026 growth), High school diploma or equivalent (typical education requirement)

755. **Library Assistants**, Clerical: $25,220 (median wage), $40,540 (90th percentile wage), 98,560 (number of positions), 9.4% (2016--2026 growth), High school diploma or equivalent (typical education requirement)

756. **Bakers**: $25,090 (median wage), $39,050 (90th percentile wage), 180,450 (number of positions), 6.3% (2016--2026 growth), No formal educational credential (typical education requirement)

757. **Tire Repairers and Changers**: $25,040 (median wage), $39,040 (90th percentile wage), 109,350 (number of positions), 0.8% (2016--2026 growth), High school diploma or equivalent (typical education requirement)

758. **Tour Guides and Escorts**: $24,920 (median wage), $43,060 (90th percentile wage), 38,660 (number of positions), 10.9% (2016--2026 growth), High school diploma or equivalent (typical education requirement)

759. **Gaming Service Workers, All Other**: $24,880 (median wage), $42,200 (90th percentile wage), 12,140 (number of positions), 0.7% (2016--2026 growth), High school diploma or equivalent (typical education requirement)

760. **Funeral Attendants**: $24,830 (median wage), $39,720 (90th percentile wage), 35,770 (number of positions), 2.7% (2016--2026 growth), High school diploma or equivalent (typical education requirement)

761. **Helpers--Production Workers**: $24,830 (median wage), $38,750 (90th percentile wage), 429,890 (number of positions), 11.6% (2016--2026 growth), High school diploma or equivalent (typical education requirement)

762. **Cooks, Institution and Cafeteria**: $24,750 (median

wage), $38,030 (90th percentile wage), 409,850 (number of positions), 7.7% (2016--2026 growth), No formal educational credential (typical education requirement)

763. **Sewers, Hand**: $24,520 (median wage), $34,460 (90th percentile wage), 6,540 (number of positions), -4% (2016--2026 growth), No formal educational credential (typical education requirement)

764. **Farmworkers, Farm, Ranch, and Aquacultural Animals**: $24,520 (median wage), $39,230 (90th percentile wage), 35,670 (number of positions), -3.8% (2016--2026 growth), No formal educational credential (typical education requirement)

765. **Meat, Poultry, and Fish Cutters and Trimmers**: $24,490 (median wage), $33,020 (90th percentile wage), 149,800 (number of positions), 0.8% (2016--2026 growth), No formal educational credential (typical education requirement)

766. **Door-to-Door Sales Workers, News and Street Vendors, and Related Workers**: $24,330 (median wage), $47,340 (90th percentile wage), 8,040 (number of positions), 6.3% (2016--2026 growth), No formal educational credential (typical education requirement)

767. **Telemarketers**: $24,300 (median wage), $39,310 (90th percentile wage), 215,290 (number of

positions), 0% (2016--2026 growth), No formal educational credential (typical education requirement)

768. **Taxi Drivers and Chauffeurs**: $24,300 (median wage), $38,500 (90th percentile wage), 188,860 (number of positions), 4.8% (2016--2026 growth), No formal educational credential (typical education requirement)

769. **Hairdressers, Hairstylists, and Cosmetologists**: $24,260 (median wage), $49,050 (90th percentile wage), 352,380 (number of positions), 10.6% (2016--2026 growth), Postsecondary nondegree award (typical education requirement)

770. **Janitors and Cleaners**, Except Maids and Housekeeping Cleaners: $24,190 (median wage), $40,760 (90th percentile wage), 2,161,740 (number of positions), 9.8% (2016--2026 growth), No formal educational credential (typical education requirement)

771. **Food Processing Workers**, All Other: $24,160 (median wage), $35,420 (90th percentile wage), 43,070 (number of positions), 5.4% (2016--2026 growth), No formal educational credential (typical education requirement)

772. **Cooks**, Restaurant: $24,140 (median wage), $35,090 (90th percentile wage), 1,217,370 (number of

positions), 11.8% (2016--2026 growth), No formal educational credential (typical education requirement)

773. **Shoe and Leather Workers and Repairers**: $23,940 (median wage), $37,350 (90th percentile wage), 7,780 (number of positions), -2.5% (2016--2026 growth), High school diploma or equivalent (typical education requirement)

774. **Recreation Workers**: $23,870 (median wage), $41,660 (90th percentile wage), 336,880 (number of positions), 8.5% (2016--2026 growth), High school diploma or equivalent (typical education requirement)

775. **Ambulance Drivers and Attendants**, Except Emergency Medical Technicians: $23,850 (median wage), $35,960 (90th percentile wage), 17,300 (number of positions), 21.9% (2016--2026 growth), High school diploma or equivalent (typical education requirement)

776. **Stock Clerks and Order Fillers**: $23,840 (median wage), $39,750 (90th percentile wage), 2,016,340 (number of positions), 5% (2016--2026 growth), High school diploma or equivalent (typical education requirement)

777. **Gaming Change Persons and Booth Cashiers**: $23,780 (median wage), $37,330 (90th percentile

wage), 23,120 (number of positions), 2.7% (2016--2026 growth), No formal educational credential (typical education requirement)

778. **Sewing Machine Operators**: $23,670 (median wage), $37,000 (90th percentile wage), 139,500 (number of positions), -14.2% (2016--2026 growth), No formal educational credential (typical education requirement)

779. **Legislators**: $23,470 (median wage), $96,500 (90th percentile wage), 53,670 (number of positions), 7.1% (2016--2026 growth), Bachelor's degree (typical education requirement)

780. **Entertainment Attendants and Related Workers, All Other**: $23,270 (median wage), $32,000 (90th percentile wage), 14,550 (number of positions), 11.4% (2016--2026 growth), High school diploma or equivalent (typical education requirement)

781. **Driver/Sales Workers**: $22,830 (median wage), $48,400 (90th percentile wage), 426,310 (number of positions), -1.2% (2016--2026 growth), High school diploma or equivalent (typical education requirement)

782. **Retail Salespersons**: $22,680 (median wage), $41,420 (90th percentile wage), 4,528,550 (number of positions), 1.9% (2016--2026 growth), No formal educational credential (typical education

requirement)

783. **Gaming and Sports Book Writers and Runners**: $22,600 (median wage), $39,520 (90th percentile wage), 11,460 (number of positions), 3.8% (2016--2026 growth), High school diploma or equivalent (typical education requirement)

784. **Home Health Aides**: $22,600 (median wage), $30,610 (90th percentile wage), 814,300 (number of positions), 46.7% (2016--2026 growth), High school diploma or equivalent (typical education requirement)

785. **Graders and Sorters, Agricultural Products**: $22,520 (median wage), $33,750 (90th percentile wage), 38,780 (number of positions), -0.9% (2016--2026 growth), No formal educational credential (typical education requirement)

786. **Automotive and Watercraft Service Attendants**: $22,420 (median wage), $34,410 (90th percentile wage), 109,790 (number of positions), 10.6% (2016--2026 growth), No formal educational credential (typical education requirement)

787. **Baggage Porters and Bellhops**: $22,260 (median wage), $36,110 (90th percentile wage), 44,750 (number of positions), 8.2% (2016--2026 growth), High school diploma or equivalent (typical education requirement)

788. **Cleaners of Vehicles and Equipment**: $22,220 (median wage), $35,630 (90th percentile wage), 348,770 (number of positions), 10.8% (2016--2026 growth), No formal educational credential (typical education requirement)

789. **Manicurists and Pedicurists**: $22,150 (median wage), $33,590 (90th percentile wage), 90,630 (number of positions), 12% (2016--2026 growth), Postsecondary nondegree award (typical education requirement)

790. **Packers and Packagers**, Hand: $22,130 (median wage), $35,410 (90th percentile wage), 705,660 (number of positions), 1.8% (2016--2026 growth), No formal educational credential (typical education requirement)

791. Motion Picture Projectionists: $22,100 (median wage), $35,030 (90th percentile wage), 5,480 (number of positions), -9.9% (2016--2026 growth), No formal educational credential (typical education requirement)

792. **Hotel, Motel, and Resort Desk Clerks**: $22,070 (median wage), $31,850 (90th percentile wage), 248,440 (number of positions), 4.5% (2016--2026 growth), High school diploma or equivalent (typical education requirement)

793. **Farmworkers and Laborers**, Crop, Nursery, and

Greenhouse: $22,000 (median wage), $30,940 (90th percentile wage), 273,450 (number of positions), 1.1% (2016--2026 growth), No formal educational credential (typical education requirement)

794. **Nonfarm Animal Caretakers**: $21,990 (median wage), $35,860 (90th percentile wage), 187,360 (number of positions), 21.9% (2016--2026 growth), High school diploma or equivalent (typical education requirement)

795. **Personal Care Aides**: $21,920 (median wage), $29,760 (90th percentile wage), 1,492,250 (number of positions), 37.4% (2016--2026 growth), High school diploma or equivalent (typical education requirement)

796. **Cooks**, Short Order: $21,890 (median wage), $30,890 (90th percentile wage), 183,990 (number of positions), -3.3% (2016--2026 growth), No formal educational credential (typical education requirement)

797. **Models**: $21,870 (median wage), $52,390 (90th percentile wage), 4,390 (number of positions), -0.9% (2016--2026 growth), No formal educational credential (typical education requirement)

798. **Maids and Housekeeping Cleaners**: $21,820 (median wage), $34,430 (90th percentile wage), 924,640 (number of positions), 5.6% (2016--2026

growth), No formal educational credential (typical education requirement)

799. **Parking Lot Attendants**: $21,730 (median wage), $30,910 (90th percentile wage), 146,350 (number of positions), 6% (2016--2026 growth), No formal educational credential (typical education requirement)

800. **Locker Room, Coatroom, and Dressing Room Attendants**: $21,720 (median wage), $36,100 (90th percentile wage), 18,040 (number of positions), 8.7% (2016--2026 growth), High school diploma or equivalent (typical education requirement)

801. **Laundry and Dry-Cleaning Workers**: $21,510 (median wage), $31,460 (90th percentile wage), 207,710 (number of positions), -0.3% (2016--2026 growth), No formal educational credential (typical education requirement)

802. **Food Preparation Workers**: $21,440 (median wage), $31,040 (90th percentile wage), 850,670 (number of positions), 7.9% (2016--2026 growth), No formal educational credential (typical education requirement)

803. **Pressers, Textile, Garment, and Related Materials**: $21,300 (median wage), $29,460 (90th percentile wage), 45,150 (number of positions), -6.7% (2016--2026 growth), No formal educational

credential (typical education requirement)

804. **Food Servers, Nonrestaurant**: $21,240 (median wage), $33,430 (90th percentile wage), 261,520 (number of positions), 10.2% (2016--2026 growth), No formal educational credential (typical education requirement)

805. **Childcare Workers**: $21,170 (median wage), $31,710 (90th percentile wage), 569,370 (number of positions), 6.7% (2016--2026 growth), High school diploma or equivalent (typical education requirement)

806. **Food Preparation and Serving Related Workers, All Other**: $21,090 (median wage), $33,450 (90th percentile wage), 59,060 (number of positions), 9.3% (2016--2026 growth), No formal educational credential (typical education requirement)

807. **Bartenders**: $20,800 (median wage), $40,230 (90th percentile wage), 603,320 (number of positions), 2.5% (2016--2026 growth), No formal educational credential (typical education requirement)

808. **Dishwashers**: $20,800 (median wage), $25,800 (90th percentile wage), 506,450 (number of positions), 4.3% (2016--2026 growth), No formal educational credential (typical education requirement)

809. **Lifeguards, Ski Patrol, and Other Recreational Protective Service Workers**: $20,290 (median wage), $31,840 (90th percentile wage), 145,100 (number of positions), 7.7% (2016--2026 growth), No formal educational credential (typical education requirement)

810. **Dining Room and Cafeteria Attendants and Bartender Helpers**: $20,200 (median wage), $30,390 (90th percentile wage), 423,080 (number of positions), 7.1% (2016--2026 growth), No formal educational credential (typical education requirement)

811. **Cashiers**: $20,180 (median wage), $28,760 (90th percentile wage), 3,541,010 (number of positions), -0.8% (2016--2026 growth), No formal educational credential (typical education requirement)

812. **Amusement and Recreation Attendants**: $20,160 (median wage), $29,660 (90th percentile wage), 286,740 (number of positions), 9.3% (2016--2026 growth), No formal educational credential (typical education requirement)

813. **Waiters and Waitresses**: $19,990 (median wage), $38,460 (90th percentile wage), 2,564,610 (number of positions), 7% (2016--2026 growth), No formal educational credential (typical education requirement)

814. **Hosts and Hostesses, Restaurant, Lounge, and Coffee Shop**: $19,980 (median wage), $28,620 (90th percentile wage), 404,360 (number of positions), 6.9% (2016--2026 growth), No formal educational credential (typical education requirement)

815. **Counter Attendants, Cafeteria, Food Concession, and Coffee Shop**: $19,970 (median wage), $28,010 (90th percentile wage), 499,550 (number of positions), 4.6% (2016--2026 growth), No formal educational credential (typical education requirement)

816. **Ushers, Lobby Attendants, and Ticket Takers**: $19,920 (median wage), $29,690 (90th percentile wage), 117,920 (number of positions), 7.5% (2016--2026 growth), No formal educational credential (typical education requirement)

817. **Cooks**, Fast Food: $19,860 (median wage), $25,290 (90th percentile wage), 513,200 (number of positions), -5.2% (2016--2026 growth), No formal educational credential (typical education requirement)

818. **Shampooers**: $19,700 (median wage), $25,750 (90th percentile wage), 15,240 (number of positions), 12.2% (2016--2026 growth), No formal educational credential (typical education requirement)

819. **Combined Food Preparation and Serving

Workers, Including Fast Food: $19,440 (median wage), $25,330 (90th percentile wage), 3,426,090 (number of positions), 16.8% (2016--2026 growth), No formal educational credential (typical education requirement)

820. **Gaming Dealers**: $19,290 (median wage), $31,780 (90th percentile wage), 94,570 (number of positions), 1.1% (2016--2026 growth), High school diploma or equivalent (typical education requirement)

4 OCCUPATIONS RANKED ALPHABETICALLY

The second main chapter of the book, this chapter presents the complete list of all the 820 detailed occupations, **ranked now alphabetically**. Recall that in the previous chapter, the same 820 occupations were presented in the descending order of the median salary of the occupations.

In the complete list of all the 820 occupations presented below, for each occupation, the following information is provided.

- Median Wage Rank

- Median Wage

- Ninetieth Percentile Wage

- Number of Existing Positions

- Projected Growth Between 2016 and 2026
- Typical Education Requirement for Entry Into the Occupation

Brief descriptions of these metrics are as follows. Note that, except for the Median Salary Rank, all other metrics are identical to those in the previous chapter.

Median Wage Rank. This the rank of the occupation according to its median salary. The list in the previous chapter was ordered by this rank.

Median Wage. At the risk of excessive repetition, we point out here once again that by the *median salary*, we mean the *salary paid to an average worker* in an occupation, or equivalently the *typical salary* paid in an occupation.

Therefore, for all purposes in this book, median salary = typical salary = salary paid to an average worker.

Ninetieth Percentile Wage. As explained in the previous chapter, the 90th percentile wage is the wage that is better than 90% of the salaries paid to workers in an occupation. Thus, it measures how well we can do beyond being an average worker.

Number of Existing Positions. This metric is pretty self-explanatory. This is the number of existing positions of an occupation in the American job market, indicating the size of the occupations and thus the demand for the occupations.

Projected Growth Between 2016 and 2026. This is the 10-year percentage growth of a given occupation between 2016 and 2026, forecasted by the U.S. Department of Labor. The data was released only in November 2017, fresh out of the oven.

For instance, the occupation of accountants and auditors had one million and four hundred thousand positions in 2016 across America, and it is projected to grow to one million five hundred and forty thousand in 2026, a 10% increase over the 10-year period.

Typical Education Needed for Entry Into the Occupation. This is the education attainment level typically required for entry positions in an occupation. Here is a list of education levels we can achieve in the U.S. These are the official categorization of education attainment levels in the employment data released by the U.S. Department of Labor:

- No formal educational credential

- High school diploma or equivalent

- Some college, no degree

- Postsecondary nondegree award

- Associate's degree

- Bachelor's degree

- Master's degree

- Doctoral or professional degree.

Now we are all set to present the full list of 820 occupations in the U.S., in an alphabetical order.

Occupations Ranked Alphabetically

1. **Accountants and Auditors**: #180 (median wage rank), $68,150 (median wage), $120,910 (90th percentile wage), 1,246,540 (number of positions), 10% (2016--2026 growth), Bachelor's degree (typical education requirement)

2. **Actors**: #505 (median wage rank), $38,896 (median wage), $64,956 (90th percentile wage), 48,620 (number of positions), 11.7% (2016--2026 growth), Some college, no degree (typical education requirement)

3. **Actuaries**: #51 (median wage rank), $100,610 (median wage), $186,250 (90th percentile wage), 19,940 (number of positions), 22.5% (2016--2026 growth), Bachelor's degree (typical education requirement)

4. **Adhesive Bonding Machine Operators and Tenders**: #641 (median wage rank), $32,290 (median wage), $50,910 (90th percentile wage), 16,940 (number of positions), -2.7% (2016--2026 growth), High school diploma or equivalent (typical

education requirement)

5. **Administrative Law Judges, Adjudicators, and Hearing Officers**: #74 (median wage rank), $92,110 (median wage), $162,400 (90th percentile wage), 14,540 (number of positions), 4% (2016--2026 growth), Doctoral or professional degree (typical education requirement)

6. **Administrative Services Managers**: #79 (median wage rank), $90,050 (median wage), $159,330 (90th percentile wage), 266,280 (number of positions), 10.1% (2016--2026 growth), Bachelor's degree (typical education requirement)

7. **Adult Basic and Secondary Education and Literacy Teachers and Instructors**: #348 (median wage rank), $50,650 (median wage), $84,740 (90th percentile wage), 58,810 (number of positions), -5.6% (2016--2026 growth), Bachelor's degree (typical education requirement)

8. **Advertising and Promotions Managers**: #50 (median wage rank), $100,810 (median wage), $168,353 (90th percentile wage), 28,860 (number of positions), 5.8% (2016--2026 growth), Bachelor's degree (typical education requirement)

9. **Advertising Sales Agents**: #354 (median wage rank), $50,380 (median wage), $115,430 (90th percentile wage), 141,100 (number of positions), -2.9% (2016--

2026 growth), High school diploma or equivalent (typical education requirement)

10. **Aerospace Engineering and Operations Technicians**: #181 (median wage rank), $68,020 (median wage), $102,000 (90th percentile wage), 11,970 (number of positions), 6.6% (2016--2026 growth), Associate's degree (typical education requirement)

11. **Aerospace Engineers**: #36 (median wage rank), $109,650 (median wage), $160,290 (90th percentile wage), 68,510 (number of positions), 6.1% (2016--2026 growth), Bachelor's degree (typical education requirement)

12. **Agents and Business Managers of Artists, Performers, and Athletes**: #225 (median wage rank), $62,080 (median wage), $194,810 (90th percentile wage), 13,470 (number of positions), 4.9% (2016--2026 growth), Bachelor's degree (typical education requirement)

13. **Agricultural and Food Science Technicians**: #538 (median wage rank), $37,550 (median wage), $61,450 (90th percentile wage), 20,420 (number of positions), 6.3% (2016--2026 growth), Associate's degree (typical education requirement)

14. **Agricultural Engineers**: #147 (median wage rank), $73,640 (median wage), $117,130 (90th percentile

wage), 1,980 (number of positions), 8.1% (2016--2026 growth), Bachelor's degree (typical education requirement)

15. **Agricultural Equipment Operators**: #686 (median wage rank), $28,850 (median wage), $43,690 (90th percentile wage), 28,700 (number of positions), 5.6% (2016--2026 growth), No formal educational credential (typical education requirement)

16. **Agricultural Inspectors**: #446 (median wage rank), $42,800 (median wage), $63,840 (90th percentile wage), 14,710 (number of positions), 4.6% (2016--2026 growth), Bachelor's degree (typical education requirement)

17. **Agricultural Sciences Teachers, Postsecondary**: #75 (median wage rank), $91,580 (median wage), $153,250 (90th percentile wage), 10,340 (number of positions), 7.5% (2016--2026 growth), Doctoral or professional degree (typical education requirement)

18. **Agricultural Workers**, All Other: #656 (median wage rank), $31,160 (median wage), $54,520 (90th percentile wage), 5,040 (number of positions), 4.5% (2016--2026 growth), No formal educational credential (typical education requirement)

19. **Air Traffic Controllers**: #23 (median wage rank), $122,410 (median wage), $172,680 (90th percentile wage), 23,240 (number of positions), 3.5% (2016--

2026 growth), Associate's degree (typical education requirement)

20. **Aircraft Cargo Handling Supervisors**: #397 (median wage rank), $47,360 (median wage), $81,620 (90th percentile wage), 7,460 (number of positions), 5.9% (2016--2026 growth), High school diploma or equivalent (typical education requirement)

21. **Aircraft Mechanics and Service Technicians**: #241 (median wage rank), $60,170 (median wage), $87,880 (90th percentile wage), 128,570 (number of positions), 4.9% (2016--2026 growth), Postsecondary nondegree award (typical education requirement)

22. **Aircraft Structure, Surfaces, Rigging, and Systems Assemblers**: #359 (median wage rank), $50,050 (median wage), $78,150 (90th percentile wage), 42,010 (number of positions), -17.4% (2016--2026 growth), High school diploma or equivalent (typical education requirement)

23. **Airfield Operations Specialists**: #378 (median wage rank), $48,910 (median wage), $90,350 (90th percentile wage), 8,760 (number of positions), 8.8% (2016--2026 growth), High school diploma or equivalent (typical education requirement)

24. **Airline Pilots, Copilots, and Flight Engineers**: #19 (median wage rank), $127,820 (median wage), $213,459 (90th percentile wage), 81,520 (number of

positions), 3.4% (2016--2026 growth), Bachelor's degree (typical education requirement)

25. **Ambulance Drivers and Attendants, Except Emergency Medical Technicians**: #775 (median wage rank), $23,850 (median wage), $35,960 (90th percentile wage), 17,300 (number of positions), 21.9% (2016--2026 growth), High school diploma or equivalent (typical education requirement)

26. **Amusement and Recreation Attendants**: #812 (median wage rank), $20,160 (median wage), $29,660 (90th percentile wage), 286,740 (number of positions), 9.3% (2016--2026 growth), No formal educational credential (typical education requirement)

27. **Anesthesiologists**: #1 (median wage rank), $247,339 (median wage), $413,057 (90th percentile wage), 30,190 (number of positions), 17.8% (2016--2026 growth), Doctoral or professional degree (typical education requirement)

28. **Animal Breeders**: #582 (median wage rank), $35,690 (median wage), $73,130 (90th percentile wage), 1,270 (number of positions), 2% (2016--2026 growth), High school diploma or equivalent (typical education requirement)

29. **Animal Control Workers**: #602 (median wage rank), $34,550 (median wage), $55,600 (90th percentile

wage), 12,970 (number of positions), 8.4% (2016--2026 growth), High school diploma or equivalent (typical education requirement)

30. **Animal Scientists**: #239 (median wage rank), $60,330 (median wage), $126,190 (90th percentile wage), 2,470 (number of positions), 6% (2016--2026 growth), Bachelor's degree (typical education requirement)

31. **Animal Trainers**: #713 (median wage rank), $27,690 (median wage), $58,050 (90th percentile wage), 13,590 (number of positions), 10.7% (2016--2026 growth), High school diploma or equivalent (typical education requirement)

32. **Anthropologists and Archeologists**: #213 (median wage rank), $63,190 (median wage), $99,590 (90th percentile wage), 6,470 (number of positions), 3.3% (2016--2026 growth), Master's degree (typical education requirement)

33. **Anthropology and Archeology Teachers, Postsecondary**: #104 (median wage rank), $81,350 (median wage), $155,500 (90th percentile wage), 5,700 (number of positions), 10% (2016--2026 growth), Doctoral or professional degree (typical education requirement)

34. **Appraisers and Assessors of Real Estate**: #334 (median wage rank), $51,850 (median wage), $97,120 (90th percentile wage), 60,770 (number of positions),

14.4% (2016--2026 growth), Bachelor's degree (typical education requirement)

35. **Arbitrators, Mediators, and Conciliators**: #244 (median wage rank), $59,770 (median wage), $123,930 (90th percentile wage), 6,300 (number of positions), 11.3% (2016--2026 growth), Bachelor's degree (typical education requirement)

36. **Architects, Except Landscape and Naval**: #127 (median wage rank), $76,930 (median wage), $129,810 (90th percentile wage), 99,860 (number of positions), 4% (2016--2026 growth), Bachelor's degree (typical education requirement)

37. **Architectural and Civil Drafters**: #340 (median wage rank), $51,640 (median wage), $78,770 (90th percentile wage), 96,810 (number of positions), 8.1% (2016--2026 growth), Associate's degree (typical education requirement)

38. **Architectural and Engineering Managers**: #16 (median wage rank), $134,730 (median wage), $207,400 (90th percentile wage), 178,390 (number of positions), 5.5% (2016--2026 growth), Bachelor's degree (typical education requirement)

39. **Architecture Teachers, Postsecondary**: #114 (median wage rank), $79,250 (median wage), $160,220 (90th percentile wage), 7,370 (number of positions), 10.6% (2016--2026 growth), Doctoral or professional degree

(typical education requirement)

40. **Archivists**: #351 (median wage rank), $50,500 (median wage), $88,160 (90th percentile wage), 5,760 (number of positions), 14.3% (2016--2026 growth), Master's degree (typical education requirement)

41. **Area, Ethnic, and Cultural Studies Teachers, Postsecondary**: #151 (median wage rank), $73,020 (median wage), $148,640 (90th percentile wage), 9,060 (number of positions), 10.5% (2016--2026 growth), Doctoral or professional degree (typical education requirement)

42. **Art Directors**: #80 (median wage rank), $89,820 (median wage), $166,400 (90th percentile wage), 36,210 (number of positions), 7.4% (2016--2026 growth), Bachelor's degree (typical education requirement)

43. **Art, Drama, and Music Teachers, Postsecondary**: #175 (median wage rank), $68,650 (median wage), $140,070 (90th percentile wage), 99,020 (number of positions), 12% (2016--2026 growth), Master's degree (typical education requirement)

44. **Artists and Related Workers**, All Other: #230 (median wage rank), $61,360 (median wage), $103,860 (90th percentile wage), 7,010 (number of positions), 6.9% (2016--2026 growth), No formal educational credential (typical education

requirement)

45. **Assemblers and Fabricators, All Other**: #697 (median wage rank), $28,550 (median wage), $47,390 (90th percentile wage), 230,310 (number of positions), -13.8% (2016--2026 growth), High school diploma or equivalent (typical education requirement)

46. **Astronomers**: #44 (median wage rank), $104,740 (median wage), $165,140 (90th percentile wage), 1,830 (number of positions), 10% (2016--2026 growth), Doctoral or professional degree (typical education requirement)

47. **Athletes and Sports Competitors**: #394 (median wage rank), $47,710 (median wage), $79,676 (90th percentile wage), 10,260 (number of positions), 7.2% (2016--2026 growth), No formal educational credential (typical education requirement)

48. **Athletic Trainers**: #420 (median wage rank), $45,630 (median wage), $69,140 (90th percentile wage), 24,130 (number of positions), 22.2% (2016--2026 growth), Bachelor's degree (typical education requirement)

49. **Atmospheric and Space Scientists**: #73 (median wage rank), $92,460 (median wage), $140,830 (90th percentile wage), 9,800 (number of positions), 12% (2016--2026 growth), Bachelor's degree (typical

education requirement)

50. **Atmospheric, Earth, Marine, and Space Sciences Teachers, Postsecondary**: #90 (median wage rank), $85,410 (median wage), $161,220 (90th percentile wage), 10,850 (number of positions), 9.5% (2016--2026 growth), Doctoral or professional degree (typical education requirement)

51. **Audio and Video Equipment Technicians**: #457 (median wage rank), $42,230 (median wage), $78,980 (90th percentile wage), 69,670 (number of positions), 12.9% (2016--2026 growth), Postsecondary nondegree award (typical education requirement)

52. **Audiologists**: #131 (median wage rank), $75,980 (median wage), $113,540 (90th percentile wage), 12,310 (number of positions), 20.4% (2016--2026 growth), Doctoral or professional degree (typical education requirement)

53. **Audio-Visual and Multimedia Collections Specialists**: #391 (median wage rank), $47,840 (median wage), $78,090 (90th percentile wage), 10,300 (number of positions), 8.7% (2016--2026 growth), Bachelor's degree (typical education requirement)

54. **Automotive and Watercraft Service Attendants**: #786 (median wage rank), $22,420 (median wage), $34,410 (90th percentile wage), 109,790 (number of

positions), 10.6% (2016--2026 growth), No formal educational credential (typical education requirement)

55. **Automotive Body and Related Repairers**: #465 (median wage rank), $41,540 (median wage), $70,620 (90th percentile wage), 143,940 (number of positions), 8.7% (2016--2026 growth), High school diploma or equivalent (typical education requirement)

56. **Automotive Glass Installers and Repairers**: #606 (median wage rank), $34,340 (median wage), $51,540 (90th percentile wage), 18,610 (number of positions), 6.6% (2016--2026 growth), High school diploma or equivalent (typical education requirement)

57. **Automotive Service Technicians and Mechanics**: #516 (median wage rank), $38,470 (median wage), $64,070 (90th percentile wage), 647,380 (number of positions), 6.3% (2016--2026 growth), Postsecondary nondegree award (typical education requirement)

58. **Avionics Technicians**: #234 (median wage rank), $60,760 (median wage), $83,260 (90th percentile wage), 17,330 (number of positions), 6% (2016--2026 growth), Associate's degree (typical education requirement)

59. **Baggage Porters and Bellhops**: #787 (median wage rank), $22,260 (median wage), $36,110 (90th

percentile wage), 44,750 (number of positions), 8.2% (2016--2026 growth), High school diploma or equivalent (typical education requirement)

60. **Bailiffs**: #448 (median wage rank), $42,670 (median wage), $74,300 (90th percentile wage), 17,880 (number of positions), -2.1% (2016--2026 growth), High school diploma or equivalent (typical education requirement)

61. **Bakers**: #756 (median wage rank), $25,090 (median wage), $39,050 (90th percentile wage), 180,450 (number of positions), 6.3% (2016--2026 growth), No formal educational credential (typical education requirement)

62. **Barbers**: #745 (median wage rank), $25,760 (median wage), $47,400 (90th percentile wage), 15,900 (number of positions), 9.2% (2016--2026 growth), Postsecondary nondegree award (typical education requirement)

63. **Bartenders**: #807 (median wage rank), $20,800 (median wage), $40,230 (90th percentile wage), 603,320 (number of positions), 2.5% (2016--2026 growth), No formal educational credential (typical education requirement)

64. **Bicycle Repairers**: #715 (median wage rank), $27,630 (median wage), $39,150 (90th percentile wage), 12,560 (number of positions), 29.4% (2016--2026

growth), High school diploma or equivalent (typical education requirement)

65. **Bill and Account Collectors**: #591 (median wage rank), $35,350 (median wage), $54,970 (90th percentile wage), 298,960 (number of positions), -3% (2016--2026 growth), High school diploma or equivalent (typical education requirement)

66. **Billing and Posting Clerks**: #574 (median wage rank), $36,150 (median wage), $52,150 (90th percentile wage), 485,220 (number of positions), 14.2% (2016--2026 growth), High school diploma or equivalent (typical education requirement)

67. **Biochemists and Biophysicists**: #100 (median wage rank), $82,180 (median wage), $158,410 (90th percentile wage), 29,200 (number of positions), 11.3% (2016--2026 growth), Doctoral or professional degree (typical education requirement)

68. **Biological Science Teachers, Postsecondary**: #130 (median wage rank), $76,650 (median wage), $157,630 (90th percentile wage), 50,820 (number of positions), 15.1% (2016--2026 growth), Doctoral or professional degree (typical education requirement)

69. **Biological Scientists**, All Other: #134 (median wage rank), $74,790 (median wage), $116,680 (90th percentile wage), 35,110 (number of positions), 7.9% (2016--2026 growth), Bachelor's degree (typical

education requirement)

70. **Biological Technicians**: #451 (median wage rank), $42,520 (median wage), $69,590 (90th percentile wage), 74,720 (number of positions), 10.2% (2016--2026 growth), Bachelor's degree (typical education requirement)

71. **Biomedical Engineers**: #89 (median wage rank), $85,620 (median wage), $134,620 (90th percentile wage), 20,590 (number of positions), 7.2% (2016--2026 growth), Bachelor's degree (typical education requirement)

72. **Boilermakers**: #227 (median wage rank), $62,060 (median wage), $85,800 (90th percentile wage), 16,660 (number of positions), 8.4% (2016--2026 growth), High school diploma or equivalent (typical education requirement)

73. **Bookkeeping, Accounting, and Auditing Clerks**: #519 (median wage rank), $38,390 (median wage), $59,630 (90th percentile wage), 1,566,960 (number of positions), -1.4% (2016--2026 growth), Some college, no degree (typical education requirement)

74. **Brickmasons and Blockmasons**: #371 (median wage rank), $49,250 (median wage), $84,100 (90th percentile wage), 64,370 (number of positions), 10.6% (2016--2026 growth), High school diploma or equivalent (typical education requirement)

75. **Bridge and Lock Tenders**: #376 (median wage rank), $49,090 (median wage), $61,740 (90th percentile wage), 3,510 (number of positions), 4.9% (2016--2026 growth), High school diploma or equivalent (typical education requirement)

76. **Broadcast News Analysts**: #284 (median wage rank), $56,680 (median wage), $163,490 (90th percentile wage), 5,070 (number of positions), -1% (2016--2026 growth), Bachelor's degree (typical education requirement)

77. **Broadcast Technicians**: #512 (median wage rank), $38,550 (median wage), $80,280 (90th percentile wage), 30,330 (number of positions), -3.2% (2016--2026 growth), Associate's degree (typical education requirement)

78. **Brokerage Clerks**: #372 (median wage rank), $49,200 (median wage), $76,390 (90th percentile wage), 59,820 (number of positions), 5% (2016--2026 growth), High school diploma or equivalent (typical education requirement)

79. **Budget Analysts**: #144 (median wage rank), $73,840 (median wage), $111,460 (90th percentile wage), 54,700 (number of positions), 6.5% (2016--2026 growth), Bachelor's degree (typical education requirement)

80. **Building Cleaning Workers**, All Other: #677

(median wage rank), $29,700 (median wage), $45,140 (90th percentile wage), 15,020 (number of positions), 12.6% (2016--2026 growth), No formal educational credential (typical education requirement)

81. **Bus and Truck Mechanics and Diesel Engine Specialists**: #424 (median wage rank), $45,170 (median wage), $67,550 (90th percentile wage), 254,280 (number of positions), 9.5% (2016--2026 growth), High school diploma or equivalent (typical education requirement)

82. **Bus Drivers, School or Special Client**: #670 (median wage rank), $30,150 (median wage), $46,390 (90th percentile wage), 515,020 (number of positions), 5.2% (2016--2026 growth), High school diploma or equivalent (typical education requirement)

83. **Bus Drivers, Transit and Intercity**: #487 (median wage rank), $39,790 (median wage), $64,290 (90th percentile wage), 169,680 (number of positions), 8.8% (2016--2026 growth), High school diploma or equivalent (typical education requirement)

84. **Business Operations Specialists**, All Other: #173 (median wage rank), $69,040 (median wage), $118,500 (90th percentile wage), 958,670 (number of positions), 8.8% (2016--2026 growth), Bachelor's degree (typical education requirement)

85. **Business Teachers, Postsecondary**: #124 (median

wage rank), $77,490 (median wage), $185,410 (90th percentile wage), 83,030 (number of positions), 18.1% (2016--2026 growth), Doctoral or professional degree (typical education requirement)

86. **Butchers and Meat Cutters**: #674 (median wage rank), $29,870 (median wage), $47,960 (90th percentile wage), 133,880 (number of positions), 5.7% (2016--2026 growth), No formal educational credential (typical education requirement)

87. **Buyers and Purchasing Agents, Farm Products**: #261 (median wage rank), $58,430 (median wage), $102,410 (90th percentile wage), 11,490 (number of positions), -5.9% (2016--2026 growth), Bachelor's degree (typical education requirement)

88. **Cabinetmakers and Bench Carpenters**: #626 (median wage rank), $33,050 (median wage), $51,470 (90th percentile wage), 97,980 (number of positions), 3.4% (2016--2026 growth), High school diploma or equivalent (typical education requirement)

89. **Camera and Photographic Equipment Repairers**: #473 (median wage rank), $41,060 (median wage), $66,150 (90th percentile wage), 3,760 (number of positions), 3.3% (2016--2026 growth), High school diploma or equivalent (typical education requirement)

90. **Camera Operators, Television, Video, and Motion**

Picture: #297 (median wage rank), $55,080 (median wage), $109,200 (90th percentile wage), 21,710 (number of positions), 6.4% (2016--2026 growth), Bachelor's degree (typical education requirement)

91. **Captains, Mates, and Pilots of Water Vessels**: #153 (median wage rank), $72,680 (median wage), $134,390 (90th percentile wage), 36,720 (number of positions), 8.8% (2016--2026 growth), Postsecondary nondegree award (typical education requirement)

92. **Cardiovascular Technologists and Technicians**: #295 (median wage rank), $55,570 (median wage), $89,450 (90th percentile wage), 53,760 (number of positions), 9.9% (2016--2026 growth), Associate's degree (typical education requirement)

93. **Career/Technical Education Teachers, Middle School**: #269 (median wage rank), $57,560 (median wage), $87,980 (90th percentile wage), 12,730 (number of positions), 7.3% (2016--2026 growth), Bachelor's degree (typical education requirement)

94. **Career/Technical Education Teachers, Secondary School**: #272 (median wage rank), $57,320 (median wage), $86,570 (90th percentile wage), 80,100 (number of positions), 6.4% (2016--2026 growth), Bachelor's degree (typical education requirement)

95. **Cargo and Freight Agents**: #461 (median wage rank), $41,920 (median wage), $64,340 (90th percentile

wage), 88,920 (number of positions), 10.4% (2016--2026 growth), High school diploma or equivalent (typical education requirement)

96. **Carpenters**: #438 (median wage rank), $43,600 (median wage), $79,480 (90th percentile wage), 676,980 (number of positions), 8.5% (2016--2026 growth), High school diploma or equivalent (typical education requirement)

97. **Carpet Installers**: #521 (median wage rank), $38,280 (median wage), $80,440 (90th percentile wage), 25,660 (number of positions), 9.8% (2016--2026 growth), No formal educational credential (typical education requirement)

98. **Cartographers and Photogrammetrists**: #216 (median wage rank), $62,750 (median wage), $99,800 (90th percentile wage), 12,100 (number of positions), 19.4% (2016--2026 growth), Bachelor's degree (typical education requirement)

99. **Cashiers**: #811 (median wage rank), $20,180 (median wage), $28,760 (90th percentile wage), 3,541,010 (number of positions), -0.8% (2016--2026 growth), No formal educational credential (typical education requirement)

100. **Cement Masons and Concrete Finishers**: #497 (median wage rank), $39,180 (median wage), $68,470 (90th percentile wage), 173,920 (number of

positions), 12.6% (2016--2026 growth), No formal educational credential (typical education requirement)

101. **Chefs and Head Cooks**: #442 (median wage rank), $43,180 (median wage), $76,280 (90th percentile wage), 134,190 (number of positions), 9.6% (2016--2026 growth), High school diploma or equivalent (typical education requirement)

102. **Chemical Engineers**: #59 (median wage rank), $98,340 (median wage), $158,800 (90th percentile wage), 31,990 (number of positions), 7.6% (2016--2026 growth), Bachelor's degree (typical education requirement)

103. **Chemical Equipment Operators and Tenders**: #393 (median wage rank), $47,780 (median wage), $77,640 (90th percentile wage), 73,840 (number of positions), -4.9% (2016--2026 growth), High school diploma or equivalent (typical education requirement)

104. **Chemical Plant and System Operators**: #243 (median wage rank), $59,920 (median wage), $81,970 (90th percentile wage), 33,300 (number of positions), -9.2% (2016--2026 growth), High school diploma or equivalent (typical education requirement)

105. **Chemical Technicians**: #412 (median wage rank), $45,840 (median wage), $76,930 (90th percentile

wage), 65,510 (number of positions), 3.9% (2016--2026 growth), Associate's degree (typical education requirement)

106. **Chemistry Teachers, Postsecondary**: #129 (median wage rank), $76,750 (median wage), $153,570 (90th percentile wage), 21,250 (number of positions), 9.9% (2016--2026 growth), Doctoral or professional degree (typical education requirement)

107. **Chemists**: #146 (median wage rank), $73,740 (median wage), $129,670 (90th percentile wage), 86,660 (number of positions), 6.5% (2016--2026 growth), Bachelor's degree (typical education requirement)

108. **Chief Executives**: #10 (median wage rank), $181,210 (median wage), $302,621 (90th percentile wage), 223,260 (number of positions), -3.5% (2016--2026 growth), Bachelor's degree (typical education requirement)

109. **Child, Family, and School Social Workers**: #440 (median wage rank), $43,250 (median wage), $75,140 (90th percentile wage), 298,840 (number of positions), 13.3% (2016--2026 growth), Bachelor's degree (typical education requirement)

110. **Childcare Workers**: #805 (median wage rank), $21,170 (median wage), $31,710 (90th percentile wage), 569,370 (number of positions), 6.7% (2016--

2026 growth), High school diploma or equivalent (typical education requirement)

111. **Chiropractors**: #186 (median wage rank), $67,520 (median wage), $141,030 (90th percentile wage), 32,960 (number of positions), 10.5% (2016--2026 growth), Doctoral or professional degree (typical education requirement)

112. **Choreographers**: #385 (median wage rank), $48,240 (median wage), $94,400 (90th percentile wage), 5,160 (number of positions), 3.2% (2016--2026 growth), High school diploma or equivalent (typical education requirement)

113. **Civil Engineering Technicians**: #362 (median wage rank), $49,980 (median wage), $77,500 (90th percentile wage), 72,150 (number of positions), 8.8% (2016--2026 growth), Associate's degree (typical education requirement)

114. **Civil Engineers**: #98 (median wage rank), $83,540 (median wage), $132,880 (90th percentile wage), 287,800 (number of positions), 10.6% (2016--2026 growth), Bachelor's degree (typical education requirement)

115. **Claims Adjusters, Examiners, and Investigators**: #206 (median wage rank), $63,680 (median wage), $95,760 (90th percentile wage), 274,420 (number of positions), -1.5% (2016--2026 growth), High school

diploma or equivalent (typical education requirement)

116. **Cleaners of Vehicles and Equipment**: #788 (median wage rank), $22,220 (median wage), $35,630 (90th percentile wage), 348,770 (number of positions), 10.8% (2016--2026 growth), No formal educational credential (typical education requirement)

117. **Cleaning, Washing, and Metal Pickling Equipment Operators and Tenders**: #696 (median wage rank), $28,550 (median wage), $45,190 (90th percentile wage), 17,860 (number of positions), 0.4% (2016--2026 growth), High school diploma or equivalent (typical education requirement)

118. **Clergy**: #417 (median wage rank), $45,740 (median wage), $79,110 (90th percentile wage), 49,320 (number of positions), 8% (2016--2026 growth), Bachelor's degree (typical education requirement)

119. **Clinical, Counseling, and School Psychologists**: #148 (median wage rank), $73,270 (median wage), $120,320 (90th percentile wage), 107,980 (number of positions), 14.2% (2016--2026 growth), Doctoral or professional degree (typical education requirement)

120. **Coaches and Scouts**: #649 (median wage rank), $31,460 (median wage), $71,940 (90th percentile wage), 230,930 (number of positions), 12.7% (2016--

2026 growth), Bachelor's degree (typical education requirement)

121. **Coating, Painting, and Spraying Machine Setters, Operators, and Tenders**: #632 (median wage rank), $32,790 (median wage), $49,440 (90th percentile wage), 85,760 (number of positions), 0.2% (2016--2026 growth), High school diploma or equivalent (typical education requirement)

122. **Coil Winders, Tapers, and Finishers**: #612 (median wage rank), $33,940 (median wage), $50,820 (90th percentile wage), 14,090 (number of positions), -20.6% (2016--2026 growth), High school diploma or equivalent (typical education requirement)

123. **Coin, Vending, and Amusement Machine Servicers and Repairers**: #625 (median wage rank), $33,070 (median wage), $51,540 (90th percentile wage), 33,600 (number of positions), -12.4% (2016--2026 growth), High school diploma or equivalent (typical education requirement)

124. **Combined Food Preparation and Serving Workers, Including Fast Food**: #819 (median wage rank), $19,440 (median wage), $25,330 (90th percentile wage), 3,426,090 (number of positions), 16.8% (2016--2026 growth), No formal educational credential (typical education requirement)

125. **Commercial and Industrial Designers**: #183

(median wage rank), $67,790 (median wage), $105,690 (90th percentile wage), 31,860 (number of positions), 5% (2016--2026 growth), Bachelor's degree (typical education requirement)

126. **Commercial Divers**: #375 (median wage rank), $49,090 (median wage), $83,730 (90th percentile wage), 3,370 (number of positions), 10.6% (2016--2026 growth), Postsecondary nondegree award (typical education requirement)

127. **Commercial Pilots**: #125 (median wage rank), $77,200 (median wage), $147,240 (90th percentile wage), 38,980 (number of positions), 3.8% (2016--2026 growth), High school diploma or equivalent (typical education requirement)

128. **Communications Equipment Operators**, All Other: #491 (median wage rank), $39,640 (median wage), $61,720 (90th percentile wage), 2,150 (number of positions), 10.4% (2016--2026 growth), High school diploma or equivalent (typical education requirement)

129. **Communications Teachers, Postsecondary**: #194 (median wage rank), $65,640 (median wage), $125,630 (90th percentile wage), 28,180 (number of positions), 10% (2016--2026 growth), Doctoral or professional degree (typical education requirement)

130. **Community and Social Service Specialists**, All

Other: #443 (median wage rank), $43,120 (median wage), $71,040 (90th percentile wage), 91,860 (number of positions), 13.2% (2016--2026 growth), Bachelor's degree (typical education requirement)

131. **Community Health Workers**: #544 (median wage rank), $37,330 (median wage), $63,880 (90th percentile wage), 51,900 (number of positions), 18.1% (2016--2026 growth), High school diploma or equivalent (typical education requirement)

132. **Compensation and Benefits Managers**: #29 (median wage rank), $116,240 (median wage), $199,950 (90th percentile wage), 15,230 (number of positions), 5% (2016--2026 growth), Bachelor's degree (typical education requirement)

133. **Compensation, Benefits, and Job Analysis Specialists**: #226 (median wage rank), $62,080 (median wage), $101,020 (90th percentile wage), 79,190 (number of positions), 8.5% (2016--2026 growth), Bachelor's degree (typical education requirement)

134. **Compliance Officers**: #191 (median wage rank), $66,540 (median wage), $105,260 (90th percentile wage), 273,910 (number of positions), 8.2% (2016--2026 growth), Bachelor's degree (typical education requirement)

135. **Computer and Information Research Scientists**:

#33 (median wage rank), $111,840 (median wage), $169,680 (90th percentile wage), 26,580 (number of positions), 19.2% (2016--2026 growth), Master's degree (typical education requirement)

136. **Computer and Information Systems Managers**: #15 (median wage rank), $135,800 (median wage), $226,786 (90th percentile wage), 352,510 (number of positions), 11.9% (2016--2026 growth), Bachelor's degree (typical education requirement)

137. **Computer Hardware Engineers**: #31 (median wage rank), $115,080 (median wage), $172,010 (90th percentile wage), 72,950 (number of positions), 5.5% (2016--2026 growth), Bachelor's degree (typical education requirement)

138. **Computer Network Architects**: #47 (median wage rank), $101,210 (median wage), $158,590 (90th percentile wage), 157,070 (number of positions), 6.4% (2016--2026 growth), Bachelor's degree (typical education requirement)

139. **Computer Network Support Specialists**: #217 (median wage rank), $62,670 (median wage), $105,910 (90th percentile wage), 188,740 (number of positions), 8.1% (2016--2026 growth), Associate's degree (typical education requirement)

140. **Computer Numerically Controlled Machine Tool Programmers, Metal and Plastic**: #349 (median wage

rank), $50,580 (median wage), $78,760 (90th percentile wage), 25,180 (number of positions), 16.3% (2016--2026 growth), Postsecondary nondegree award (typical education requirement)

141. **Computer Occupations**, All Other: #87 (median wage rank), $86,510 (median wage), $133,890 (90th percentile wage), 261,210 (number of positions), 9% (2016--2026 growth), Bachelor's degree (typical education requirement)

142. **Computer Operators**: #456 (median wage rank), $42,270 (median wage), $63,430 (90th percentile wage), 46,810 (number of positions), -22.9% (2016--2026 growth), High school diploma or equivalent (typical education requirement)

143. **Computer Programmers**: #110 (median wage rank), $79,840 (median wage), $130,360 (90th percentile wage), 271,200 (number of positions), -7.6% (2016--2026 growth), Bachelor's degree (typical education requirement)

144. **Computer Science Teachers, Postsecondary**: #123 (median wage rank), $77,570 (median wage), $155,580 (90th percentile wage), 32,540 (number of positions), 8% (2016--2026 growth), Doctoral or professional degree (typical education requirement)

145. **Computer Systems Analysts**: #85 (median wage rank), $87,220 (median wage), $137,690 (90th

percentile wage), 568,960 (number of positions), 8.8% (2016--2026 growth), Bachelor's degree (typical education requirement)

146. **Computer User Support Specialists**: #369 (median wage rank), $49,390 (median wage), $82,160 (90th percentile wage), 602,840 (number of positions), 11.2% (2016--2026 growth), Some college, no degree (typical education requirement)

147. **Computer, Automated Teller, and Office Machine Repairers**: #547 (median wage rank), $37,100 (median wage), $60,260 (90th percentile wage), 102,170 (number of positions), -0.7% (2016--2026 growth), Some college, no degree (typical education requirement)

148. **Computer-Controlled Machine Tool Operators, Metal and Plastic**: #529 (median wage rank), $37,880 (median wage), $57,750 (90th percentile wage), 146,190 (number of positions), 1.1% (2016--2026 growth), High school diploma or equivalent (typical education requirement)

149. **Concierges**: #680 (median wage rank), $29,250 (median wage), $46,750 (90th percentile wage), 32,020 (number of positions), 11.3% (2016--2026 growth), High school diploma or equivalent (typical education requirement)

150. **Conservation Scientists**: #228 (median wage

rank), $61,810 (median wage), $95,970 (90th percentile wage), 20,470 (number of positions), 6.5% (2016--2026 growth), Bachelor's degree (typical education requirement)

151. **Construction and Building Inspectors**: #259 (median wage rank), $58,480 (median wage), $94,220 (90th percentile wage), 94,960 (number of positions), 9.9% (2016--2026 growth), High school diploma or equivalent (typical education requirement)

152. **Construction and Related Workers**, All Other: #558 (median wage rank), $36,890 (median wage), $61,940 (90th percentile wage), 35,340 (number of positions), 9.9% (2016--2026 growth), High school diploma or equivalent (typical education requirement)

153. **Construction Laborers**: #620 (median wage rank), $33,430 (median wage), $62,600 (90th percentile wage), 912,100 (number of positions), 12.6% (2016--2026 growth), No formal educational credential (typical education requirement)

154. **Construction Managers**: #82 (median wage rank), $89,300 (median wage), $158,330 (90th percentile wage), 249,650 (number of positions), 11.4% (2016--2026 growth), Bachelor's degree (typical education requirement)

155. **Continuous Mining Machine Operators**: #336

(median wage rank), $51,840 (median wage), $74,240 (90th percentile wage), 12,030 (number of positions), -3.9% (2016--2026 growth), No formal educational credential (typical education requirement)

156. **Control and Valve Installers and Repairers, Except Mechanical Door**: #303 (median wage rank), $54,520 (median wage), $86,420 (90th percentile wage), 45,740 (number of positions), 5% (2016--2026 growth), High school diploma or equivalent (typical education requirement)

157. **Conveyor Operators and Tenders**: #650 (median wage rank), $31,410 (median wage), $49,880 (90th percentile wage), 28,590 (number of positions), -1.2% (2016--2026 growth), No formal educational credential (typical education requirement)

158. **Cooks, All Other**: #724 (median wage rank), $27,120 (median wage), $43,580 (90th percentile wage), 15,490 (number of positions), 9% (2016--2026 growth), No formal educational credential (typical education requirement)

159. **Cooks, Fast Food**: #817 (median wage rank), $19,860 (median wage), $25,290 (90th percentile wage), 513,200 (number of positions), -5.2% (2016--2026 growth), No formal educational credential (typical education requirement)

160. **Cooks, Institution and Cafeteria**: #762 (median

wage rank), $24,750 (median wage), $38,030 (90th percentile wage), 409,850 (number of positions), 7.7% (2016--2026 growth), No formal educational credential (typical education requirement)

161. **Cooks, Private Household**: #645 (median wage rank), $32,060 (median wage), $62,730 (90th percentile wage), 370 (number of positions), 5.7% (2016--2026 growth), Postsecondary nondegree award (typical education requirement)

162. **Cooks, Restaurant**: #772 (median wage rank), $24,140 (median wage), $35,090 (90th percentile wage), 1,217,370 (number of positions), 11.8% (2016--2026 growth), No formal educational credential (typical education requirement)

163. **Cooks, Short Order**: #796 (median wage rank), $21,890 (median wage), $30,890 (90th percentile wage), 183,990 (number of positions), -3.3% (2016--2026 growth), No formal educational credential (typical education requirement)

164. **Cooling and Freezing Equipment Operators and Tenders**: #681 (median wage rank), $29,190 (median wage), $50,210 (90th percentile wage), 8,170 (number of positions), 1.9% (2016--2026 growth), High school diploma or equivalent (typical education requirement)

165. **Correctional Officers and Jailers**: #445 (median

wage rank), $42,820 (median wage), $74,630 (90th percentile wage), 431,600 (number of positions), -7.7% (2016--2026 growth), High school diploma or equivalent (typical education requirement)

166. **Correspondence Clerks**: #570 (median wage rank), $36,370 (median wage), $53,630 (90th percentile wage), 6,780 (number of positions), 2.1% (2016--2026 growth), High school diploma or equivalent (typical education requirement)

167. **Cost Estimators**: #229 (median wage rank), $61,790 (median wage), $103,250 (90th percentile wage), 214,610 (number of positions), 10.6% (2016--2026 growth), Bachelor's degree (typical education requirement)

168. **Costume Attendants**: #410 (median wage rank), $45,900 (median wage), $87,310 (90th percentile wage), 6,640 (number of positions), 9.7% (2016--2026 growth), High school diploma or equivalent (typical education requirement)

169. **Counselors**, All Other: #430 (median wage rank), $44,350 (median wage), $74,810 (90th percentile wage), 28,380 (number of positions), 14.3% (2016--2026 growth), Master's degree (typical education requirement)

170. **Counter and Rental Clerks**: #750 (median wage rank), $25,550 (median wage), $46,740 (90th

percentile wage), 450,330 (number of positions), 5.5% (2016--2026 growth), No formal educational credential (typical education requirement)

171. **Counter Attendants, Cafeteria, Food Concession, and Coffee Shop**: #815 (median wage rank), $19,970 (median wage), $28,010 (90th percentile wage), 499,550 (number of positions), 4.6% (2016--2026 growth), No formal educational credential (typical education requirement)

172. **Couriers and Messengers**: #708 (median wage rank), $28,170 (median wage), $44,440 (90th percentile wage), 74,120 (number of positions), 8.4% (2016--2026 growth), High school diploma or equivalent (typical education requirement)

173. **Court Reporters**: #342 (median wage rank), $51,320 (median wage), $95,990 (90th percentile wage), 17,700 (number of positions), 3.3% (2016--2026 growth), Postsecondary nondegree award (typical education requirement)

174. **Court, Municipal, and License Clerks**: #563 (median wage rank), $36,670 (median wage), $57,420 (90th percentile wage), 128,620 (number of positions), 6.6% (2016--2026 growth), High school diploma or equivalent (typical education requirement)

175. **Craft Artists**: #619 (median wage rank), $33,440

(median wage), $65,080 (90th percentile wage), 5,070 (number of positions), 6.3% (2016--2026 growth), No formal educational credential (typical education requirement)

176. **Crane and Tower Operators**: #331 (median wage rank), $52,170 (median wage), $82,600 (90th percentile wage), 45,020 (number of positions), 8.6% (2016--2026 growth), High school diploma or equivalent (typical education requirement)

177. **Credit Analysts**: #165 (median wage rank), $69,930 (median wage), $137,730 (90th percentile wage), 72,930 (number of positions), 8.4% (2016--2026 growth), Bachelor's degree (typical education requirement)

178. **Credit Authorizers, Checkers, and Clerks**: #556 (median wage rank), $36,930 (median wage), $58,800 (90th percentile wage), 37,680 (number of positions), -2.8% (2016--2026 growth), High school diploma or equivalent (typical education requirement)

179. **Credit Counselors**: #428 (median wage rank), $44,380 (median wage), $75,220 (90th percentile wage), 34,110 (number of positions), 13.9% (2016--2026 growth), Bachelor's degree (typical education requirement)

180. **Criminal Justice and Law Enforcement Teachers, Postsecondary**: #247 (median wage rank), $59,590

(median wage), $105,210 (90th percentile wage), 14,620 (number of positions), 12.5% (2016--2026 growth), Doctoral or professional degree (typical education requirement)

181. **Crossing Guards**: #729 (median wage rank), $26,700 (median wage), $42,210 (90th percentile wage), 72,900 (number of positions), 8.5% (2016--2026 growth), No formal educational credential (typical education requirement)

182. **Crushing, Grinding, and Polishing Machine Setters, Operators, and Tenders**: #604 (median wage rank), $34,390 (median wage), $52,060 (90th percentile wage), 29,830 (number of positions), -6.7% (2016--2026 growth), High school diploma or equivalent (typical education requirement)

183. **Curators**: #317 (median wage rank), $53,360 (median wage), $94,430 (90th percentile wage), 11,170 (number of positions), 14% (2016--2026 growth), Master's degree (typical education requirement)

184. **Customer Service Representatives**: #640 (median wage rank), $32,300 (median wage), $53,730 (90th percentile wage), 2,707,040 (number of positions), 4.9% (2016--2026 growth), High school diploma or equivalent (typical education requirement)

185. **Cutters and Trimmers, Hand**: #716 (median wage

rank), $27,600 (median wage), $42,450 (90th percentile wage), 14,250 (number of positions), -10% (2016--2026 growth), No formal educational credential (typical education requirement)

186. **Cutting and Slicing Machine Setters, Operators, and Tenders**: #631 (median wage rank), $32,870 (median wage), $48,840 (90th percentile wage), 61,330 (number of positions), -3.9% (2016--2026 growth), High school diploma or equivalent (typical education requirement)

187. **Cutting, Punching, and Press Machine Setters, Operators, and Tenders, Metal and Plastic**: #639 (median wage rank), $32,370 (median wage), $50,330 (90th percentile wage), 192,800 (number of positions), -8.7% (2016--2026 growth), High school diploma or equivalent (typical education requirement)

188. **Dancers**: #694 (median wage rank), $28,579 (median wage), $69,347 (90th percentile wage), 10,060 (number of positions), 5% (2016--2026 growth), No formal educational credential (typical education requirement)

189. **Data Entry Keyers**: #671 (median wage rank), $30,100 (median wage), $45,360 (90th percentile wage), 194,810 (number of positions), -21.1% (2016--2026 growth), High school diploma or equivalent

(typical education requirement)

190. **Database Administrators**: #92 (median wage rank), $84,950 (median wage), $129,930 (90th percentile wage), 113,730 (number of positions), 11.5% (2016--2026 growth), Bachelor's degree (typical education requirement)

191. **Demonstrators and Product Promoters**: #748 (median wage rank), $25,610 (median wage), $48,480 (90th percentile wage), 86,500 (number of positions), 7% (2016--2026 growth), No formal educational credential (typical education requirement)

192. **Dental Assistants**: #555 (median wage rank), $36,940 (median wage), $52,000 (90th percentile wage), 327,290 (number of positions), 19.5% (2016--2026 growth), Postsecondary nondegree award (typical education requirement)

193. **Dental Hygienists**: #152 (median wage rank), $72,910 (median wage), $100,170 (90th percentile wage), 204,990 (number of positions), 19.6% (2016--2026 growth), Associate's degree (typical education requirement)

194. **Dental Laboratory Technicians**: #535 (median wage rank), $37,680 (median wage), $61,970 (90th percentile wage), 37,110 (number of positions), 14.5% (2016--2026 growth), High school diploma or equivalent (typical education requirement)

195. **Dentists, All Other Specialists:** #11 (median wage rank), $173,000 (median wage), $288,910 (90th percentile wage), 5,380 (number of positions), 12% (2016--2026 growth), Doctoral or professional degree (typical education requirement)

196. **Dentists, General:** #14 (median wage rank), $153,900 (median wage), $257,013 (90th percentile wage), 105,620 (number of positions), 17.5% (2016--2026 growth), Doctoral or professional degree (typical education requirement)

197. **Derrick Operators, Oil and Gas:** #387 (median wage rank), $48,130 (median wage), $75,520 (90th percentile wage), 11,580 (number of positions), 25.7% (2016--2026 growth), No formal educational credential (typical education requirement)

198. **Designers, All Other:** #316 (median wage rank), $53,380 (median wage), $116,250 (90th percentile wage), 7,230 (number of positions), 6.4% (2016--2026 growth), Bachelor's degree (typical education requirement)

199. **Desktop Publishers:** #470 (median wage rank), $41,090 (median wage), $70,290 (90th percentile wage), 13,090 (number of positions), -13.9% (2016--2026 growth), Associate's degree (typical education requirement)

200. **Detectives and Criminal Investigators:** #122

(median wage rank), $78,120 (median wage), $131,200 (90th percentile wage), 104,980 (number of positions), 4.5% (2016--2026 growth), High school diploma or equivalent (typical education requirement)

201. **Diagnostic Medical Sonographers**: #167 (median wage rank), $69,650 (median wage), $99,100 (90th percentile wage), 65,790 (number of positions), 23.2% (2016--2026 growth), Associate's degree (typical education requirement)

202. **Dietetic Technicians**: #735 (median wage rank), $26,350 (median wage), $45,960 (90th percentile wage), 32,240 (number of positions), 9.3% (2016--2026 growth), Associate's degree (typical education requirement)

203. **Dietitians and Nutritionists**: #255 (median wage rank), $58,920 (median wage), $82,410 (90th percentile wage), 61,430 (number of positions), 14.1% (2016--2026 growth), Bachelor's degree (typical education requirement)

204. **Dining Room and Cafeteria Attendants and Bartender Helpers**: #810 (median wage rank), $20,200 (median wage), $30,390 (90th percentile wage), 423,080 (number of positions), 7.1% (2016--2026 growth), No formal educational credential (typical education requirement)

205. **Directors, Religious Activities and Education:** #511 (median wage rank), $38,610 (median wage), $79,380 (90th percentile wage), 20,590 (number of positions), 7.3% (2016--2026 growth), Bachelor's degree (typical education requirement)

206. **Dishwashers:** #808 (median wage rank), $20,800 (median wage), $25,800 (90th percentile wage), 506,450 (number of positions), 4.3% (2016--2026 growth), No formal educational credential (typical education requirement)

207. **Dispatchers, Except Police, Fire, and Ambulance:** #528 (median wage rank), $37,940 (median wage), $63,420 (90th percentile wage), 197,910 (number of positions), 0% (2016--2026 growth), High school diploma or equivalent (typical education requirement)

208. **Door-to-Door Sales Workers, News and Street Vendors, and Related Workers:** #766 (median wage rank), $24,330 (median wage), $47,340 (90th percentile wage), 8,040 (number of positions), 6.3% (2016--2026 growth), No formal educational credential (typical education requirement)

209. **Drafters, All Other:** #353 (median wage rank), $50,470 (median wage), $82,680 (90th percentile wage), 15,530 (number of positions), 7.9% (2016--2026 growth), Associate's degree (typical education

requirement)

210. **Dredge Operators**: #454 (median wage rank), $42,420 (median wage), $70,510 (90th percentile wage), 1,760 (number of positions), 5.3% (2016--2026 growth), High school diploma or equivalent (typical education requirement)

211. **Drilling and Boring Machine Tool Setters, Operators, and Tenders, Metal and Plastic**: #569 (median wage rank), $36,410 (median wage), $57,660 (90th percentile wage), 12,290 (number of positions), -19.4% (2016--2026 growth), High school diploma or equivalent (typical education requirement)

212. **Driver/Sales Workers**: #781 (median wage rank), $22,830 (median wage), $48,400 (90th percentile wage), 426,310 (number of positions), -1.2% (2016--2026 growth), High school diploma or equivalent (typical education requirement)

213. **Drywall and Ceiling Tile Installers**: #469 (median wage rank), $41,090 (median wage), $79,660 (90th percentile wage), 93,180 (number of positions), 1.2% (2016--2026 growth), No formal educational credential (typical education requirement)

214. **Earth Drillers, Except Oil and Gas**: #429 (median wage rank), $44,360 (median wage), $75,880 (90th percentile wage), 18,500 (number of positions), 19.7% (2016--2026 growth), High school diploma or

equivalent (typical education requirement)

215. **Economics Teachers, Postsecondary**: #65 (median wage rank), $95,770 (median wage), $195,730 (90th percentile wage), 13,060 (number of positions), 10.6% (2016--2026 growth), Doctoral or professional degree (typical education requirement)

216. **Economists**: #48 (median wage rank), $101,050 (median wage), $181,060 (90th percentile wage), 19,380 (number of positions), 6% (2016--2026 growth), Master's degree (typical education requirement)

217. **Editors**: #274 (median wage rank), $57,210 (median wage), $111,610 (90th percentile wage), 97,170 (number of positions), -0.1% (2016--2026 growth), Bachelor's degree (typical education requirement)

218. **Education Administrators, All Other**: #121 (median wage rank), $78,210 (median wage), $131,410 (90th percentile wage), 34,140 (number of positions), 10.4% (2016--2026 growth), Bachelor's degree (typical education requirement)

219. **Education Administrators, Elementary and Secondary School**: #72 (median wage rank), $92,510 (median wage), $135,770 (90th percentile wage), 242,970 (number of positions), 7.8% (2016--2026 growth), Master's degree (typical education requirement)

220. **Education Administrators, Postsecondary**: #77 (median wage rank), $90,760 (median wage), $179,250 (90th percentile wage), 138,430 (number of positions), 10% (2016--2026 growth), Master's degree (typical education requirement)

221. **Education Administrators, Preschool and Childcare Center/Program**: #415 (median wage rank), $45,790 (median wage), $82,790 (90th percentile wage), 48,530 (number of positions), 10.6% (2016--2026 growth), Bachelor's degree (typical education requirement)

222. **Education Teachers, Postsecondary**: #219 (median wage rank), $62,520 (median wage), $118,160 (90th percentile wage), 58,850 (number of positions), 10.3% (2016--2026 growth), Doctoral or professional degree (typical education requirement)

223. **Education, Training, and Library Workers**, All Other: #449 (median wage rank), $42,600 (median wage), $78,270 (90th percentile wage), 100,640 (number of positions), 10.5% (2016--2026 growth), Bachelor's degree (typical education requirement)

224. **Educational, Guidance, School, and Vocational Counselors**: #302 (median wage rank), $54,560 (median wage), $90,030 (90th percentile wage), 260,670 (number of positions), 11.3% (2016--2026 growth), Master's degree (typical education

requirement)

225. **Electric Motor, Power Tool, and Related Repairers**: #464 (median wage rank), $41,570 (median wage), $71,260 (90th percentile wage), 17,050 (number of positions), 7% (2016--2026 growth), High school diploma or equivalent (typical education requirement)

226. **Electrical and Electronic Equipment Assemblers**: #653 (median wage rank), $31,310 (median wage), $49,600 (90th percentile wage), 218,530 (number of positions), -20.7% (2016--2026 growth), High school diploma or equivalent (typical education requirement)

227. **Electrical and Electronics Drafters**: #242 (median wage rank), $59,970 (median wage), $96,820 (90th percentile wage), 26,750 (number of positions), 6.7% (2016--2026 growth), Associate's degree (typical education requirement)

228. **Electrical and Electronics Engineering Technicians**: #224 (median wage rank), $62,190 (median wage), $91,640 (90th percentile wage), 134,870 (number of positions), 2% (2016--2026 growth), Associate's degree (typical education requirement)

229. **Electrical and Electronics Installers and Repairers, Transportation Equipment**: #250 (median

wage rank), $59,280 (median wage), $83,450 (90th percentile wage), 13,960 (number of positions), 2.9% (2016--2026 growth), Postsecondary nondegree award (typical education requirement)

230. **Electrical and Electronics Repairers, Commercial and Industrial Equipment**: #289 (median wage rank), $56,250 (median wage), $80,160 (90th percentile wage), 67,390 (number of positions), 2.4% (2016--2026 growth), Postsecondary nondegree award (typical education requirement)

231. **Electrical and Electronics Repairers, Powerhouse, Substation, and Relay**: #133 (median wage rank), $75,670 (median wage), $98,890 (90th percentile wage), 23,060 (number of positions), 3.7% (2016--2026 growth), Postsecondary nondegree award (typical education requirement)

232. **Electrical Engineers**: #67 (median wage rank), $94,210 (median wage), $149,040 (90th percentile wage), 183,770 (number of positions), 8.6% (2016--2026 growth), Bachelor's degree (typical education requirement)

233. **Electrical Power-Line Installers and Repairers**: #182 (median wage rank), $68,010 (median wage), $98,190 (90th percentile wage), 117,670 (number of positions), 13.9% (2016--2026 growth), High school diploma or equivalent (typical education

requirement)

234. **Electricians**: #321 (median wage rank), $52,720 (median wage), $90,420 (90th percentile wage), 607,120 (number of positions), 9% (2016--2026 growth), High school diploma or equivalent (typical education requirement)

235. **Electromechanical Equipment Assemblers**: #622 (median wage rank), $33,350 (median wage), $51,080 (90th percentile wage), 45,540 (number of positions), -21.3% (2016--2026 growth), High school diploma or equivalent (typical education requirement)

236. **Electro-Mechanical Technicians**: #294 (median wage rank), $55,610 (median wage), $85,440 (90th percentile wage), 13,710 (number of positions), 3.5% (2016--2026 growth), Associate's degree (typical education requirement)

237. **Electronic Equipment Installers and Repairers, Motor Vehicles**: #642 (median wage rank), $32,220 (median wage), $50,770 (90th percentile wage), 11,750 (number of positions), -25.2% (2016--2026 growth), High school diploma or equivalent (typical education requirement)

238. **Electronic Home Entertainment Equipment Installers and Repairers**: #540 (median wage rank), $37,410 (median wage), $59,640 (90th percentile wage), 25,550 (number of positions), 1.2% (2016--

2026 growth), Postsecondary nondegree award (typical education requirement)

239. **Electronics Engineers, Except Computer**: #58 (median wage rank), $99,210 (median wage), $155,330 (90th percentile wage), 132,100 (number of positions), 3.7% (2016--2026 growth), Bachelor's degree (typical education requirement)

240. **Elementary School Teachers, Except Special Education**: #293 (median wage rank), $55,800 (median wage), $88,590 (90th percentile wage), 1,392,660 (number of positions), 7.4% (2016--2026 growth), Bachelor's degree (typical education requirement)

241. **Elevator Installers and Repairers**: #119 (median wage rank), $78,890 (median wage), $114,980 (90th percentile wage), 22,240 (number of positions), 12.1% (2016--2026 growth), High school diploma or equivalent (typical education requirement)

242. **Eligibility Interviewers, Government Programs**: #439 (median wage rank), $43,350 (median wage), $58,810 (90th percentile wage), 135,940 (number of positions), 6% (2016--2026 growth), High school diploma or equivalent (typical education requirement)

243. **Embalmers**: #483 (median wage rank), $40,150 (median wage), $63,090 (90th percentile wage), 3,710

(number of positions), -0.8% (2016--2026 growth), Associate's degree (typical education requirement)

244. **Emergency Management Directors**: #163 (median wage rank), $70,500 (median wage), $133,880 (90th percentile wage), 9,570 (number of positions), 7.7% (2016--2026 growth), Bachelor's degree (typical education requirement)

245. **Emergency Medical Technicians and Paramedics**: #634 (median wage rank), $32,670 (median wage), $56,310 (90th percentile wage), 244,960 (number of positions), 15.1% (2016--2026 growth), Postsecondary nondegree award (typical education requirement)

246. **Engine and Other Machine Assemblers**: #468 (median wage rank), $41,210 (median wage), $61,800 (90th percentile wage), 38,150 (number of positions), -17.2% (2016--2026 growth), High school diploma or equivalent (typical education requirement)

247. **Engineering Teachers, Postsecondary**: #60 (median wage rank), $97,530 (median wage), $176,560 (90th percentile wage), 38,000 (number of positions), 14.5% (2016--2026 growth), Doctoral or professional degree (typical education requirement)

248. **Engineering Technicians, Except Drafters, All Other**: #221 (median wage rank), $62,330 (median wage), $95,960 (90th percentile wage), 74,290 (number of positions), 5.2% (2016--2026 growth),

Associate's degree (typical education requirement)

249. **Engineers**, All Other: #61 (median wage rank), $97,300 (median wage), $152,970 (90th percentile wage), 123,390 (number of positions), 6.2% (2016--2026 growth), Bachelor's degree (typical education requirement)

250. **English Language and Literature Teachers, Postsecondary**: #205 (median wage rank), $63,730 (median wage), $130,890 (90th percentile wage), 71,270 (number of positions), 9.8% (2016--2026 growth), Doctoral or professional degree (typical education requirement)

251. **Entertainers and Performers, Sports and Related Workers**, All Other: #576 (median wage rank), $36,067 (median wage), $82,222 (90th percentile wage), 13,150 (number of positions), 8% (2016--2026 growth), No formal educational credential (typical education requirement)

252. **Entertainment Attendants and Related Workers**, All Other: #780 (median wage rank), $23,270 (median wage), $32,000 (90th percentile wage), 14,550 (number of positions), 11.4% (2016--2026 growth), High school diploma or equivalent (typical education requirement)

253. **Environmental Engineering Technicians**: #373 (median wage rank), $49,170 (median wage), $80,780

(90th percentile wage), 16,550 (number of positions), 12.9% (2016--2026 growth), Associate's degree (typical education requirement)

254. **Environmental Engineers:** #93 (median wage rank), $84,890 (median wage), $130,120 (90th percentile wage), 52,280 (number of positions), 8.3% (2016--2026 growth), Bachelor's degree (typical education requirement)

255. **Environmental Science and Protection Technicians, Including Health:** #433 (median wage rank), $44,190 (median wage), $75,980 (90th percentile wage), 32,950 (number of positions), 11.9% (2016--2026 growth), Associate's degree (typical education requirement)

256. **Environmental Science Teachers, Postsecondary:** #120 (median wage rank), $78,340 (median wage), $150,890 (90th percentile wage), 5,520 (number of positions), 9.6% (2016--2026 growth), Doctoral or professional degree (typical education requirement)

257. **Environmental Scientists and Specialists, Including Health:** #174 (median wage rank), $68,910 (median wage), $120,320 (90th percentile wage), 84,250 (number of positions), 11.1% (2016--2026 growth), Bachelor's degree (typical education requirement)

258. **Epidemiologists:** #160 (median wage rank),

$70,820 (median wage), $114,510 (90th percentile wage), 5,690 (number of positions), 8.7% (2016--2026 growth), Master's degree (typical education requirement)

259. **Etchers and Engravers**: #657 (median wage rank), $31,110 (median wage), $51,270 (90th percentile wage), 9,520 (number of positions), 1% (2016--2026 growth), High school diploma or equivalent (typical education requirement)

260. **Excavating and Loading Machine and Dragline Operators**: #475 (median wage rank), $41,030 (median wage), $69,280 (90th percentile wage), 48,320 (number of positions), 8.4% (2016--2026 growth), High school diploma or equivalent (typical education requirement)

261. **Executive Secretaries and Executive Administrative Assistants**: #292 (median wage rank), $55,860 (median wage), $83,070 (90th percentile wage), 631,610 (number of positions), -17.4% (2016--2026 growth), High school diploma or equivalent (typical education requirement)

262. **Exercise Physiologists**: #399 (median wage rank), $47,340 (median wage), $74,330 (90th percentile wage), 6,880 (number of positions), 12.9% (2016--2026 growth), Bachelor's degree (typical education requirement)

263. **Explosives Workers, Ordnance Handling Experts, and Blasters**: #330 (median wage rank), $52,170 (median wage), $78,660 (90th percentile wage), 6,310 (number of positions), 7.1% (2016--2026 growth), High school diploma or equivalent (typical education requirement)

264. **Extraction Workers, All Other**: #381 (median wage rank), $48,750 (median wage), $74,700 (90th percentile wage), 4,320 (number of positions), 15.9% (2016--2026 growth), High school diploma or equivalent (typical education requirement)

265. **Extruding and Drawing Machine Setters, Operators, and Tenders, Metal and Plastic**: #613 (median wage rank), $33,870 (median wage), $50,260 (90th percentile wage), 71,960 (number of positions), -15.2% (2016--2026 growth), High school diploma or equivalent (typical education requirement)

266. **Extruding and Forming Machine Setters, Operators, and Tenders, Synthetic and Glass Fibers**: #608 (median wage rank), $34,240 (median wage), $49,810 (90th percentile wage), 19,340 (number of positions), -8.5% (2016--2026 growth), High school diploma or equivalent (typical education requirement)

267. **Extruding, Forming, Pressing, and Compacting Machine Setters, Operators, and Tenders**: #636

(median wage rank), $32,510 (median wage), $50,330 (90th percentile wage), 71,260 (number of positions), -5.4% (2016--2026 growth), High school diploma or equivalent (typical education requirement)

268. **Fabric and Apparel Patternmakers**: #490 (median wage rank), $39,650 (median wage), $86,960 (90th percentile wage), 5,310 (number of positions), -15% (2016--2026 growth), High school diploma or equivalent (typical education requirement)

269. **Fabric Menders, Except Garment**: #727 (median wage rank), $26,920 (median wage), $37,430 (90th percentile wage), 550 (number of positions), -7.6% (2016--2026 growth), High school diploma or equivalent (typical education requirement)

270. **Fallers**: #541 (median wage rank), $37,370 (median wage), $71,590 (90th percentile wage), 5,370 (number of positions), -10.5% (2016--2026 growth), High school diploma or equivalent (typical education requirement)

271. **Family and General Practitioners**: #9 (median wage rank), $190,490 (median wage), $318,118 (90th percentile wage), 122,970 (number of positions), 16.5% (2016--2026 growth), Doctoral or professional degree (typical education requirement)

272. **Farm and Home Management Advisors**: #368 (median wage rank), $49,490 (median wage), $80,900

(90th percentile wage), 8,620 (number of positions), 7.3% (2016--2026 growth), Master's degree (typical education requirement)

273. **Farm Equipment Mechanics and Service Technicians**: #532 (median wage rank), $37,820 (median wage), $57,420 (90th percentile wage), 35,110 (number of positions), 7.4% (2016--2026 growth), High school diploma or equivalent (typical education requirement)

274. **Farm Labor Contractors**: #594 (median wage rank), $35,160 (median wage), $95,360 (90th percentile wage), 810 (number of positions), 8% (2016--2026 growth), No formal educational credential (typical education requirement)

275. **Farmers, Ranchers, and Other Agricultural Managers**: #192 (median wage rank), $66,360 (median wage), $126,070 (90th percentile wage), 4,560 (number of positions), 6.7% (2016--2026 growth), High school diploma or equivalent (typical education requirement)

276. **Farmworkers and Laborers, Crop, Nursery, and Greenhouse**: #793 (median wage rank), $22,000 (median wage), $30,940 (90th percentile wage), 273,450 (number of positions), 1.1% (2016--2026 growth), No formal educational credential (typical education requirement)

277. **Farmworkers, Farm, Ranch, and Aquacultural Animals**: #764 (median wage rank), $24,520 (median wage), $39,230 (90th percentile wage), 35,670 (number of positions), -3.8% (2016--2026 growth), No formal educational credential (typical education requirement)

278. **Fashion Designers**: #198 (median wage rank), $65,170 (median wage), $130,050 (90th percentile wage), 19,230 (number of positions), 3.1% (2016--2026 growth), Bachelor's degree (typical education requirement)

279. **Fence Erectors**: #624 (median wage rank), $33,150 (median wage), $58,080 (90th percentile wage), 21,500 (number of positions), 11.2% (2016--2026 growth), No formal educational credential (typical education requirement)

280. **Fiberglass Laminators and Fabricators**: #660 (median wage rank), $30,870 (median wage), $47,670 (90th percentile wage), 19,400 (number of positions), -1.3% (2016--2026 growth), High school diploma or equivalent (typical education requirement)

281. **File Clerks**: #683 (median wage rank), $29,090 (median wage), $47,410 (90th percentile wage), 130,950 (number of positions), -10.3% (2016--2026 growth), High school diploma or equivalent (typical education requirement)

282. **Film and Video Editors**: #215 (median wage rank), $62,760 (median wage), $162,260 (90th percentile wage), 29,880 (number of positions), 16.3% (2016--2026 growth), Bachelor's degree (typical education requirement)

283. **Financial Analysts**: #103 (median wage rank), $81,760 (median wage), $165,100 (90th percentile wage), 281,610 (number of positions), 10.8% (2016--2026 growth), Bachelor's degree (typical education requirement)

284. **Financial Clerks**, All Other: #493 (median wage rank), $39,540 (median wage), $60,950 (90th percentile wage), 34,540 (number of positions), 9.9% (2016--2026 growth), High school diploma or equivalent (typical education requirement)

285. **Financial Examiners**: #113 (median wage rank), $79,280 (median wage), $148,390 (90th percentile wage), 49,750 (number of positions), 9.8% (2016--2026 growth), Bachelor's degree (typical education requirement)

286. **Financial Managers**: #25 (median wage rank), $121,750 (median wage), $203,323 (90th percentile wage), 543,300 (number of positions), 18.7% (2016--2026 growth), Bachelor's degree (typical education requirement)

287. **Financial Specialists**, All Other: #169 (median

wage rank), $69,470 (median wage), $118,780 (90th percentile wage), 123,270 (number of positions), 8.7% (2016--2026 growth), Bachelor's degree (typical education requirement)

288. **Fine Artists, Including Painters, Sculptors, and Illustrators**: #346 (median wage rank), $50,790 (median wage), $103,680 (90th percentile wage), 11,520 (number of positions), 8.6% (2016--2026 growth), Bachelor's degree (typical education requirement)

289. **Fire Inspectors and Investigators**: #260 (median wage rank), $58,440 (median wage), $95,270 (90th percentile wage), 11,910 (number of positions), 7.3% (2016--2026 growth), Postsecondary nondegree award (typical education requirement)

290. **Firefighters**: #389 (median wage rank), $48,030 (median wage), $81,110 (90th percentile wage), 315,910 (number of positions), 7.2% (2016--2026 growth), Postsecondary nondegree award (typical education requirement)

291. **First-Line Supervisors of Construction Trades and Extraction Workers**: #214 (median wage rank), $62,980 (median wage), $102,880 (90th percentile wage), 538,220 (number of positions), 12.7% (2016--2026 growth), High school diploma or equivalent (typical education requirement)

292. **First-Line Supervisors of Correctional Officers**: #235 (median wage rank), $60,560 (median wage), $98,290 (90th percentile wage), 43,230 (number of positions), -7.8% (2016--2026 growth), High school diploma or equivalent (typical education requirement)

293. **First-Line Supervisors of Farming, Fishing, and Forestry Workers**: #422 (median wage rank), $45,320 (median wage), $76,270 (90th percentile wage), 19,550 (number of positions), 4.6% (2016--2026 growth), High school diploma or equivalent (typical education requirement)

294. **First-Line Supervisors of Fire Fighting and Prevention Workers**: #137 (median wage rank), $74,540 (median wage), $117,800 (90th percentile wage), 57,170 (number of positions), 7.2% (2016--2026 growth), Postsecondary nondegree award (typical education requirement)

295. **First-Line Supervisors of Food Preparation and Serving Workers**: #648 (median wage rank), $31,480 (median wage), $54,510 (90th percentile wage), 908,550 (number of positions), 9.3% (2016--2026 growth), High school diploma or equivalent (typical education requirement)

296. **First-Line Supervisors of Helpers, Laborers, and Material Movers, Hand**: #400 (median wage rank),

$47,230 (median wage), $77,060 (90th percentile wage), 183,620 (number of positions), 8.5% (2016--2026 growth), High school diploma or equivalent (typical education requirement)

297. **First-Line Supervisors of Housekeeping and Janitorial Workers**: #523 (median wage rank), $38,190 (median wage), $63,350 (90th percentile wage), 161,140 (number of positions), 8.6% (2016--2026 growth), High school diploma or equivalent (typical education requirement)

298. **First-Line Supervisors of Landscaping, Lawn Service, and Groundskeeping Workers**: #418 (median wage rank), $45,740 (median wage), $75,060 (90th percentile wage), 103,070 (number of positions), 9.6% (2016--2026 growth), High school diploma or equivalent (typical education requirement)

299. **First-Line Supervisors of Mechanics, Installers, and Repairers**: #208 (median wage rank), $63,540 (median wage), $100,480 (90th percentile wage), 453,330 (number of positions), 7.1% (2016--2026 growth), High school diploma or equivalent (typical education requirement)

300. **First-Line Supervisors of Non-Retail Sales Workers**: #149 (median wage rank), $73,150 (median wage), $150,400 (90th percentile wage), 252,670

(number of positions), 6.4% (2016--2026 growth), High school diploma or equivalent (typical education requirement)

301. **First-Line Supervisors of Office and Administrative Support Workers**: #308 (median wage rank), $54,340 (median wage), $87,690 (90th percentile wage), 1,443,150 (number of positions), 3.4% (2016--2026 growth), High school diploma or equivalent (typical education requirement)

302. **First-Line Supervisors of Personal Service Workers**: #562 (median wage rank), $36,700 (median wage), $61,850 (90th percentile wage), 190,420 (number of positions), 13% (2016--2026 growth), High school diploma or equivalent (typical education requirement)

303. **First-Line Supervisors of Police and Detectives**: #94 (median wage rank), $84,840 (median wage), $134,810 (90th percentile wage), 100,200 (number of positions), 6.6% (2016--2026 growth), High school diploma or equivalent (typical education requirement)

304. **First-Line Supervisors of Production and Operating Workers**: #266 (median wage rank), $57,780 (median wage), $95,800 (90th percentile wage), 610,480 (number of positions), -0.1% (2016--2026 growth), High school diploma or equivalent

4 OCCUPATIONS RANKED ALPHABETICALLY

(typical education requirement)

305. **First-Line Supervisors of Protective Service Workers**, All Other: #392 (median wage rank), $47,820 (median wage), $78,740 (90th percentile wage), 72,880 (number of positions), 4.6% (2016--2026 growth), High school diploma or equivalent (typical education requirement)

306. **First-Line Supervisors of Retail Sales Workers**: #498 (median wage rank), $39,040 (median wage), $66,480 (90th percentile wage), 1,194,220 (number of positions), 5% (2016--2026 growth), High school diploma or equivalent (typical education requirement)

307. **First-Line Supervisors of Transportation and Material-Moving Machine and Vehicle Operators**: #273 (median wage rank), $57,270 (median wage), $89,670 (90th percentile wage), 202,760 (number of positions), 6.6% (2016--2026 growth), High school diploma or equivalent (typical education requirement)

308. **Fish and Game Wardens**: #339 (median wage rank), $51,730 (median wage), $77,440 (90th percentile wage), 6,610 (number of positions), 4.3% (2016--2026 growth), Bachelor's degree (typical education requirement)

309. **Fishers and Related Fishing Workers**: #725

(median wage rank), $27,110 (median wage), $48,080 (90th percentile wage), 520 (number of positions), 2016--2026 growth project not available, typical education requirement not available

310. **Fitness Trainers and Aerobics Instructors**: #524 (median wage rank), $38,160 (median wage), $72,980 (90th percentile wage), 257,410 (number of positions), 9.8% (2016--2026 growth), High school diploma or equivalent (typical education requirement)

311. **Flight Attendants**: #384 (median wage rank), $48,500 (median wage), $78,650 (90th percentile wage), 113,390 (number of positions), 10.2% (2016--2026 growth), High school diploma or equivalent (typical education requirement)

312. **Floor Layers, Except Carpet, Wood, and Hard Tiles**: #530 (median wage rank), $37,840 (median wage), $68,720 (90th percentile wage), 10,340 (number of positions), 10% (2016--2026 growth), No formal educational credential (typical education requirement)

313. **Floor Sanders and Finishers**: #559 (median wage rank), $36,860 (median wage), $59,660 (90th percentile wage), 4,590 (number of positions), 9.8% (2016--2026 growth), No formal educational credential (typical education requirement)

314. **Floral Designers**: #743 (median wage rank), $25,850 (median wage), $39,130 (90th percentile wage), 43,990 (number of positions), -5.9% (2016--2026 growth), High school diploma or equivalent (typical education requirement)

315. **Food and Tobacco Roasting, Baking, and Drying Machine Operators and Tenders**: #695 (median wage rank), $28,570 (median wage), $48,550 (90th percentile wage), 20,080 (number of positions), -0.6% (2016--2026 growth), No formal educational credential (typical education requirement)

316. **Food Batchmakers**: #712 (median wage rank), $27,810 (median wage), $46,010 (90th percentile wage), 148,540 (number of positions), 1.3% (2016--2026 growth), High school diploma or equivalent (typical education requirement)

317. **Food Cooking Machine Operators and Tenders**: #704 (median wage rank), $28,350 (median wage), $45,830 (90th percentile wage), 36,520 (number of positions), 2.6% (2016--2026 growth), High school diploma or equivalent (typical education requirement)

318. **Food Preparation and Serving Related Workers**, All Other: #806 (median wage rank), $21,090 (median wage), $33,450 (90th percentile wage), 59,060 (number of positions), 9.3% (2016--2026 growth), No

formal educational credential (typical education requirement)

319. **Food Preparation Workers**: #802 (median wage rank), $21,440 (median wage), $31,040 (90th percentile wage), 850,670 (number of positions), 7.9% (2016--2026 growth), No formal educational credential (typical education requirement)

320. **Food Processing Workers, All Other**: #771 (median wage rank), $24,160 (median wage), $35,420 (90th percentile wage), 43,070 (number of positions), 5.4% (2016--2026 growth), No formal educational credential (typical education requirement)

321. **Food Scientists and Technologists**: #204 (median wage rank), $63,950 (median wage), $117,480 (90th percentile wage), 14,200 (number of positions), 6% (2016--2026 growth), Bachelor's degree (typical education requirement)

322. **Food Servers, Nonrestaurant**: #804 (median wage rank), $21,240 (median wage), $33,430 (90th percentile wage), 261,520 (number of positions), 10.2% (2016--2026 growth), No formal educational credential (typical education requirement)

323. **Food Service Managers**: #345 (median wage rank), $50,820 (median wage), $87,120 (90th percentile wage), 201,470 (number of positions), 8.8% (2016--2026 growth), High school diploma or equivalent

(typical education requirement)

324. **Foreign Language and Literature Teachers, Postsecondary**: #210 (median wage rank), $63,500 (median wage), $125,580 (90th percentile wage), 28,720 (number of positions), 11.8% (2016--2026 growth), Doctoral or professional degree (typical education requirement)

325. **Forensic Science Technicians**: #281 (median wage rank), $56,750 (median wage), $97,400 (90th percentile wage), 14,800 (number of positions), 16.8% (2016--2026 growth), Bachelor's degree (typical education requirement)

326. **Forest and Conservation Technicians**: #587 (median wage rank), $35,560 (median wage), $55,510 (90th percentile wage), 30,090 (number of positions), 3.8% (2016--2026 growth), Associate's degree (typical education requirement)

327. **Forest and Conservation Workers**: #726 (median wage rank), $26,940 (median wage), $49,150 (90th percentile wage), 7,170 (number of positions), -1.3% (2016--2026 growth), High school diploma or equivalent (typical education requirement)

328. **Forest Fire Inspectors and Prevention Specialists**: #572 (median wage rank), $36,230 (median wage), $76,660 (90th percentile wage), 1,650 (number of positions), 26.6% (2016--2026 growth), High school

diploma or equivalent (typical education requirement)

329. **Foresters**: #256 (median wage rank), $58,700 (median wage), $82,400 (90th percentile wage), 8,420 (number of positions), 5.2% (2016--2026 growth), Bachelor's degree (typical education requirement)

330. **Forestry and Conservation Science Teachers, Postsecondary**: #88 (median wage rank), $85,880 (median wage), $144,820 (90th percentile wage), 1,750 (number of positions), 7.7% (2016--2026 growth), Doctoral or professional degree (typical education requirement)

331. **Forging Machine Setters, Operators, and Tenders, Metal and Plastic**: #557 (median wage rank), $36,930 (median wage), $57,860 (90th percentile wage), 19,160 (number of positions), -19.2% (2016--2026 growth), High school diploma or equivalent (typical education requirement)

332. **Foundry Mold and Coremakers**: #599 (median wage rank), $34,790 (median wage), $49,970 (90th percentile wage), 12,810 (number of positions), -24% (2016--2026 growth), High school diploma or equivalent (typical education requirement)

333. **Fundraisers**: #309 (median wage rank), $54,130 (median wage), $91,530 (90th percentile wage), 68,910 (number of positions), 14.6% (2016--2026

growth), Bachelor's degree (typical education requirement)

334. **Funeral Attendants**: #760 (median wage rank), $24,830 (median wage), $39,720 (90th percentile wage), 35,770 (number of positions), 2.7% (2016--2026 growth), High school diploma or equivalent (typical education requirement)

335. **Funeral Service Managers**: #145 (median wage rank), $73,830 (median wage), $147,990 (90th percentile wage), 8,370 (number of positions), 6.4% (2016--2026 growth), Associate's degree (typical education requirement)

336. **Furnace, Kiln, Oven, Drier, and Kettle Operators and Tenders**: #577 (median wage rank), $36,040 (median wage), $56,040 (90th percentile wage), 19,520 (number of positions), -5% (2016--2026 growth), High school diploma or equivalent (typical education requirement)

337. **Furniture Finishers**: #666 (median wage rank), $30,550 (median wage), $47,890 (90th percentile wage), 17,370 (number of positions), 2.5% (2016--2026 growth), High school diploma or equivalent (typical education requirement)

338. **Gaming and Sports Book Writers and Runners**: #783 (median wage rank), $22,600 (median wage), $39,520 (90th percentile wage), 11,460 (number of

positions), 3.8% (2016--2026 growth), High school diploma or equivalent (typical education requirement)

339. **Gaming Cage Workers**: #740 (median wage rank), $25,990 (median wage), $40,640 (90th percentile wage), 18,810 (number of positions), 1.4% (2016--2026 growth), High school diploma or equivalent (typical education requirement)

340. **Gaming Change Persons and Booth Cashiers**: #777 (median wage rank), $23,780 (median wage), $37,330 (90th percentile wage), 23,120 (number of positions), 2.7% (2016--2026 growth), No formal educational credential (typical education requirement)

341. **Gaming Dealers**: #820 (median wage rank), $19,290 (median wage), $31,780 (90th percentile wage), 94,570 (number of positions), 1.1% (2016--2026 growth), High school diploma or equivalent (typical education requirement)

342. **Gaming Managers**: #171 (median wage rank), $69,180 (median wage), $124,400 (90th percentile wage), 4,280 (number of positions), 2.5% (2016--2026 growth), High school diploma or equivalent (typical education requirement)

343. **Gaming Service Workers**, All Other: #759 (median wage rank), $24,880 (median wage), $42,200 (90th

percentile wage), 12,140 (number of positions), 0.7% (2016--2026 growth), High school diploma or equivalent (typical education requirement)

344. **Gaming Supervisors**: #350 (median wage rank), $50,520 (median wage), $74,660 (90th percentile wage), 22,130 (number of positions), 3.5% (2016--2026 growth), High school diploma or equivalent (typical education requirement)

345. **Gaming Surveillance Officers and Gaming Investigators**: #635 (median wage rank), $32,630 (median wage), $52,500 (90th percentile wage), 10,460 (number of positions), 3.5% (2016--2026 growth), High school diploma or equivalent (typical education requirement)

346. **Gas Compressor and Gas Pumping Station Operators**: #237 (median wage rank), $60,470 (median wage), $78,920 (90th percentile wage), 3,890 (number of positions), 3.3% (2016--2026 growth), High school diploma or equivalent (typical education requirement)

347. **Gas Plant Operators**: #185 (median wage rank), $67,580 (median wage), $95,030 (90th percentile wage), 17,350 (number of positions), 0% (2016--2026 growth), High school diploma or equivalent (typical education requirement)

348. **General and Operations Managers**: #57 (median

wage rank), $99,310 (median wage), $165,848 (90th percentile wage), 2,188,870 (number of positions), 9.1% (2016--2026 growth), Bachelor's degree (typical education requirement)

349. **Genetic Counselors**: #142 (median wage rank), $74,120 (median wage), $104,770 (90th percentile wage), 2,720 (number of positions), 28.3% (2016--2026 growth), Master's degree (typical education requirement)

350. **Geographers**: #140 (median wage rank), $74,260 (median wage), $101,370 (90th percentile wage), 1,370 (number of positions), 6.2% (2016--2026 growth), Bachelor's degree (typical education requirement)

351. **Geography Teachers, Postsecondary**: #128 (median wage rank), $76,810 (median wage), $134,010 (90th percentile wage), 4,140 (number of positions), 8.4% (2016--2026 growth), Doctoral or professional degree (typical education requirement)

352. **Geological and Petroleum Technicians**: #287 (median wage rank), $56,470 (median wage), $103,080 (90th percentile wage), 15,100 (number of positions), 16.4% (2016--2026 growth), Associate's degree (typical education requirement)

353. **Geoscientists, Except Hydrologists and Geographers**: #81 (median wage rank), $89,780

(median wage), $189,020 (90th percentile wage), 30,420 (number of positions), 13.9% (2016--2026 growth), Bachelor's degree (typical education requirement)

354. **Glaziers**: #460 (median wage rank), $41,920 (median wage), $81,050 (90th percentile wage), 47,140 (number of positions), 10.6% (2016--2026 growth), High school diploma or equivalent (typical education requirement)

355. **Graders and Sorters, Agricultural Products**: #785 (median wage rank), $22,520 (median wage), $33,750 (90th percentile wage), 38,780 (number of positions), -0.9% (2016--2026 growth), No formal educational credential (typical education requirement)

356. **Graduate Teaching Assistants**: #607 (median wage rank), $34,240 (median wage), $55,080 (90th percentile wage), 135,130 (number of positions), 7.7% (2016--2026 growth), Bachelor's degree (typical education requirement)

357. **Graphic Designers**: #395 (median wage rank), $47,640 (median wage), $82,020 (90th percentile wage), 210,710 (number of positions), 4.7% (2016--2026 growth), Bachelor's degree (typical education requirement)

358. **Grinding and Polishing Workers, Hand**: #693 (median wage rank), $28,720 (median wage), $45,440

(90th percentile wage), 26,670 (number of positions), -20.5% (2016--2026 growth), No formal educational credential (typical education requirement)

359. **Grinding, Lapping, Polishing, and Buffing Machine Tool Setters, Operators, and Tenders, Metal and Plastic**: #630 (median wage rank), $32,890 (median wage), $50,640 (90th percentile wage), 74,600 (number of positions), -10% (2016--2026 growth), High school diploma or equivalent (typical education requirement)

360. **Grounds Maintenance Workers**, All Other: #700 (median wage rank), $28,470 (median wage), $56,430 (90th percentile wage), 15,170 (number of positions), 8.5% (2016--2026 growth), No formal educational credential (typical education requirement)

361. **Hairdressers, Hairstylists, and Cosmetologists**: #769 (median wage rank), $24,260 (median wage), $49,050 (90th percentile wage), 352,380 (number of positions), 10.6% (2016--2026 growth), Postsecondary nondegree award (typical education requirement)

362. **Hazardous Materials Removal Workers**: #479 (median wage rank), $40,640 (median wage), $74,160 (90th percentile wage), 44,280 (number of positions), 17.1% (2016--2026 growth), High school diploma or equivalent (typical education requirement)

363. **Health and Safety Engineers, Except Mining**

Safety Engineers and Inspectors: #86 (median wage rank), $86,720 (median wage), $134,110 (90th percentile wage), 25,410 (number of positions), 8.6% (2016--2026 growth), Bachelor's degree (typical education requirement)

364. **Health Diagnosing and Treating Practitioners**, All Other: #138 (median wage rank), $74,530 (median wage), $135,650 (90th percentile wage), 36,280 (number of positions), 11.4% (2016--2026 growth), Master's degree (typical education requirement)

365. **Health Educators**: #320 (median wage rank), $53,070 (median wage), $95,730 (90th percentile wage), 57,570 (number of positions), 14.5% (2016--2026 growth), Bachelor's degree (typical education requirement)

366. **Health Specialties Teachers, Postsecondary**: #56 (median wage rank), $99,360 (median wage), $165,931 (90th percentile wage), 186,740 (number of positions), 25.9% (2016--2026 growth), Doctoral or professional degree (typical education requirement)

367. **Health Technologists and Technicians**, All Other: #471 (median wage rank), $41,070 (median wage), $71,280 (90th percentile wage), 122,170 (number of positions), 19.4% (2016--2026 growth), Postsecondary nondegree award (typical education requirement)

368. **Healthcare Practitioners and Technical Workers**,

All Other: #379 (median wage rank), $48,820 (median wage), $104,050 (90th percentile wage), 36,000 (number of positions), 12.1% (2016--2026 growth), Postsecondary nondegree award (typical education requirement)

369. **Healthcare Social Workers**: #312 (median wage rank), $53,760 (median wage), $80,020 (90th percentile wage), 159,310 (number of positions), 18.5% (2016--2026 growth), Master's degree (typical education requirement)

370. **Healthcare Support Workers, All Other**: #571 (median wage rank), $36,330 (median wage), $54,240 (90th percentile wage), 93,830 (number of positions), 11.6% (2016--2026 growth), High school diploma or equivalent (typical education requirement)

371. **Hearing Aid Specialists**: #355 (median wage rank), $50,250 (median wage), $80,940 (90th percentile wage), 6,740 (number of positions), 19.2% (2016--2026 growth), High school diploma or equivalent (typical education requirement)

372. **Heat Treating Equipment Setters, Operators, and Tenders, Metal and Plastic**: #546 (median wage rank), $37,180 (median wage), $57,290 (90th percentile wage), 19,780 (number of positions), -14.1% (2016--2026 growth), High school diploma or equivalent (typical education requirement)

373. **Heating, Air Conditioning, and Refrigeration Mechanics and Installers**: #409 (median wage rank), $45,910 (median wage), $73,350 (90th percentile wage), 294,730 (number of positions), 14.7% (2016--2026 growth), Postsecondary nondegree award (typical education requirement)

374. **Heavy and Tractor-Trailer Truck Drivers**: #467 (median wage rank), $41,340 (median wage), $63,140 (90th percentile wage), 1,704,520 (number of positions), 6.1% (2016--2026 growth), Postsecondary nondegree award (typical education requirement)

375. **Helpers, Construction Trades**, All Other: #679 (median wage rank), $29,270 (median wage), $46,220 (90th percentile wage), 21,820 (number of positions), 12.1% (2016--2026 growth), No formal educational credential (typical education requirement)

376. **Helpers--Brickmasons, Blockmasons, Stonemasons, and Tile and Marble Setters**: #665 (median wage rank), $30,570 (median wage), $49,990 (90th percentile wage), 23,950 (number of positions), 12.1% (2016--2026 growth), No formal educational credential (typical education requirement)

377. **Helpers--Carpenters**: #688 (median wage rank), $28,810 (median wage), $43,030 (90th percentile wage), 35,890 (number of positions), 12.8% (2016--2026 growth), No formal educational credential

(typical education requirement)

378. **Helpers--Electricians**: #678 (median wage rank), $29,530 (median wage), $44,450 (90th percentile wage), 71,890 (number of positions), 10.6% (2016--2026 growth), High school diploma or equivalent (typical education requirement)

379. **Helpers--Extraction Workers**: #579 (median wage rank), $35,790 (median wage), $51,220 (90th percentile wage), 17,660 (number of positions), 19.7% (2016--2026 growth), High school diploma or equivalent (typical education requirement)

380. **Helpers--Installation, Maintenance, and Repair Workers**: #717 (median wage rank), $27,510 (median wage), $43,680 (90th percentile wage), 118,720 (number of positions), 11.1% (2016--2026 growth), High school diploma or equivalent (typical education requirement)

381. **Helpers--Painters, Paperhangers, Plasterers, and Stucco Masons**: #720 (median wage rank), $27,310 (median wage), $39,670 (90th percentile wage), 10,780 (number of positions), 4.1% (2016--2026 growth), No formal educational credential (typical education requirement)

382. **Helpers--Pipelayers, Plumbers, Pipefitters, and Steamfitters**: #684 (median wage rank), $29,030 (median wage), $43,470 (90th percentile wage),

54,080 (number of positions), 18.6% (2016--2026 growth), High school diploma or equivalent (typical education requirement)

383. **Helpers--Production Workers**: #761 (median wage rank), $24,830 (median wage), $38,750 (90th percentile wage), 429,890 (number of positions), 11.6% (2016--2026 growth), High school diploma or equivalent (typical education requirement)

384. **Helpers--Roofers**: #714 (median wage rank), $27,670 (median wage), $39,110 (90th percentile wage), 10,190 (number of positions), 12.4% (2016--2026 growth), No formal educational credential (typical education requirement)

385. **Highway Maintenance Workers**: #525 (median wage rank), $38,130 (median wage), $56,820 (90th percentile wage), 143,320 (number of positions), 6.9% (2016--2026 growth), High school diploma or equivalent (typical education requirement)

386. **Historians**: #296 (median wage rank), $55,110 (median wage), $102,830 (90th percentile wage), 2,950 (number of positions), 5.4% (2016--2026 growth), Master's degree (typical education requirement)

387. **History Teachers, Postsecondary**: #156 (median wage rank), $71,820 (median wage), $130,530 (90th percentile wage), 21,800 (number of positions), 10.3%

(2016--2026 growth), Doctoral or professional degree (typical education requirement)

388. **Hoist and Winch Operators**: #450 (median wage rank), $42,530 (median wage), $91,330 (90th percentile wage), 2,960 (number of positions), -0.7% (2016--2026 growth), No formal educational credential (typical education requirement)

389. **Home Appliance Repairers**: #537 (median wage rank), $37,570 (median wage), $62,600 (90th percentile wage), 33,480 (number of positions), -0.9% (2016--2026 growth), High school diploma or equivalent (typical education requirement)

390. **Home Economics Teachers, Postsecondary**: #170 (median wage rank), $69,190 (median wage), $115,910 (90th percentile wage), 2,970 (number of positions), 7.8% (2016--2026 growth), Master's degree (typical education requirement)

391. **Home Health Aides**: #784 (median wage rank), $22,600 (median wage), $30,610 (90th percentile wage), 814,300 (number of positions), 46.7% (2016--2026 growth), High school diploma or equivalent (typical education requirement)

392. **Hosts and Hostesses, Restaurant, Lounge, and Coffee Shop**: #814 (median wage rank), $19,980 (median wage), $28,620 (90th percentile wage), 404,360 (number of positions), 6.9% (2016--2026

growth), No formal educational credential (typical education requirement)

393. **Hotel, Motel, and Resort Desk Clerks**: #792 (median wage rank), $22,070 (median wage), $31,850 (90th percentile wage), 248,440 (number of positions), 4.5% (2016--2026 growth), High school diploma or equivalent (typical education requirement)

394. **Human Resources Assistants, Except Payroll and Timekeeping**: #499 (median wage rank), $39,020 (median wage), $56,440 (90th percentile wage), 137,150 (number of positions), -1.8% (2016--2026 growth), Associate's degree (typical education requirement)

395. **Human Resources Managers**: #38 (median wage rank), $106,910 (median wage), $193,550 (90th percentile wage), 129,810 (number of positions), 8.9% (2016--2026 growth), Bachelor's degree (typical education requirement)

396. **Human Resources Specialists**: #251 (median wage rank), $59,180 (median wage), $101,420 (90th percentile wage), 524,800 (number of positions), 7.1% (2016--2026 growth), Bachelor's degree (typical education requirement)

397. **Hydrologists**: #108 (median wage rank), $80,480 (median wage), $120,100 (90th percentile wage),

6,300 (number of positions), 9.9% (2016--2026 growth), Bachelor's degree (typical education requirement)

398. **Industrial Engineering Technicians**: #319 (median wage rank), $53,330 (median wage), $86,430 (90th percentile wage), 63,220 (number of positions), 0.6% (2016--2026 growth), Associate's degree (typical education requirement)

399. **Industrial Engineers**: #96 (median wage rank), $84,310 (median wage), $129,390 (90th percentile wage), 256,550 (number of positions), 9.7% (2016--2026 growth), Bachelor's degree (typical education requirement)

400. **Industrial Machinery Mechanics**: #360 (median wage rank), $50,040 (median wage), $76,110 (90th percentile wage), 334,490 (number of positions), 6.8% (2016--2026 growth), High school diploma or equivalent (typical education requirement)

401. **Industrial Production Managers**: #62 (median wage rank), $97,140 (median wage), $165,450 (90th percentile wage), 168,400 (number of positions), -0.2% (2016--2026 growth), Bachelor's degree (typical education requirement)

402. **Industrial Truck and Tractor Operators**: #638 (median wage rank), $32,460 (median wage), $48,850 (90th percentile wage), 542,750 (number of

positions), 6.6% (2016--2026 growth), No formal educational credential (typical education requirement)

403. **Industrial-Organizational Psychologists**: #99 (median wage rank), $82,760 (median wage), $184,380 (90th percentile wage), 1,020 (number of positions), 5.6% (2016--2026 growth), Master's degree (typical education requirement)

404. **Information and Record Clerks**, All Other: #495 (median wage rank), $39,260 (median wage), $56,650 (90th percentile wage), 166,850 (number of positions), 7.6% (2016--2026 growth), High school diploma or equivalent (typical education requirement)

405. **Information Security Analysts**: #71 (median wage rank), $92,600 (median wage), $147,290 (90th percentile wage), 96,870 (number of positions), 28.4% (2016--2026 growth), Bachelor's degree (typical education requirement)

406. **Inspectors, Testers, Sorters, Samplers, and Weighers**: #560 (median wage rank), $36,780 (median wage), $63,590 (90th percentile wage), 518,950 (number of positions), -10.7% (2016--2026 growth), High school diploma or equivalent (typical education requirement)

407. **Installation, Maintenance, and Repair Workers**,

All Other: #513 (median wage rank), $38,480 (median wage), $64,560 (90th percentile wage), 146,460 (number of positions), 8% (2016--2026 growth), High school diploma or equivalent (typical education requirement)

408. **Instructional Coordinators**: #220 (median wage rank), $62,460 (median wage), $100,320 (90th percentile wage), 147,330 (number of positions), 10.1% (2016--2026 growth), Master's degree (typical education requirement)

409. **Insulation Workers, Floor, Ceiling, and Wall**: #584 (median wage rank), $35,660 (median wage), $61,520 (90th percentile wage), 29,500 (number of positions), 1.3% (2016--2026 growth), No formal educational credential (typical education requirement)

410. **Insulation Workers, Mechanical**: #421 (median wage rank), $45,430 (median wage), $84,230 (90th percentile wage), 27,270 (number of positions), 9.7% (2016--2026 growth), High school diploma or equivalent (typical education requirement)

411. **Insurance Appraisers, Auto Damage**: #209 (median wage rank), $63,510 (median wage), $95,000 (90th percentile wage), 15,130 (number of positions), 4.9% (2016--2026 growth), Postsecondary nondegree award (typical education requirement)

4 OCCUPATIONS RANKED ALPHABETICALLY

412. **Insurance Claims and Policy Processing Clerks**: #517 (median wage rank), $38,430 (median wage), $59,310 (90th percentile wage), 274,350 (number of positions), 11% (2016--2026 growth), High school diploma or equivalent (typical education requirement)

413. **Insurance Sales Agents**: #361 (median wage rank), $49,990 (median wage), $128,070 (90th percentile wage), 385,700 (number of positions), 9.7% (2016--2026 growth), High school diploma or equivalent (typical education requirement)

414. **Insurance Underwriters**: #184 (median wage rank), $67,680 (median wage), $121,430 (90th percentile wage), 91,650 (number of positions), -5.2% (2016--2026 growth), Bachelor's degree (typical education requirement)

415. **Interior Designers**: #363 (median wage rank), $49,810 (median wage), $91,230 (90th percentile wage), 53,160 (number of positions), 4.9% (2016--2026 growth), Bachelor's degree (typical education requirement)

416. **Internists, General**: #7 (median wage rank), $196,380 (median wage), $327,955 (90th percentile wage), 45,290 (number of positions), 16.9% (2016--2026 growth), Doctoral or professional degree (typical education requirement)

417. **Interpreters and Translators**: #407 (median wage rank), $46,120 (median wage), $83,010 (90th percentile wage), 51,350 (number of positions), 16.7% (2016--2026 growth), Bachelor's degree (typical education requirement)

418. **Interviewers, Except Eligibility and Loan**: #643 (median wage rank), $32,150 (median wage), $48,420 (90th percentile wage), 186,030 (number of positions), 5.7% (2016--2026 growth), High school diploma or equivalent (typical education requirement)

419. **Janitors and Cleaners, Except Maids and Housekeeping Cleaners**: #770 (median wage rank), $24,190 (median wage), $40,760 (90th percentile wage), 2,161,740 (number of positions), 9.8% (2016--2026 growth), No formal educational credential (typical education requirement)

420. **Jewelers and Precious Stone and Metal Workers**: #522 (median wage rank), $38,200 (median wage), $66,110 (90th percentile wage), 26,480 (number of positions), -3.1% (2016--2026 growth), High school diploma or equivalent (typical education requirement)

421. **Judges, Magistrate Judges, and Magistrates**: #21 (median wage rank), $125,880 (median wage), $183,570 (90th percentile wage), 27,210 (number of

positions), 5.6% (2016--2026 growth), Doctoral or professional degree (typical education requirement)

422. **Judicial Law Clerks**: #338 (median wage rank), $51,760 (median wage), $106,640 (90th percentile wage), 13,410 (number of positions), 5.5% (2016--2026 growth), Doctoral or professional degree (typical education requirement)

423. **Kindergarten Teachers, Except Special Education**: #322 (median wage rank), $52,620 (median wage), $81,210 (90th percentile wage), 151,290 (number of positions), 7.9% (2016--2026 growth), Bachelor's degree (typical education requirement)

424. **Labor Relations Specialists**: #222 (median wage rank), $62,310 (median wage), $114,340 (90th percentile wage), 79,430 (number of positions), -7.8% (2016--2026 growth), Bachelor's degree (typical education requirement)

425. **Laborers and Freight, Stock, and Material Movers, Hand**: #741 (median wage rank), $25,980 (median wage), $42,690 (90th percentile wage), 2,587,900 (number of positions), 7.6% (2016--2026 growth), No formal educational credential (typical education requirement)

426. **Landscape Architects**: #211 (median wage rank), $63,480 (median wage), $106,770 (90th percentile

wage), 19,420 (number of positions), 6.2% (2016--2026 growth), Bachelor's degree (typical education requirement)

427. **Landscaping and Groundskeeping Workers**: #736 (median wage rank), $26,320 (median wage), $41,070 (90th percentile wage), 906,570 (number of positions), 10.3% (2016--2026 growth), No formal educational credential (typical education requirement)

428. **Lathe and Turning Machine Tool Setters, Operators, and Tenders, Metal and Plastic**: #515 (median wage rank), $38,480 (median wage), $56,990 (90th percentile wage), 33,850 (number of positions), -8.4% (2016--2026 growth), High school diploma or equivalent (typical education requirement)

429. **Laundry and Dry-Cleaning Workers**: #801 (median wage rank), $21,510 (median wage), $31,460 (90th percentile wage), 207,710 (number of positions), -0.3% (2016--2026 growth), No formal educational credential (typical education requirement)

430. **Law Teachers, Postsecondary**: #35 (median wage rank), $111,210 (median wage), $185,721 (90th percentile wage), 16,010 (number of positions), 12.2% (2016--2026 growth), Doctoral or professional degree (typical education requirement)

431. **Lawyers**: #27 (median wage rank), $118,160 (median wage), $197,327 (90th percentile wage), 619,530 (number of positions), 9.4% (2016--2026 growth), Doctoral or professional degree (typical education requirement)

432. **Layout Workers, Metal and Plastic**: #413 (median wage rank), $45,820 (median wage), $66,010 (90th percentile wage), 9,070 (number of positions), -6.8% (2016--2026 growth), High school diploma or equivalent (typical education requirement)

433. **Legal Secretaries**: #434 (median wage rank), $44,180 (median wage), $75,530 (90th percentile wage), 191,200 (number of positions), -19.1% (2016--2026 growth), High school diploma or equivalent (typical education requirement)

434. **Legal Support Workers**, All Other: #301 (median wage rank), $54,650 (median wage), $127,650 (90th percentile wage), 44,960 (number of positions), 3.6% (2016--2026 growth), Associate's degree (typical education requirement)

435. **Legislators**: #779 (median wage rank), $23,470 (median wage), $96,500 (90th percentile wage), 53,670 (number of positions), 7.1% (2016--2026 growth), Bachelor's degree (typical education requirement)

436. **Librarians**: #267 (median wage rank), $57,680

(median wage), $90,140 (90th percentile wage), 129,350 (number of positions), 8.9% (2016--2026 growth), Master's degree (typical education requirement)

437. **Library Assistants, Clerical**: #755 (median wage rank), $25,220 (median wage), $40,540 (90th percentile wage), 98,560 (number of positions), 9.4% (2016--2026 growth), High school diploma or equivalent (typical education requirement)

438. **Library Science Teachers, Postsecondary**: #178 (median wage rank), $68,410 (median wage), $106,960 (90th percentile wage), 4,870 (number of positions), 9% (2016--2026 growth), Doctoral or professional degree (typical education requirement)

439. **Library Technicians**: #629 (median wage rank), $32,890 (median wage), $52,880 (90th percentile wage), 93,410 (number of positions), 9.1% (2016--2026 growth), Postsecondary nondegree award (typical education requirement)

440. **Licensed Practical and Licensed Vocational Nurses**: #436 (median wage rank), $44,090 (median wage), $60,420 (90th percentile wage), 702,400 (number of positions), 12.2% (2016--2026 growth), Postsecondary nondegree award (typical education requirement)

441. **Life Scientists**, All Other: #143 (median wage

rank), $73,860 (median wage), $136,370 (90th percentile wage), 7,890 (number of positions), 9% (2016--2026 growth), Bachelor's degree (typical education requirement)

442. **Life, Physical, and Social Science Technicians, All Other**: #408 (median wage rank), $46,040 (median wage), $77,010 (90th percentile wage), 68,540 (number of positions), 9.6% (2016--2026 growth), Associate's degree (typical education requirement)

443. **Lifeguards, Ski Patrol, and Other Recreational Protective Service Workers**: #809 (median wage rank), $20,290 (median wage), $31,840 (90th percentile wage), 145,100 (number of positions), 7.7% (2016--2026 growth), No formal educational credential (typical education requirement)

444. **Light Truck or Delivery Services Drivers**: #664 (median wage rank), $30,580 (median wage), $60,630 (90th percentile wage), 858,710 (number of positions), 6.8% (2016--2026 growth), High school diploma or equivalent (typical education requirement)

445. **Loading Machine Operators, Underground Mining**: #315 (median wage rank), $53,420 (median wage), $67,100 (90th percentile wage), 2,550 (number of positions), -3.2% (2016--2026 growth), No formal educational credential (typical education

requirement)

446. **Loan Interviewers and Clerks**: #510 (median wage rank), $38,630 (median wage), $58,630 (90th percentile wage), 224,340 (number of positions), 12.4% (2016--2026 growth), High school diploma or equivalent (typical education requirement)

447. **Loan Officers**: #207 (median wage rank), $63,650 (median wage), $132,290 (90th percentile wage), 305,700 (number of positions), 11.5% (2016--2026 growth), Bachelor's degree (typical education requirement)

448. **Locker Room, Coatroom, and Dressing Room Attendants**: #800 (median wage rank), $21,720 (median wage), $36,100 (90th percentile wage), 18,040 (number of positions), 8.7% (2016--2026 growth), High school diploma or equivalent (typical education requirement)

449. **Locksmiths and Safe Repairers**: #481 (median wage rank), $40,420 (median wage), $62,960 (90th percentile wage), 18,640 (number of positions), -3.2% (2016--2026 growth), High school diploma or equivalent (typical education requirement)

450. **Locomotive Engineers**: #268 (median wage rank), $57,670 (median wage), $85,290 (90th percentile wage), 39,900 (number of positions), -2.8% (2016--2026 growth), High school diploma or equivalent

4 OCCUPATIONS RANKED ALPHABETICALLY

(typical education requirement)

451. **Locomotive Firers**: #262 (median wage rank), $58,230 (median wage), $97,820 (90th percentile wage), 1,210 (number of positions), -78.6% (2016--2026 growth), High school diploma or equivalent (typical education requirement)

452. **Lodging Managers**: #335 (median wage rank), $51,840 (median wage), $96,570 (90th percentile wage), 35,410 (number of positions), 5.9% (2016--2026 growth), High school diploma or equivalent (typical education requirement)

453. **Log Graders and Scalers**: #548 (median wage rank), $37,090 (median wage), $53,110 (90th percentile wage), 3,020 (number of positions), 2.7% (2016--2026 growth), High school diploma or equivalent (typical education requirement)

454. **Logging Equipment Operators**: #539 (median wage rank), $37,490 (median wage), $56,110 (90th percentile wage), 27,250 (number of positions), -7% (2016--2026 growth), High school diploma or equivalent (typical education requirement)

455. **Logging Workers**, All Other: #502 (median wage rank), $38,950 (median wage), $57,430 (90th percentile wage), 3,010 (number of positions), -9.5% (2016--2026 growth), High school diploma or equivalent (typical education requirement)

456. **Logisticians**: #141 (median wage rank), $74,170 (median wage), $117,310 (90th percentile wage), 146,060 (number of positions), 6.9% (2016--2026 growth), Bachelor's degree (typical education requirement)

457. **Machine Feeders and Offbearers**: #701 (median wage rank), $28,410 (median wage), $46,140 (90th percentile wage), 88,070 (number of positions), 1.8% (2016--2026 growth), No formal educational credential (typical education requirement)

458. **Machinists**: #462 (median wage rank), $41,700 (median wage), $62,590 (90th percentile wage), 391,120 (number of positions), 2.1% (2016--2026 growth), High school diploma or equivalent (typical education requirement)

459. **Magnetic Resonance Imaging Technologists**: #177 (median wage rank), $68,420 (median wage), $95,890 (90th percentile wage), 35,850 (number of positions), 13.6% (2016--2026 growth), Associate's degree (typical education requirement)

460. **Maids and Housekeeping Cleaners**: #798 (median wage rank), $21,820 (median wage), $34,430 (90th percentile wage), 924,640 (number of positions), 5.6% (2016--2026 growth), No formal educational credential (typical education requirement)

461. **Mail Clerks and Mail Machine Operators, Except**

Postal Service: #682 (median wage rank), $29,160 (median wage), $45,220 (90th percentile wage), 91,530 (number of positions), -7.5% (2016--2026 growth), High school diploma or equivalent (typical education requirement)

462. **Maintenance and Repair Workers, General**: #554 (median wage rank), $36,940 (median wage), $60,660 (90th percentile wage), 1,332,480 (number of positions), 7.9% (2016--2026 growth), High school diploma or equivalent (typical education requirement)

463. **Maintenance Workers, Machinery**: #427 (median wage rank), $44,550 (median wage), $66,240 (90th percentile wage), 89,630 (number of positions), 5.6% (2016--2026 growth), High school diploma or equivalent (typical education requirement)

464. **Makeup Artists, Theatrical and Performance**: #233 (median wage rank), $60,970 (median wage), $124,960 (90th percentile wage), 3,600 (number of positions), 11.2% (2016--2026 growth), Postsecondary nondegree award (typical education requirement)

465. **Management Analysts**: #105 (median wage rank), $81,330 (median wage), $149,720 (90th percentile wage), 637,690 (number of positions), 12% (2016--2026 growth), Bachelor's degree (typical education requirement)

466. **Managers, All Other**: #43 (median wage rank), $104,970 (median wage), $172,570 (90th percentile wage), 403,670 (number of positions), 7.6% (2016--2026 growth), Bachelor's degree (typical education requirement)

467. **Manicurists and Pedicurists**: #789 (median wage rank), $22,150 (median wage), $33,590 (90th percentile wage), 90,630 (number of positions), 12% (2016--2026 growth), Postsecondary nondegree award (typical education requirement)

468. **Manufactured Building and Mobile Home Installers**: #675 (median wage rank), $29,810 (median wage), $43,400 (90th percentile wage), 3,200 (number of positions), -8.8% (2016--2026 growth), High school diploma or equivalent (typical education requirement)

469. **Marine Engineers and Naval Architects**: #69 (median wage rank), $93,350 (median wage), $152,450 (90th percentile wage), 8,120 (number of positions), 11.5% (2016--2026 growth), Bachelor's degree (typical education requirement)

470. **Market Research Analysts and Marketing Specialists**: #218 (median wage rank), $62,560 (median wage), $121,720 (90th percentile wage), 558,630 (number of positions), 22.8% (2016--2026 growth), Bachelor's degree (typical education

requirement)

471. **Marketing Managers**: #17 (median wage rank), $131,180 (median wage), $219,071 (90th percentile wage), 205,900 (number of positions), 10% (2016--2026 growth), Bachelor's degree (typical education requirement)

472. **Marriage and Family Therapists**: #374 (median wage rank), $49,170 (median wage), $81,960 (90th percentile wage), 36,960 (number of positions), 20.2% (2016--2026 growth), Master's degree (typical education requirement)

473. **Massage Therapists**: #485 (median wage rank), $39,860 (median wage), $74,870 (90th percentile wage), 95,830 (number of positions), 23.5% (2016--2026 growth), Postsecondary nondegree award (typical education requirement)

474. **Material Moving Workers**, All Other: #703 (median wage rank), $28,370 (median wage), $58,840 (90th percentile wage), 23,880 (number of positions), 9.3% (2016--2026 growth), No formal educational credential (typical education requirement)

475. **Materials Engineers**: #70 (median wage rank), $93,310 (median wage), $148,840 (90th percentile wage), 26,800 (number of positions), 1.6% (2016--2026 growth), Bachelor's degree (typical education requirement)

476. **Materials Scientists**: #55 (median wage rank), $99,430 (median wage), $157,750 (90th percentile wage), 7,750 (number of positions), 7.1% (2016--2026 growth), Bachelor's degree (typical education requirement)

477. **Mathematical Science Occupations, All Other**: #199 (median wage rank), $65,050 (median wage), $157,600 (90th percentile wage), 2,000 (number of positions), 10.7% (2016--2026 growth), Bachelor's degree (typical education requirement)

478. **Mathematical Science Teachers, Postsecondary**: #168 (median wage rank), $69,520 (median wage), $147,700 (90th percentile wage), 52,020 (number of positions), 9.2% (2016--2026 growth), Doctoral or professional degree (typical education requirement)

479. **Mathematical Technicians**: #365 (median wage rank), $49,660 (median wage), $100,730 (90th percentile wage), 510 (number of positions), 7.5% (2016--2026 growth), Bachelor's degree (typical education requirement)

480. **Mathematicians**: #42 (median wage rank), $105,810 (median wage), $160,310 (90th percentile wage), 2,730 (number of positions), 29.4% (2016--2026 growth), Master's degree (typical education requirement)

481. **Meat, Poultry, and Fish Cutters and Trimmers**:

#765 (median wage rank), $24,490 (median wage), $33,020 (90th percentile wage), 149,800 (number of positions), 0.8% (2016--2026 growth), No formal educational credential (typical education requirement)

482. **Mechanical Door Repairers**: #514 (median wage rank), $38,480 (median wage), $58,000 (90th percentile wage), 19,840 (number of positions), 10.4% (2016--2026 growth), High school diploma or equivalent (typical education requirement)

483. **Mechanical Drafters**: #304 (median wage rank), $54,480 (median wage), $85,920 (90th percentile wage), 63,630 (number of positions), 5.1% (2016--2026 growth), Associate's degree (typical education requirement)

484. **Mechanical Engineering Technicians**: #305 (median wage rank), $54,480 (median wage), $82,810 (90th percentile wage), 45,510 (number of positions), 5% (2016--2026 growth), Associate's degree (typical education requirement)

485. **Mechanical Engineers**: #97 (median wage rank), $84,190 (median wage), $131,350 (90th percentile wage), 285,790 (number of positions), 8.8% (2016--2026 growth), Bachelor's degree (typical education requirement)

486. **Media and Communication Equipment Workers**,

All Other: #132 (median wage rank), $75,700 (median wage), $118,840 (90th percentile wage), 18,620 (number of positions), 7.9% (2016--2026 growth), High school diploma or equivalent (typical education requirement)

487. **Media and Communication Workers, All Other**: #437 (median wage rank), $43,600 (median wage), $91,820 (90th percentile wage), 23,310 (number of positions), 8.7% (2016--2026 growth), High school diploma or equivalent (typical education requirement)

488. **Medical and Clinical Laboratory Technicians**: #501 (median wage rank), $38,950 (median wage), $61,720 (90th percentile wage), 160,190 (number of positions), 14% (2016--2026 growth), Associate's degree (typical education requirement)

489. **Medical and Clinical Laboratory Technologists**: #232 (median wage rank), $61,070 (median wage), $85,160 (90th percentile wage), 166,730 (number of positions), 11.5% (2016--2026 growth), Bachelor's degree (typical education requirement)

490. **Medical and Health Services Managers**: #63 (median wage rank), $96,540 (median wage), $172,240 (90th percentile wage), 332,150 (number of positions), 19.8% (2016--2026 growth), Bachelor's degree (typical education requirement)

491. **Medical Appliance Technicians**: #578 (median wage rank), $35,980 (median wage), $62,720 (90th percentile wage), 14,570 (number of positions), 13.7% (2016--2026 growth), High school diploma or equivalent (typical education requirement)

492. **Medical Assistants**: #647 (median wage rank), $31,540 (median wage), $45,310 (90th percentile wage), 623,560 (number of positions), 29.1% (2016--2026 growth), Postsecondary nondegree award (typical education requirement)

493. **Medical Equipment Preparers**: #603 (median wage rank), $34,400 (median wage), $50,620 (90th percentile wage), 52,500 (number of positions), 10.9% (2016--2026 growth), High school diploma or equivalent (typical education requirement)

494. **Medical Equipment Repairers**: #388 (median wage rank), $48,070 (median wage), $78,520 (90th percentile wage), 43,370 (number of positions), 5.3% (2016--2026 growth), Associate's degree (typical education requirement)

495. **Medical Records and Health Information Technicians**: #526 (median wage rank), $38,040 (median wage), $62,840 (90th percentile wage), 200,140 (number of positions), 13.5% (2016--2026 growth), Postsecondary nondegree award (typical education requirement)

496. **Medical Scientists, Except Epidemiologists**: #106 (median wage rank), $80,530 (median wage), $159,570 (90th percentile wage), 108,870 (number of positions), 13.2% (2016--2026 growth), Doctoral or professional degree (typical education requirement)

497. **Medical Secretaries**: #617 (median wage rank), $33,730 (median wage), $49,730 (90th percentile wage), 556,820 (number of positions), 22.5% (2016--2026 growth), High school diploma or equivalent (typical education requirement)

498. **Medical Transcriptionists**: #581 (median wage rank), $35,720 (median wage), $51,640 (90th percentile wage), 54,070 (number of positions), -3.5% (2016--2026 growth), Postsecondary nondegree award (typical education requirement)

499. **Meeting, Convention, and Event Planners**: #398 (median wage rank), $47,350 (median wage), $83,030 (90th percentile wage), 95,850 (number of positions), 10.2% (2016--2026 growth), Bachelor's degree (typical education requirement)

500. **Mental Health and Substance Abuse Social Workers**: #447 (median wage rank), $42,700 (median wage), $74,650 (90th percentile wage), 114,040 (number of positions), 17.9% (2016--2026 growth), Master's degree (typical education requirement)

501. **Mental Health Counselors**: #444 (median wage

rank), $42,840 (median wage), $70,100 (90th percentile wage), 139,820 (number of positions), 19.8% (2016--2026 growth), Master's degree (typical education requirement)

502. **Merchandise Displayers and Window Trimmers**: #730 (median wage rank), $26,700 (median wage), $47,150 (90th percentile wage), 114,690 (number of positions), 3.8% (2016--2026 growth), High school diploma or equivalent (typical education requirement)

503. **Metal Workers and Plastic Workers**, All Other: #623 (median wage rank), $33,280 (median wage), $56,490 (90th percentile wage), 22,930 (number of positions), -6.6% (2016--2026 growth), High school diploma or equivalent (typical education requirement)

504. **Metal-Refining Furnace Operators and Tenders**: #474 (median wage rank), $41,040 (median wage), $59,980 (90th percentile wage), 17,730 (number of positions), -8.1% (2016--2026 growth), High school diploma or equivalent (typical education requirement)

505. **Meter Readers, Utilities**: #503 (median wage rank), $38,940 (median wage), $65,970 (90th percentile wage), 34,070 (number of positions), -4.4% (2016--2026 growth), High school diploma or

equivalent (typical education requirement)

506. **Microbiologists**: #189 (median wage rank), $66,850 (median wage), $128,190 (90th percentile wage), 21,670 (number of positions), 8% (2016--2026 growth), Bachelor's degree (typical education requirement)

507. **Middle School Teachers, Except Special and Career/Technical Education**: #282 (median wage rank), $56,720 (median wage), $89,120 (90th percentile wage), 626,310 (number of positions), 7.5% (2016--2026 growth), Bachelor's degree (typical education requirement)

508. **Milling and Planing Machine Setters, Operators, and Tenders, Metal and Plastic**: #486 (median wage rank), $39,840 (median wage), $60,930 (90th percentile wage), 17,560 (number of positions), -19.3% (2016--2026 growth), High school diploma or equivalent (typical education requirement)

509. **Millwrights**: #327 (median wage rank), $52,440 (median wage), $78,390 (90th percentile wage), 39,670 (number of positions), 9.8% (2016--2026 growth), High school diploma or equivalent (typical education requirement)

510. **Mine Cutting and Channeling Machine Operators**: #333 (median wage rank), $51,900 (median wage), $73,280 (90th percentile wage), 5,930

(number of positions), -4.7% (2016--2026 growth), High school diploma or equivalent (typical education requirement)

511. **Mine Shuttle Car Operators**: #288 (median wage rank), $56,450 (median wage), $68,080 (90th percentile wage), 1,590 (number of positions), -21.9% (2016--2026 growth), No formal educational credential (typical education requirement)

512. **Mining and Geological Engineers, Including Mining Safety Engineers**: #68 (median wage rank), $93,720 (median wage), $160,510 (90th percentile wage), 6,940 (number of positions), 7.2% (2016--2026 growth), Bachelor's degree (typical education requirement)

513. **Mining Machine Operators**, All Other: #390 (median wage rank), $48,010 (median wage), $73,920 (90th percentile wage), 2,160 (number of positions), 0.1% (2016--2026 growth), High school diploma or equivalent (typical education requirement)

514. **Mixing and Blending Machine Setters, Operators, and Tenders**: #583 (median wage rank), $35,680 (median wage), $55,960 (90th percentile wage), 130,480 (number of positions), -3.1% (2016--2026 growth), High school diploma or equivalent (typical education requirement)

515. **Mobile Heavy Equipment Mechanics, Except**

Engines: #370 (median wage rank), $49,370 (median wage), $72,740 (90th percentile wage), 123,570 (number of positions), 8.2% (2016--2026 growth), High school diploma or equivalent (typical education requirement)

516. **Model Makers, Metal and Plastic**: #383 (median wage rank), $48,550 (median wage), $78,010 (90th percentile wage), 6,250 (number of positions), -12.2% (2016--2026 growth), High school diploma or equivalent (typical education requirement)

517. **Model Makers, Wood**: #477 (median wage rank), $40,890 (median wage), $76,480 (90th percentile wage), 1,040 (number of positions), 3.6% (2016--2026 growth), High school diploma or equivalent (typical education requirement)

518. **Models**: #797 (median wage rank), $21,870 (median wage), $52,390 (90th percentile wage), 4,390 (number of positions), -0.9% (2016--2026 growth), No formal educational credential (typical education requirement)

519. **Molders, Shapers, and Casters, Except Metal and Plastic**: #662 (median wage rank), $30,610 (median wage), $47,720 (90th percentile wage), 39,450 (number of positions), -1% (2016--2026 growth), High school diploma or equivalent (typical education requirement)

520. **Molding, Coremaking, and Casting Machine Setters, Operators, and Tenders, Metal and Plastic**: #667 (median wage rank), $30,480 (median wage), $48,550 (90th percentile wage), 145,560 (number of positions), -15% (2016--2026 growth), High school diploma or equivalent (typical education requirement)

521. **Morticians, Undertakers, and Funeral Directors**: #358 (median wage rank), $50,090 (median wage), $83,980 (90th percentile wage), 25,850 (number of positions), 4.6% (2016--2026 growth), Associate's degree (typical education requirement)

522. **Motion Picture Projectionists**: #791 (median wage rank), $22,100 (median wage), $35,030 (90th percentile wage), 5,480 (number of positions), -9.9% (2016--2026 growth), No formal educational credential (typical education requirement)

523. **Motor Vehicle Operators**, All Other: #723 (median wage rank), $27,150 (median wage), $53,880 (90th percentile wage), 53,680 (number of positions), 10.3% (2016--2026 growth), No formal educational credential (typical education requirement)

524. **Motorboat Mechanics and Service Technicians**: #508 (median wage rank), $38,780 (median wage), $61,200 (90th percentile wage), 20,260 (number of positions), 0.6% (2016--2026 growth), High school

diploma or equivalent (typical education requirement)

525. **Motorboat Operators**: #482 (median wage rank), $40,210 (median wage), $72,820 (90th percentile wage), 3,290 (number of positions), 7.6% (2016--2026 growth), Postsecondary nondegree award (typical education requirement)

526. **Motorcycle Mechanics**: #600 (median wage rank), $34,720 (median wage), $56,350 (90th percentile wage), 16,000 (number of positions), 1.4% (2016--2026 growth), Postsecondary nondegree award (typical education requirement)

527. **Multimedia Artists and Animators**: #197 (median wage rank), $65,300 (median wage), $115,960 (90th percentile wage), 29,810 (number of positions), 10.4% (2016--2026 growth), Bachelor's degree (typical education requirement)

528. **Multiple Machine Tool Setters, Operators, and Tenders, Metal and Plastic**: #605 (median wage rank), $34,340 (median wage), $53,090 (90th percentile wage), 117,300 (number of positions), -2.6% (2016--2026 growth), High school diploma or equivalent (typical education requirement)

529. **Museum Technicians and Conservators**: #484 (median wage rank), $40,040 (median wage), $73,080 (90th percentile wage), 10,970 (number of positions),

12.4% (2016--2026 growth), Bachelor's degree (typical education requirement)

530. **Music Directors and Composers**: #357 (median wage rank), $50,110 (median wage), $106,700 (90th percentile wage), 18,380 (number of positions), 6.1% (2016--2026 growth), Bachelor's degree (typical education requirement)

531. **Musical Instrument Repairers and Tuners**: #596 (median wage rank), $35,010 (median wage), $59,350 (90th percentile wage), 7,980 (number of positions), 2.3% (2016--2026 growth), High school diploma or equivalent (typical education requirement)

532. **Musicians and Singers**: #328 (median wage rank), $52,291 (median wage), $141,710 (90th percentile wage), 40,110 (number of positions), 6.6% (2016--2026 growth), No formal educational credential (typical education requirement)

533. **Natural Sciences Managers**: #26 (median wage rank), $119,850 (median wage), $200,150 (90th percentile wage), 54,780 (number of positions), 9.9% (2016--2026 growth), Bachelor's degree (typical education requirement)

534. **Network and Computer Systems Administrators**: #112 (median wage rank), $79,700 (median wage), $127,610 (90th percentile wage), 376,820 (number of positions), 6.1% (2016--2026 growth), Bachelor's

degree (typical education requirement)

535. **New Accounts Clerks**: #597 (median wage rank), $34,990 (median wage), $50,010 (90th percentile wage), 41,630 (number of positions), -6.2% (2016--2026 growth), High school diploma or equivalent (typical education requirement)

536. **Nonfarm Animal Caretakers**: #794 (median wage rank), $21,990 (median wage), $35,860 (90th percentile wage), 187,360 (number of positions), 21.9% (2016--2026 growth), High school diploma or equivalent (typical education requirement)

537. **Nuclear Engineers**: #45 (median wage rank), $102,220 (median wage), $152,420 (90th percentile wage), 17,680 (number of positions), 3.8% (2016--2026 growth), Bachelor's degree (typical education requirement)

538. **Nuclear Medicine Technologists**: #139 (median wage rank), $74,350 (median wage), $101,850 (90th percentile wage), 19,650 (number of positions), 9.8% (2016--2026 growth), Associate's degree (typical education requirement)

539. **Nuclear Power Reactor Operators**: #76 (median wage rank), $91,170 (median wage), $121,570 (90th percentile wage), 7,170 (number of positions), -10.2% (2016--2026 growth), High school diploma or equivalent (typical education requirement)

540. **Nuclear Technicians**: #117 (median wage rank), $79,140 (median wage), $106,950 (90th percentile wage), 6,840 (number of positions), 0.6% (2016--2026 growth), Associate's degree (typical education requirement)

541. **Nurse Anesthetists**: #13 (median wage rank), $160,270 (median wage), $267,651 (90th percentile wage), 39,860 (number of positions), 16% (2016--2026 growth), Master's degree (typical education requirement)

542. **Nurse Midwives**: #54 (median wage rank), $99,770 (median wage), $142,510 (90th percentile wage), 6,270 (number of positions), 20.6% (2016--2026 growth), Master's degree (typical education requirement)

543. **Nurse Practitioners**: #49 (median wage rank), $100,910 (median wage), $140,930 (90th percentile wage), 150,230 (number of positions), 36% (2016--2026 growth), Master's degree (typical education requirement)

544. **Nursing Assistants**: #733 (median wage rank), $26,590 (median wage), $37,900 (90th percentile wage), 1,443,150 (number of positions), 10.9% (2016--2026 growth), Postsecondary nondegree award (typical education requirement)

545. **Nursing Instructors and Teachers,**

Postsecondary: #172 (median wage rank), $69,130 (median wage), $117,540 (90th percentile wage), 56,210 (number of positions), 24% (2016--2026 growth), Doctoral or professional degree (typical education requirement)

546. **Obstetricians and Gynecologists**: #3 (median wage rank), $214,963 (median wage), $358,989 (90th percentile wage), 19,800 (number of positions), 17.9% (2016--2026 growth), Doctoral or professional degree (typical education requirement)

547. **Occupational Health and Safety Specialists**: #159 (median wage rank), $70,920 (median wage), $104,460 (90th percentile wage), 76,630 (number of positions), 7.6% (2016--2026 growth), Bachelor's degree (typical education requirement)

548. **Occupational Health and Safety Technicians**: #380 (median wage rank), $48,820 (median wage), $79,990 (90th percentile wage), 16,560 (number of positions), 9.5% (2016--2026 growth), High school diploma or equivalent (typical education requirement)

549. **Occupational Therapists**: #101 (median wage rank), $81,910 (median wage), $119,720 (90th percentile wage), 118,070 (number of positions), 21.2% (2016--2026 growth), Master's degree (typical education requirement)

550. **Occupational Therapy Aides**: #705 (median wage rank), $28,330 (median wage), $51,180 (90th percentile wage), 7,210 (number of positions), 24.7% (2016--2026 growth), High school diploma or equivalent (typical education requirement)

551. **Occupational Therapy Assistants**: #254 (median wage rank), $59,010 (median wage), $80,090 (90th percentile wage), 38,170 (number of positions), 28.9% (2016--2026 growth), Associate's degree (typical education requirement)

552. **Office and Administrative Support Workers**, All Other: #610 (median wage rank), $34,020 (median wage), $55,210 (90th percentile wage), 216,650 (number of positions), 9.2% (2016--2026 growth), High school diploma or equivalent (typical education requirement)

553. **Office Clerks, General**: #663 (median wage rank), $30,580 (median wage), $50,410 (90th percentile wage), 2,955,550 (number of positions), -1% (2016--2026 growth), High school diploma or equivalent (typical education requirement)

554. **Office Machine Operators, Except Computer**: #668 (median wage rank), $30,460 (median wage), $48,240 (90th percentile wage), 58,160 (number of positions), -15.6% (2016--2026 growth), High school diploma or equivalent (typical education

requirement)

555. **Operating Engineers and Other Construction Equipment Operators**: #411 (median wage rank), $45,890 (median wage), $80,200 (90th percentile wage), 356,750 (number of positions), 12.4% (2016--2026 growth), High school diploma or equivalent (typical education requirement)

556. **Operations Research Analysts**: #116 (median wage rank), $79,200 (median wage), $132,660 (90th percentile wage), 109,150 (number of positions), 27.4% (2016--2026 growth), Bachelor's degree (typical education requirement)

557. **Ophthalmic Laboratory Technicians**: #661 (median wage rank), $30,640 (median wage), $51,830 (90th percentile wage), 28,570 (number of positions), 11.9% (2016--2026 growth), High school diploma or equivalent (typical education requirement)

558. **Ophthalmic Medical Technicians**: #590 (median wage rank), $35,530 (median wage), $51,330 (90th percentile wage), 43,990 (number of positions), 19.4% (2016--2026 growth), Postsecondary nondegree award (typical education requirement)

559. **Opticians, Dispensing**: #589 (median wage rank), $35,530 (median wage), $57,180 (90th percentile wage), 75,270 (number of positions), 14.5% (2016--2026 growth), High school diploma or equivalent

(typical education requirement)

560. **Optometrists**: #40 (median wage rank), $106,140 (median wage), $192,050 (90th percentile wage), 36,430 (number of positions), 17.3% (2016--2026 growth), Doctoral or professional degree (typical education requirement)

561. **Oral and Maxillofacial Surgeons**: #4 (median wage rank), $213,642 (median wage), $356,782 (90th percentile wage), 5,380 (number of positions), 17.2% (2016--2026 growth), Doctoral or professional degree (typical education requirement)

562. **Order Clerks**: #621 (median wage rank), $33,370 (median wage), $52,130 (90th percentile wage), 176,850 (number of positions), -2% (2016--2026 growth), High school diploma or equivalent (typical education requirement)

563. **Orderlies**: #731 (median wage rank), $26,690 (median wage), $40,180 (90th percentile wage), 52,940 (number of positions), 8.1% (2016--2026 growth), High school diploma or equivalent (typical education requirement)

564. **Orthodontists**: #5 (median wage rank), $209,890 (median wage), $350,516 (90th percentile wage), 5,200 (number of positions), 17.3% (2016--2026 growth), Doctoral or professional degree (typical education requirement)

565. **Orthotists and Prosthetists**: #195 (median wage rank), $65,630 (median wage), $104,010 (90th percentile wage), 7,500 (number of positions), 21.9% (2016--2026 growth), Master's degree (typical education requirement)

566. **Outdoor Power Equipment and Other Small Engine Mechanics**: #616 (median wage rank), $33,730 (median wage), $51,360 (90th percentile wage), 33,020 (number of positions), 11.4% (2016--2026 growth), High school diploma or equivalent (typical education requirement)

567. **Packaging and Filling Machine Operators and Tenders**: #706 (median wage rank), $28,290 (median wage), $47,620 (90th percentile wage), 386,520 (number of positions), 1.7% (2016--2026 growth), High school diploma or equivalent (typical education requirement)

568. **Packers and Packagers, Hand**: #790 (median wage rank), $22,130 (median wage), $35,410 (90th percentile wage), 705,660 (number of positions), 1.8% (2016--2026 growth), No formal educational credential (typical education requirement)

569. **Painters, Construction and Maintenance**: #536 (median wage rank), $37,570 (median wage), $63,670 (90th percentile wage), 217,280 (number of positions), 6.1% (2016--2026 growth), No formal

educational credential (typical education requirement)

570. **Painters, Transportation Equipment**: #458 (median wage rank), $42,150 (median wage), $70,580 (90th percentile wage), 54,860 (number of positions), 6.9% (2016--2026 growth), High school diploma or equivalent (typical education requirement)

571. **Painting, Coating, and Decorating Workers**: #673 (median wage rank), $30,030 (median wage), $47,560 (90th percentile wage), 15,450 (number of positions), 1.1% (2016--2026 growth), No formal educational credential (typical education requirement)

572. **Paper Goods Machine Setters, Operators, and Tenders**: #551 (median wage rank), $36,990 (median wage), $58,720 (90th percentile wage), 93,100 (number of positions), -9% (2016--2026 growth), High school diploma or equivalent (typical education requirement)

573. **Paperhangers**: #614 (median wage rank), $33,770 (median wage), $53,560 (90th percentile wage), 3,190 (number of positions), 5% (2016--2026 growth), No formal educational credential (typical education requirement)

574. **Paralegals and Legal Assistants**: #367 (median wage rank), $49,500 (median wage), $80,260 (90th percentile wage), 277,310 (number of positions),

14.6% (2016--2026 growth), Associate's degree (typical education requirement)

575. **Parking Enforcement Workers**: #527 (median wage rank), $37,950 (median wage), $60,110 (90th percentile wage), 8,920 (number of positions), -35.3% (2016--2026 growth), High school diploma or equivalent (typical education requirement)

576. **Parking Lot Attendants**: #799 (median wage rank), $21,730 (median wage), $30,910 (90th percentile wage), 146,350 (number of positions), 6% (2016--2026 growth), No formal educational credential (typical education requirement)

577. **Parts Salespersons**: #676 (median wage rank), $29,780 (median wage), $52,430 (90th percentile wage), 248,740 (number of positions), 5.1% (2016--2026 growth), No formal educational credential (typical education requirement)

578. **Patternmakers, Metal and Plastic**: #432 (median wage rank), $44,210 (median wage), $62,590 (90th percentile wage), 3,420 (number of positions), -15.5% (2016--2026 growth), High school diploma or equivalent (typical education requirement)

579. **Patternmakers, Wood**: #404 (median wage rank), $46,510 (median wage), $72,950 (90th percentile wage), 970 (number of positions), 3.9% (2016--2026 growth), High school diploma or equivalent (typical

education requirement)

580. **Paving, Surfacing, and Tamping Equipment Operators**: #500 (median wage rank), $38,970 (median wage), $70,270 (90th percentile wage), 51,880 (number of positions), 12.1% (2016--2026 growth), High school diploma or equivalent (typical education requirement)

581. **Payroll and Timekeeping Clerks**: #455 (median wage rank), $42,390 (median wage), $62,030 (90th percentile wage), 159,650 (number of positions), -0.9% (2016--2026 growth), High school diploma or equivalent (typical education requirement)

582. **Pediatricians, General**: #12 (median wage rank), $168,990 (median wage), $282,213 (90th percentile wage), 26,960 (number of positions), 17.8% (2016--2026 growth), Doctoral or professional degree (typical education requirement)

583. **Personal Care Aides**: #795 (median wage rank), $21,920 (median wage), $29,760 (90th percentile wage), 1,492,250 (number of positions), 37.4% (2016--2026 growth), High school diploma or equivalent (typical education requirement)

584. **Personal Care and Service Workers**, All Other: #751 (median wage rank), $25,420 (median wage), $38,460 (90th percentile wage), 54,520 (number of positions), 6.8% (2016--2026 growth), High school

diploma or equivalent (typical education requirement)

585. **Personal Financial Advisors**: #78 (median wage rank), $90,530 (median wage), $151,185 (90th percentile wage), 201,850 (number of positions), 14.4% (2016--2026 growth), Bachelor's degree (typical education requirement)

586. **Pest Control Workers**: #628 (median wage rank), $33,040 (median wage), $50,920 (90th percentile wage), 72,830 (number of positions), 8% (2016--2026 growth), High school diploma or equivalent (typical education requirement)

587. **Pesticide Handlers, Sprayers, and Applicators, Vegetation**: #615 (median wage rank), $33,740 (median wage), $51,030 (90th percentile wage), 25,230 (number of positions), 7% (2016--2026 growth), High school diploma or equivalent (typical education requirement)

588. **Petroleum Engineers**: #18 (median wage rank), $128,230 (median wage), $214,144 (90th percentile wage), 32,780 (number of positions), 14.5% (2016--2026 growth), Bachelor's degree (typical education requirement)

589. **Petroleum Pump System Operators, Refinery Operators, and Gaugers**: #187 (median wage rank), $67,400 (median wage), $96,070 (90th percentile

wage), 41,630 (number of positions), 2.8% (2016-2026 growth), High school diploma or equivalent (typical education requirement)

590. **Pharmacists**: #24 (median wage rank), $122,230 (median wage), $157,950 (90th percentile wage), 305,510 (number of positions), 5.6% (2016--2026 growth), Doctoral or professional degree (typical education requirement)

591. **Pharmacy Aides**: #754 (median wage rank), $25,240 (median wage), $44,380 (90th percentile wage), 36,660 (number of positions), -4.8% (2016--2026 growth), High school diploma or equivalent (typical education requirement)

592. **Pharmacy Technicians**: #659 (median wage rank), $30,920 (median wage), $45,710 (90th percentile wage), 398,390 (number of positions), 11.8% (2016--2026 growth), High school diploma or equivalent (typical education requirement)

593. **Philosophy and Religion Teachers, Postsecondary**: #179 (median wage rank), $68,360 (median wage), $127,740 (90th percentile wage), 23,180 (number of positions), 12.3% (2016--2026 growth), Doctoral or professional degree (typical education requirement)

594. **Phlebotomists**: #633 (median wage rank), $32,710 (median wage), $46,850 (90th percentile wage),

120,970 (number of positions), 24.4% (2016--2026 growth), Postsecondary nondegree award (typical education requirement)

595. **Photographers**: #609 (median wage rank), $34,070 (median wage), $76,220 (90th percentile wage), 48,660 (number of positions), -8.4% (2016--2026 growth), High school diploma or equivalent (typical education requirement)

596. **Photographic Process Workers and Processing Machine Operators**: #734 (median wage rank), $26,470 (median wage), $48,030 (90th percentile wage), 26,430 (number of positions), -18.4% (2016--2026 growth), High school diploma or equivalent (typical education requirement)

597. **Physical Scientists**, All Other: #64 (median wage rank), $96,070 (median wage), $155,000 (90th percentile wage), 18,960 (number of positions), 6.4% (2016--2026 growth), Bachelor's degree (typical education requirement)

598. **Physical Therapist Aides**: #746 (median wage rank), $25,680 (median wage), $38,340 (90th percentile wage), 50,030 (number of positions), 29.1% (2016--2026 growth), High school diploma or equivalent (typical education requirement)

599. **Physical Therapist Assistants**: #285 (median wage rank), $56,610 (median wage), $79,040 (90th

percentile wage), 85,580 (number of positions), 30.8% (2016--2026 growth), Associate's degree (typical education requirement)

600. **Physical Therapists**: #91 (median wage rank), $85,400 (median wage), $122,130 (90th percentile wage), 216,920 (number of positions), 25% (2016--2026 growth), Doctoral or professional degree (typical education requirement)

601. **Physician Assistants**: #46 (median wage rank), $101,480 (median wage), $142,210 (90th percentile wage), 104,050 (number of positions), 37.4% (2016--2026 growth), Master's degree (typical education requirement)

602. **Physicians and Surgeons**, All Other: #6 (median wage rank), $206,920 (median wage), $345,556 (90th percentile wage), 338,620 (number of positions), 13.3% (2016--2026 growth), Doctoral or professional degree (typical education requirement)

603. **Physicists**: #30 (median wage rank), $115,870 (median wage), $189,560 (90th percentile wage), 16,680 (number of positions), 14.5% (2016--2026 growth), Doctoral or professional degree (typical education requirement)

604. **Physics Teachers, Postsecondary**: #95 (median wage rank), $84,570 (median wage), $164,130 (90th percentile wage), 14,160 (number of positions), 10%

THE COMPLETE LIST OF AMERICAN JOBS

(2016--2026 growth), Doctoral or professional degree (typical education requirement)

605. **Pile-Driver Operators**: #298 (median wage rank), $55,070 (median wage), $98,840 (90th percentile wage), 3,570 (number of positions), 14.7% (2016--2026 growth), High school diploma or equivalent (typical education requirement)

606. **Pipelayers**: #518 (median wage rank), $38,410 (median wage), $67,550 (90th percentile wage), 39,620 (number of positions), 17.3% (2016--2026 growth), No formal educational credential (typical education requirement)

607. **Plant and System Operators, All Other**: #300 (median wage rank), $54,930 (median wage), $78,630 (90th percentile wage), 11,970 (number of positions), 1.9% (2016--2026 growth), High school diploma or equivalent (typical education requirement)

608. **Plasterers and Stucco Masons**: #506 (median wage rank), $38,890 (median wage), $71,290 (90th percentile wage), 22,810 (number of positions), 4% (2016--2026 growth), No formal educational credential (typical education requirement)

609. **Plating and Coating Machine Setters, Operators, and Tenders, Metal and Plastic**: #654 (median wage rank), $31,280 (median wage), $50,290 (90th percentile wage), 35,570 (number of positions), -

13.8% (2016--2026 growth), High school diploma or equivalent (typical education requirement)

610. **Plumbers, Pipefitters, and Steamfitters**: #341 (median wage rank), $51,450 (median wage), $90,530 (90th percentile wage), 411,870 (number of positions), 15.8% (2016--2026 growth), High school diploma or equivalent (typical education requirement)

611. **Podiatrists**: #22 (median wage rank), $124,830 (median wage), $208,466 (90th percentile wage), 9,800 (number of positions), 9.7% (2016--2026 growth), Doctoral or professional degree (typical education requirement)

612. **Police and Sheriff's Patrol Officers**: #246 (median wage rank), $59,680 (median wage), $98,510 (90th percentile wage), 657,690 (number of positions), 7% (2016--2026 growth), High school diploma or equivalent (typical education requirement)

613. **Police, Fire, and Ambulance Dispatchers**: #507 (median wage rank), $38,870 (median wage), $61,270 (90th percentile wage), 95,170 (number of positions), 8.3% (2016--2026 growth), High school diploma or equivalent (typical education requirement)

614. **Political Science Teachers, Postsecondary**: #115 (median wage rank), $79,210 (median wage), $164,830 (90th percentile wage), 16,720 (number of

positions), 10.5% (2016--2026 growth), Doctoral or professional degree (typical education requirement)

615. **Political Scientists**: #32 (median wage rank), $114,290 (median wage), $160,290 (90th percentile wage), 6,350 (number of positions), 2.1% (2016--2026 growth), Master's degree (typical education requirement)

616. **Postal Service Clerks**: #279 (median wage rank), $56,790 (median wage), $57,990 (90th percentile wage), 82,030 (number of positions), -12.1% (2016--2026 growth), High school diploma or equivalent (typical education requirement)

617. **Postal Service Mail Carriers**: #263 (median wage rank), $58,110 (median wage), $61,100 (90th percentile wage), 328,950 (number of positions), -12.1% (2016--2026 growth), High school diploma or equivalent (typical education requirement)

618. **Postal Service Mail Sorters, Processors, and Processing Machine Operators**: #291 (median wage rank), $56,220 (median wage), $57,300 (90th percentile wage), 110,770 (number of positions), -16.5% (2016--2026 growth), High school diploma or equivalent (typical education requirement)

619. **Postmasters and Mail Superintendents**: #157 (median wage rank), $71,670 (median wage), $89,930 (90th percentile wage), 14,720 (number of positions),

-20.9% (2016--2026 growth), High school diploma or equivalent (typical education requirement)

620. **Postsecondary Teachers, All Other:** #202 (median wage rank), $64,400 (median wage), $130,090 (90th percentile wage), 194,870 (number of positions), 9.4% (2016--2026 growth), Doctoral or professional degree (typical education requirement)

621. **Pourers and Casters, Metal:** #573 (median wage rank), $36,180 (median wage), $52,590 (90th percentile wage), 8,560 (number of positions), -23.4% (2016--2026 growth), High school diploma or equivalent (typical education requirement)

622. **Power Distributors and Dispatchers:** #102 (median wage rank), $81,900 (median wage), $110,340 (90th percentile wage), 11,380 (number of positions), -2.5% (2016--2026 growth), High school diploma or equivalent (typical education requirement)

623. **Power Plant Operators:** #135 (median wage rank), $74,690 (median wage), $101,590 (90th percentile wage), 35,010 (number of positions), 1.3% (2016--2026 growth), High school diploma or equivalent (typical education requirement)

624. **Precision Instrument and Equipment Repairers,** All Other: #290 (median wage rank), $56,230 (median wage), $81,310 (90th percentile wage), 11,640

(number of positions), 2.9% (2016--2026 growth), High school diploma or equivalent (typical education requirement)

625. **Prepress Technicians and Workers**: #504 (median wage rank), $38,930 (median wage), $60,590 (90th percentile wage), 33,340 (number of positions), -19% (2016--2026 growth), Postsecondary nondegree award (typical education requirement)

626. **Preschool Teachers, Except Special Education**: #690 (median wage rank), $28,790 (median wage), $54,310 (90th percentile wage), 385,550 (number of positions), 10.5% (2016--2026 growth), Associate's degree (typical education requirement)

627. **Pressers, Textile, Garment, and Related Materials**: #803 (median wage rank), $21,300 (median wage), $29,460 (90th percentile wage), 45,150 (number of positions), -6.7% (2016--2026 growth), No formal educational credential (typical education requirement)

628. **Print Binding and Finishing Workers**: #651 (median wage rank), $31,410 (median wage), $49,320 (90th percentile wage), 52,730 (number of positions), -11.3% (2016--2026 growth), High school diploma or equivalent (typical education requirement)

629. **Printing Press Operators**: #588 (median wage rank), $35,530 (median wage), $57,610 (90th

percentile wage), 169,910 (number of positions), -9.4% (2016--2026 growth), High school diploma or equivalent (typical education requirement)

630. **Private Detectives and Investigators**: #386 (median wage rank), $48,190 (median wage), $87,070 (90th percentile wage), 28,490 (number of positions), 10.5% (2016--2026 growth), High school diploma or equivalent (typical education requirement)

631. **Probation Officers and Correctional Treatment Specialists**: #356 (median wage rank), $50,160 (median wage), $88,930 (90th percentile wage), 87,500 (number of positions), 5.7% (2016--2026 growth), Bachelor's degree (typical education requirement)

632. **Procurement Clerks**: #466 (median wage rank), $41,410 (median wage), $58,110 (90th percentile wage), 72,120 (number of positions), -4.2% (2016--2026 growth), High school diploma or equivalent (typical education requirement)

633. **Producers and Directors**: #158 (median wage rank), $70,950 (median wage), $189,870 (90th percentile wage), 114,510 (number of positions), 12% (2016--2026 growth), Bachelor's degree (typical education requirement)

634. **Production Workers**, All Other: #691 (median wage rank), $28,770 (median wage), $51,470 (90th

percentile wage), 251,670 (number of positions), 4.9% (2016--2026 growth), High school diploma or equivalent (typical education requirement)

635. **Production, Planning, and Expediting Clerks**: #403 (median wage rank), $46,760 (median wage), $74,340 (90th percentile wage), 321,780 (number of positions), 5.4% (2016--2026 growth), High school diploma or equivalent (typical education requirement)

636. **Proofreaders and Copy Markers**: #553 (median wage rank), $36,960 (median wage), $60,530 (90th percentile wage), 11,430 (number of positions), 2.2% (2016--2026 growth), Bachelor's degree (typical education requirement)

637. **Property, Real Estate, and Community Association Managers**: #277 (median wage rank), $57,040 (median wage), $126,390 (90th percentile wage), 180,290 (number of positions), 10.7% (2016--2026 growth), High school diploma or equivalent (typical education requirement)

638. **Prosthodontists**: #20 (median wage rank), $126,050 (median wage), $210,504 (90th percentile wage), 750 (number of positions), 17.2% (2016--2026 growth), Doctoral or professional degree (typical education requirement)

639. **Protective Service Workers**, All Other: #692

(median wage rank), $28,720 (median wage), $53,460 (90th percentile wage), 135,120 (number of positions), 8.4% (2016--2026 growth), High school diploma or equivalent (typical education requirement)

640. **Psychiatric Aides**: #728 (median wage rank), $26,720 (median wage), $42,220 (90th percentile wage), 67,410 (number of positions), 5.2% (2016--2026 growth), High school diploma or equivalent (typical education requirement)

641. **Psychiatric Technicians**: #658 (median wage rank), $30,970 (median wage), $59,960 (90th percentile wage), 61,720 (number of positions), 5.9% (2016--2026 growth), Postsecondary nondegree award (typical education requirement)

642. **Psychiatrists**: #8 (median wage rank), $194,740 (median wage), $325,216 (90th percentile wage), 24,820 (number of positions), 13.1% (2016--2026 growth), Doctoral or professional degree (typical education requirement)

643. **Psychologists**, All Other: #66 (median wage rank), $95,710 (median wage), $127,710 (90th percentile wage), 13,310 (number of positions), 9.1% (2016--2026 growth), Master's degree (typical education requirement)

644. **Psychology Teachers, Postsecondary**: #150

(median wage rank), $73,140 (median wage), $148,470 (90th percentile wage), 37,640 (number of positions), 15.1% (2016--2026 growth), Doctoral or professional degree (typical education requirement)

645. **Public Address System and Other Announcers**: #685 (median wage rank), $28,940 (median wage), $77,640 (90th percentile wage), 8,020 (number of positions), 3.2% (2016--2026 growth), High school diploma or equivalent (typical education requirement)

646. **Public Relations and Fundraising Managers**: #37 (median wage rank), $107,320 (median wage), $205,110 (90th percentile wage), 63,970 (number of positions), 10.4% (2016--2026 growth), Bachelor's degree (typical education requirement)

647. **Public Relations Specialists**: #265 (median wage rank), $58,020 (median wage), $110,560 (90th percentile wage), 226,940 (number of positions), 9% (2016--2026 growth), Bachelor's degree (typical education requirement)

648. **Pump Operators, Except Wellhead Pumpers**: #452 (median wage rank), $42,470 (median wage), $73,750 (90th percentile wage), 12,030 (number of positions), 13.8% (2016--2026 growth), High school diploma or equivalent (typical education requirement)

649. **Purchasing Agents, Except Wholesale, Retail, and**

Farm Products: #212 (median wage rank), $63,300 (median wage), $101,770 (90th percentile wage), 297,600 (number of positions), -5.6% (2016--2026 growth), Bachelor's degree (typical education requirement)

650. **Purchasing Managers**: #34 (median wage rank), $111,590 (median wage), $177,560 (90th percentile wage), 71,750 (number of positions), 5.6% (2016--2026 growth), Bachelor's degree (typical education requirement)

651. **Radiation Therapists**: #109 (median wage rank), $80,160 (median wage), $123,710 (90th percentile wage), 17,450 (number of positions), 11.9% (2016--2026 growth), Associate's degree (typical education requirement)

652. **Radio and Television Announcers**: #652 (median wage rank), $31,400 (median wage), $89,720 (90th percentile wage), 29,210 (number of positions), -10.9% (2016--2026 growth), Bachelor's degree (typical education requirement)

653. **Radio Operators**: #406 (median wage rank), $46,250 (median wage), $73,930 (90th percentile wage), 870 (number of positions), -1% (2016--2026 growth), High school diploma or equivalent (typical education requirement)

654. **Radio, Cellular, and Tower Equipment Installers**

and Repairers: #325 (median wage rank), $52,480 (median wage), $78,930 (90th percentile wage), 14,120 (number of positions), 5.5% (2016--2026 growth), Associate's degree (typical education requirement)

655. **Radiologic Technologists**: #271 (median wage rank), $57,450 (median wage), $82,590 (90th percentile wage), 200,650 (number of positions), 12.3% (2016--2026 growth), Associate's degree (typical education requirement)

656. **Rail Car Repairers**: #299 (median wage rank), $55,000 (median wage), $76,220 (90th percentile wage), 22,090 (number of positions), 5.1% (2016--2026 growth), High school diploma or equivalent (typical education requirement)

657. **Rail Transportation Workers, All Other**: #238 (median wage rank), $60,420 (median wage), $90,580 (90th percentile wage), 4,470 (number of positions), 3.2% (2016--2026 growth), High school diploma or equivalent (typical education requirement)

658. **Rail Yard Engineers, Dinkey Operators, and Hostlers**: #352 (median wage rank), $50,470 (median wage), $87,770 (90th percentile wage), 4,530 (number of positions), 3.7% (2016--2026 growth), High school diploma or equivalent (typical education requirement)

659. **Railroad Brake, Signal, and Switch Operators**: #286 (median wage rank), $56,570 (median wage), $76,110 (90th percentile wage), 19,860 (number of positions), -1.6% (2016--2026 growth), High school diploma or equivalent (typical education requirement)

660. **Railroad Conductors and Yardmasters**: #270 (median wage rank), $57,480 (median wage), $79,620 (90th percentile wage), 42,880 (number of positions), -2.1% (2016--2026 growth), High school diploma or equivalent (typical education requirement)

661. **Rail-Track Laying and Maintenance Equipment Operators**: #310 (median wage rank), $53,970 (median wage), $72,810 (90th percentile wage), 14,250 (number of positions), 8.6% (2016--2026 growth), High school diploma or equivalent (typical education requirement)

662. **Real Estate Brokers**: #278 (median wage rank), $56,790 (median wage), $162,260 (90th percentile wage), 40,850 (number of positions), 5.4% (2016--2026 growth), High school diploma or equivalent (typical education requirement)

663. **Real Estate Sales Agents**: #435 (median wage rank), $44,090 (median wage), $112,570 (90th percentile wage), 151,840 (number of positions), 6.2% (2016--2026 growth), High school diploma or

equivalent (typical education requirement)

664. **Receptionists and Information Clerks:** #711 (median wage rank), $27,920 (median wage), $40,380 (90th percentile wage), 997,770 (number of positions), 9.1% (2016--2026 growth), High school diploma or equivalent (typical education requirement)

665. **Recreation and Fitness Studies Teachers, Postsecondary:** #252 (median wage rank), $59,180 (median wage), $119,830 (90th percentile wage), 17,390 (number of positions), 9.6% (2016--2026 growth), Doctoral or professional degree (typical education requirement)

666. **Recreation Workers:** #774 (median wage rank), $23,870 (median wage), $41,660 (90th percentile wage), 336,880 (number of positions), 8.5% (2016--2026 growth), High school diploma or equivalent (typical education requirement)

667. **Recreational Therapists:** #405 (median wage rank), $46,410 (median wage), $72,340 (90th percentile wage), 18,100 (number of positions), 6.5% (2016--2026 growth), Bachelor's degree (typical education requirement)

668. **Recreational Vehicle Service Technicians:** #567 (median wage rank), $36,430 (median wage), $56,610 (90th percentile wage), 13,520 (number of positions),

-1.1% (2016--2026 growth), High school diploma or equivalent (typical education requirement)

669. **Refractory Materials Repairers, Except Brickmasons**: #423 (median wage rank), $45,230 (median wage), $66,710 (90th percentile wage), 1,540 (number of positions), -3.5% (2016--2026 growth), High school diploma or equivalent (typical education requirement)

670. **Refuse and Recyclable Material Collectors**: #592 (median wage rank), $35,270 (median wage), $60,500 (90th percentile wage), 114,680 (number of positions), 13% (2016--2026 growth), No formal educational credential (typical education requirement)

671. **Registered Nurses**: #176 (median wage rank), $68,450 (median wage), $102,990 (90th percentile wage), 2,857,180 (number of positions), 14.8% (2016--2026 growth), Bachelor's degree (typical education requirement)

672. **Rehabilitation Counselors**: #601 (median wage rank), $34,670 (median wage), $62,010 (90th percentile wage), 103,030 (number of positions), 9.7% (2016--2026 growth), Master's degree (typical education requirement)

673. **Reinforcing Iron and Rebar Workers**: #396 (median wage rank), $47,600 (median wage), $89,980

(90th percentile wage), 20,020 (number of positions), 12.1% (2016--2026 growth), High school diploma or equivalent (typical education requirement)

674. **Religious Workers, All Other**: #687 (median wage rank), $28,820 (median wage), $58,970 (90th percentile wage), 8,250 (number of positions), 7.7% (2016--2026 growth), Bachelor's degree (typical education requirement)

675. **Reporters and Correspondents**: #531 (median wage rank), $37,820 (median wage), $86,610 (90th percentile wage), 40,090 (number of positions), -10.7% (2016--2026 growth), Bachelor's degree (typical education requirement)

676. **Reservation and Transportation Ticket Agents and Travel Clerks**: #593 (median wage rank), $35,230 (median wage), $59,270 (90th percentile wage), 146,350 (number of positions), 3.7% (2016--2026 growth), High school diploma or equivalent (typical education requirement)

677. **Residential Advisors**: #749 (median wage rank), $25,570 (median wage), $39,960 (90th percentile wage), 110,330 (number of positions), 12.9% (2016--2026 growth), High school diploma or equivalent (typical education requirement)

678. **Respiratory Therapists**: #257 (median wage rank), $58,670 (median wage), $81,550 (90th percentile

wage), 126,770 (number of positions), 23.4% (2016--2026 growth), Associate's degree (typical education requirement)

679. **Respiratory Therapy Technicians**: #364 (median wage rank), $49,780 (median wage), $72,970 (90th percentile wage), 10,600 (number of positions), -56.3% (2016--2026 growth), Associate's degree (typical education requirement)

680. **Retail Salespersons**: #782 (median wage rank), $22,680 (median wage), $41,420 (90th percentile wage), 4,528,550 (number of positions), 1.9% (2016--2026 growth), No formal educational credential (typical education requirement)

681. **Riggers**: #419 (median wage rank), $45,690 (median wage), $74,750 (90th percentile wage), 21,020 (number of positions), 9.8% (2016--2026 growth), High school diploma or equivalent (typical education requirement)

682. **Rock Splitters, Quarry**: #611 (median wage rank), $34,020 (median wage), $49,370 (90th percentile wage), 3,770 (number of positions), -6.3% (2016--2026 growth), No formal educational credential (typical education requirement)

683. **Rolling Machine Setters, Operators, and Tenders, Metal and Plastic**: #478 (median wage rank), $40,680 (median wage), $60,750 (90th percentile wage),

29,060 (number of positions), -12.9% (2016--2026 growth), High school diploma or equivalent (typical education requirement)

684. **Roof Bolters, Mining**: #280 (median wage rank), $56,780 (median wage), $76,640 (90th percentile wage), 3,930 (number of positions), -5.2% (2016--2026 growth), High school diploma or equivalent (typical education requirement)

685. **Roofers**: #533 (median wage rank), $37,760 (median wage), $64,630 (90th percentile wage), 116,410 (number of positions), 11.3% (2016--2026 growth), No formal educational credential (typical education requirement)

686. **Rotary Drill Operators, Oil and Gas**: #307 (median wage rank), $54,430 (median wage), $87,170 (90th percentile wage), 17,400 (number of positions), 24.2% (2016--2026 growth), No formal educational credential (typical education requirement)

687. **Roustabouts, Oil and Gas**: #542 (median wage rank), $37,340 (median wage), $60,600 (90th percentile wage), 51,290 (number of positions), 24.5% (2016--2026 growth), No formal educational credential (typical education requirement)

688. **Sailors and Marine Oilers**: #459 (median wage rank), $42,060 (median wage), $72,100 (90th percentile wage), 32,530 (number of positions), 7.6%

(2016--2026 growth), No formal educational credential (typical education requirement)

689. **Sales and Related Workers**, All Other: #545 (median wage rank), $37,190 (median wage), $73,000 (90th percentile wage), 81,080 (number of positions), 9.8% (2016--2026 growth), High school diploma or equivalent (typical education requirement)

690. **Sales Engineers**: #53 (median wage rank), $100,000 (median wage), $166,500 (90th percentile wage), 74,330 (number of positions), 6.9% (2016--2026 growth), Bachelor's degree (typical education requirement)

691. **Sales Managers**: #28 (median wage rank), $117,960 (median wage), $196,993 (90th percentile wage), 365,230 (number of positions), 7.4% (2016--2026 growth), Bachelor's degree (typical education requirement)

692. **Sales Representatives, Services**, All Other: #324 (median wage rank), $52,490 (median wage), $113,950 (90th percentile wage), 953,870 (number of positions), 9.6% (2016--2026 growth), High school diploma or equivalent (typical education requirement)

693. **Sales Representatives, Wholesale and Manufacturing, Except Technical and Scientific Products**: #275 (median wage rank), $57,140 (median

wage), $121,080 (90th percentile wage), 1,404,050 (number of positions), 5.5% (2016--2026 growth), High school diploma or equivalent (typical education requirement)

694. **Sales Representatives, Wholesale and Manufacturing, Technical and Scientific Products:** #118 (median wage rank), $78,980 (median wage), $160,940 (90th percentile wage), 328,370 (number of positions), 5.5% (2016--2026 growth), Bachelor's degree (typical education requirement)

695. **Sawing Machine Setters, Operators, and Tenders, Wood:** #702 (median wage rank), $28,380 (median wage), $43,530 (90th percentile wage), 50,640 (number of positions), 0.8% (2016--2026 growth), High school diploma or equivalent (typical education requirement)

696. **Secondary School Teachers, Except Special and Career/Technical Education:** #264 (median wage rank), $58,030 (median wage), $92,920 (90th percentile wage), 1,003,250 (number of positions), 7.5% (2016--2026 growth), Bachelor's degree (typical education requirement)

697. **Secretaries and Administrative Assistants, Except Legal, Medical, and Executive:** #598 (median wage rank), $34,820 (median wage), $53,060 (90th percentile wage), 2,295,510 (number of positions), -

6.5% (2016--2026 growth), High school diploma or equivalent (typical education requirement)

698. **Securities, Commodities, and Financial Services Sales Agents**: #188 (median wage rank), $67,310 (median wage), $112,408 (90th percentile wage), 353,780 (number of positions), 6.1% (2016--2026 growth), Bachelor's degree (typical education requirement)

699. **Security and Fire Alarm Systems Installers**: #431 (median wage rank), $44,330 (median wage), $65,470 (90th percentile wage), 67,700 (number of positions), 14.4% (2016--2026 growth), High school diploma or equivalent (typical education requirement)

700. **Security Guards**: #744 (median wage rank), $25,770 (median wage), $47,260 (90th percentile wage), 1,103,120 (number of positions), 6.3% (2016--2026 growth), High school diploma or equivalent (typical education requirement)

701. **Segmental Pavers**: #618 (median wage rank), $33,530 (median wage), $50,900 (90th percentile wage), 1,720 (number of positions), 12.4% (2016--2026 growth), High school diploma or equivalent (typical education requirement)

702. **Self-Enrichment Education Teachers**: #543 (median wage rank), $37,330 (median wage), $74,700 (90th percentile wage), 229,840 (number of

positions), 14.9% (2016--2026 growth), High school diploma or equivalent (typical education requirement)

703. **Semiconductor Processors**: #586 (median wage rank), $35,660 (median wage), $53,540 (90th percentile wage), 24,430 (number of positions), -5.1% (2016--2026 growth), High school diploma or equivalent (typical education requirement)

704. **Separating, Filtering, Clarifying, Precipitating, and Still Machine Setters, Operators, and Tenders**: #520 (median wage rank), $38,360 (median wage), $63,020 (90th percentile wage), 47,160 (number of positions), 0.2% (2016--2026 growth), High school diploma or equivalent (typical education requirement)

705. **Septic Tank Servicers and Sewer Pipe Cleaners**: #568 (median wage rank), $36,430 (median wage), $59,290 (90th percentile wage), 26,320 (number of positions), 16.9% (2016--2026 growth), High school diploma or equivalent (typical education requirement)

706. **Service Unit Operators, Oil, Gas, and Mining**: #382 (median wage rank), $48,610 (median wage), $79,770 (90th percentile wage), 42,890 (number of positions), 23.4% (2016--2026 growth), No formal educational credential (typical education

requirement)

707. **Set and Exhibit Designers**: #344 (median wage rank), $50,990 (median wage), $97,320 (90th percentile wage), 12,060 (number of positions), 10.9% (2016--2026 growth), Bachelor's degree (typical education requirement)

708. **Sewers, Hand**: #763 (median wage rank), $24,520 (median wage), $34,460 (90th percentile wage), 6,540 (number of positions), -4% (2016--2026 growth), No formal educational credential (typical education requirement)

709. **Sewing Machine Operators**: #778 (median wage rank), $23,670 (median wage), $37,000 (90th percentile wage), 139,500 (number of positions), -14.2% (2016--2026 growth), No formal educational credential (typical education requirement)

710. **Shampooers**: #818 (median wage rank), $19,700 (median wage), $25,750 (90th percentile wage), 15,240 (number of positions), 12.2% (2016--2026 growth), No formal educational credential (typical education requirement)

711. **Sheet Metal Workers**: #401 (median wage rank), $46,940 (median wage), $85,340 (90th percentile wage), 134,450 (number of positions), 8.7% (2016--2026 growth), High school diploma or equivalent (typical education requirement)

712. **Ship Engineers**: #162 (median wage rank), $70,570 (median wage), $119,690 (90th percentile wage), 9,750 (number of positions), 6.5% (2016--2026 growth), Postsecondary nondegree award (typical education requirement)

713. **Shipping, Receiving, and Traffic Clerks**: #655 (median wage rank), $31,180 (median wage), $48,760 (90th percentile wage), 676,990 (number of positions), 0% (2016--2026 growth), High school diploma or equivalent (typical education requirement)

714. **Shoe and Leather Workers and Repairers**: #773 (median wage rank), $23,940 (median wage), $37,350 (90th percentile wage), 7,780 (number of positions), -2.5% (2016--2026 growth), High school diploma or equivalent (typical education requirement)

715. **Shoe Machine Operators and Tenders**: #737 (median wage rank), $26,150 (median wage), $36,400 (90th percentile wage), 3,500 (number of positions), -8.5% (2016--2026 growth), High school diploma or equivalent (typical education requirement)

716. **Signal and Track Switch Repairers**: #196 (median wage rank), $65,350 (median wage), $82,800 (90th percentile wage), 8,680 (number of positions), 1.1% (2016--2026 growth), High school diploma or equivalent (typical education requirement)

717. **Skincare Specialists**: #669 (median wage rank), $30,270 (median wage), $59,780 (90th percentile wage), 43,980 (number of positions), 12.6% (2016--2026 growth), Postsecondary nondegree award (typical education requirement)

718. **Slaughterers and Meat Packers**: #732 (median wage rank), $26,590 (median wage), $36,170 (90th percentile wage), 80,780 (number of positions), 0.5% (2016--2026 growth), No formal educational credential (typical education requirement)

719. **Slot Supervisors**: #575 (median wage rank), $36,080 (median wage), $60,630 (90th percentile wage), 7,640 (number of positions), 4.3% (2016--2026 growth), High school diploma or equivalent (typical education requirement)

720. **Social and Community Service Managers**: #200 (median wage rank), $64,680 (median wage), $110,970 (90th percentile wage), 126,230 (number of positions), 15.7% (2016--2026 growth), Bachelor's degree (typical education requirement)

721. **Social and Human Service Assistants**: #646 (median wage rank), $31,810 (median wage), $50,640 (90th percentile wage), 360,650 (number of positions), 16.4% (2016--2026 growth), High school diploma or equivalent (typical education requirement)

722. **Social Science Research Assistants**: #441 (median wage rank), $43,190 (median wage), $74,900 (90th percentile wage), 30,030 (number of positions), 4.1% (2016--2026 growth), Bachelor's degree (typical education requirement)

723. **Social Sciences Teachers, Postsecondary**, All Other: #161 (median wage rank), $70,740 (median wage), $166,830 (90th percentile wage), 13,320 (number of positions), 10% (2016--2026 growth), Doctoral or professional degree (typical education requirement)

724. **Social Scientists and Related Workers**, All Other: #126 (median wage rank), $77,020 (median wage), $119,800 (90th percentile wage), 36,380 (number of positions), 5.9% (2016--2026 growth), Bachelor's degree (typical education requirement)

725. **Social Work Teachers, Postsecondary**: #203 (median wage rank), $64,030 (median wage), $130,520 (90th percentile wage), 11,860 (number of positions), 9.9% (2016--2026 growth), Doctoral or professional degree (typical education requirement)

726. **Social Workers**, All Other: #240 (median wage rank), $60,230 (median wage), $85,190 (90th percentile wage), 59,540 (number of positions), 7.9% (2016--2026 growth), Bachelor's degree (typical education requirement)

727. **Sociologists**: #111 (median wage rank), $79,750 (median wage), $146,860 (90th percentile wage), 2,870 (number of positions), 0.1% (2016--2026 growth), Master's degree (typical education requirement)

728. **Sociology Teachers, Postsecondary**: #155 (median wage rank), $71,840 (median wage), $133,740 (90th percentile wage), 14,580 (number of positions), 9.8% (2016--2026 growth), Doctoral or professional degree (typical education requirement)

729. **Software Developers, Applications**: #52 (median wage rank), $100,080 (median wage), $157,590 (90th percentile wage), 794,000 (number of positions), 30.5% (2016--2026 growth), Bachelor's degree (typical education requirement)

730. **Software Developers, Systems Software**: #39 (median wage rank), $106,860 (median wage), $163,220 (90th percentile wage), 409,820 (number of positions), 10.8% (2016--2026 growth), Bachelor's degree (typical education requirement)

731. **Soil and Plant Scientists**: #223 (median wage rank), $62,300 (median wage), $114,390 (90th percentile wage), 14,690 (number of positions), 9% (2016--2026 growth), Bachelor's degree (typical education requirement)

732. **Solar Photovoltaic Installers**: #496 (median wage

rank), $39,240 (median wage), $60,570 (90th percentile wage), 8,870 (number of positions), 105.3% (2016--2026 growth), High school diploma or equivalent (typical education requirement)

733. **Sound Engineering Technicians**: #313 (median wage rank), $53,680 (median wage), $121,630 (90th percentile wage), 15,210 (number of positions), 6.3% (2016--2026 growth), Postsecondary nondegree award (typical education requirement)

734. **Special Education Teachers, All Other**: #311 (median wage rank), $53,860 (median wage), $93,620 (90th percentile wage), 40,190 (number of positions), 9.8% (2016--2026 growth), Bachelor's degree (typical education requirement)

735. **Special Education Teachers, Kindergarten and Elementary School**: #276 (median wage rank), $57,040 (median wage), $90,260 (90th percentile wage), 190,530 (number of positions), 7.4% (2016--2026 growth), Bachelor's degree (typical education requirement)

736. **Special Education Teachers, Middle School**: #258 (median wage rank), $58,560 (median wage), $93,260 (90th percentile wage), 90,250 (number of positions), 7.1% (2016--2026 growth), Bachelor's degree (typical education requirement)

737. **Special Education Teachers, Preschool**: #326

(median wage rank), $52,460 (median wage), $89,290 (90th percentile wage), 28,140 (number of positions), 11.2% (2016--2026 growth), Bachelor's degree (typical education requirement)

738. **Special Education Teachers, Secondary School**: #245 (median wage rank), $59,700 (median wage), $96,930 (90th percentile wage), 132,490 (number of positions), 7.4% (2016--2026 growth), Bachelor's degree (typical education requirement)

739. **Speech-Language Pathologists**: #136 (median wage rank), $74,680 (median wage), $116,810 (90th percentile wage), 135,980 (number of positions), 17.5% (2016--2026 growth), Master's degree (typical education requirement)

740. **Stationary Engineers and Boiler Operators**: #248 (median wage rank), $59,400 (median wage), $93,300 (90th percentile wage), 33,720 (number of positions), 4.8% (2016--2026 growth), High school diploma or equivalent (typical education requirement)

741. **Statistical Assistants**: #402 (median wage rank), $46,850 (median wage), $69,480 (90th percentile wage), 10,900 (number of positions), 9.2% (2016--2026 growth), Bachelor's degree (typical education requirement)

742. **Statisticians**: #107 (median wage rank), $80,500 (median wage), $130,090 (90th percentile wage),

33,440 (number of positions), 33.4% (2016--2026 growth), Master's degree (typical education requirement)

743. **Stock Clerks and Order Fillers**: #776 (median wage rank), $23,840 (median wage), $39,750 (90th percentile wage), 2,016,340 (number of positions), 5% (2016--2026 growth), High school diploma or equivalent (typical education requirement)

744. **Stonemasons**: #488 (median wage rank), $39,780 (median wage), $65,790 (90th percentile wage), 13,190 (number of positions), 9.8% (2016--2026 growth), High school diploma or equivalent (typical education requirement)

745. **Structural Iron and Steel Workers**: #337 (median wage rank), $51,800 (median wage), $91,830 (90th percentile wage), 69,440 (number of positions), 12.8% (2016--2026 growth), High school diploma or equivalent (typical education requirement)

746. **Structural Metal Fabricators and Fitters**: #534 (median wage rank), $37,730 (median wage), $58,900 (90th percentile wage), 77,270 (number of positions), -15.3% (2016--2026 growth), High school diploma or equivalent (typical education requirement)

747. **Substance Abuse and Behavioral Disorder Counselors**: #472 (median wage rank), $41,070 (median wage), $65,080 (90th percentile wage),

91,040 (number of positions), 19.9% (2016--2026 growth), Bachelor's degree (typical education requirement)

748. **Substitute Teachers**: #710 (median wage rank), $28,010 (median wage), $46,140 (90th percentile wage), 609,960 (number of positions), 2016--2026 growth not available, typical education requirement not available

749. **Subway and Streetcar Operators**: #201 (median wage rank), $64,680 (median wage), $80,910 (90th percentile wage), 12,350 (number of positions), 4.1% (2016--2026 growth), High school diploma or equivalent (typical education requirement)

750. **Surgeons**: #2 (median wage rank), $232,028 (median wage), $387,486 (90th percentile wage), 41,190 (number of positions), 16.8% (2016--2026 growth), Doctoral or professional degree (typical education requirement)

751. **Surgical Technologists**: #425 (median wage rank), $45,160 (median wage), $64,800 (90th percentile wage), 105,720 (number of positions), 11.7% (2016--2026 growth), Postsecondary nondegree award (typical education requirement)

752. **Survey Researchers**: #306 (median wage rank), $54,470 (median wage), $100,250 (90th percentile wage), 11,930 (number of positions), 0.9% (2016--

2026 growth), Master's degree (typical education requirement)

753. **Surveying and Mapping Technicians**: #453 (median wage rank), $42,450 (median wage), $70,280 (90th percentile wage), 53,920 (number of positions), 10.6% (2016--2026 growth), High school diploma or equivalent (typical education requirement)

754. **Surveyors**: #249 (median wage rank), $59,390 (median wage), $98,360 (90th percentile wage), 43,340 (number of positions), 11.2% (2016--2026 growth), Bachelor's degree (typical education requirement)

755. **Switchboard Operators, Including Answering Service**: #709 (median wage rank), $28,030 (median wage), $42,090 (90th percentile wage), 90,910 (number of positions), -19.9% (2016--2026 growth), High school diploma or equivalent (typical education requirement)

756. **Tailors, Dressmakers, and Custom Sewers**: #707 (median wage rank), $28,240 (median wage), $46,960 (90th percentile wage), 21,660 (number of positions), -0.3% (2016--2026 growth), No formal educational credential (typical education requirement)

757. **Tank Car, Truck, and Ship Loaders**: #580 (median wage rank), $35,770 (median wage), $66,190 (90th percentile wage), 10,920 (number of positions), 5.2%

(2016--2026 growth), No formal educational credential (typical education requirement)

758. **Tapers**: #377 (median wage rank), $48,990 (median wage), $90,260 (90th percentile wage), 18,480 (number of positions), 0.6% (2016--2026 growth), No formal educational credential (typical education requirement)

759. **Tax Examiners and Collectors, and Revenue Agents**: #332 (median wage rank), $52,060 (median wage), $97,440 (90th percentile wage), 58,450 (number of positions), -0.6% (2016--2026 growth), Bachelor's degree (typical education requirement)

760. **Tax Preparers**: #565 (median wage rank), $36,550 (median wage), $80,250 (90th percentile wage), 70,030 (number of positions), 10.8% (2016--2026 growth), High school diploma or equivalent (typical education requirement)

761. **Taxi Drivers and Chauffeurs**: #768 (median wage rank), $24,300 (median wage), $38,500 (90th percentile wage), 188,860 (number of positions), 4.8% (2016--2026 growth), No formal educational credential (typical education requirement)

762. **Teacher Assistants**: #752 (median wage rank), $25,410 (median wage), $38,820 (90th percentile wage), 1,263,820 (number of positions), 8.4% (2016--2026 growth), Some college, no degree (typical

education requirement)

763. **Teachers and Instructors, All Other, Except Substitute Teachers**: #492 (median wage rank), $39,570 (median wage), $82,960 (90th percentile wage), 292,950 (number of positions), 2016--2026 growth not available, typical education requirement not available

764. **Team Assemblers**: #672 (median wage rank), $30,060 (median wage), $50,980 (90th percentile wage), 1,112,780 (number of positions), -12.6% (2016--2026 growth), High school diploma or equivalent (typical education requirement)

765. **Technical Writers**: #166 (median wage rank), $69,850 (median wage), $111,260 (90th percentile wage), 49,780 (number of positions), 10.9% (2016--2026 growth), Bachelor's degree (typical education requirement)

766. **Telecommunications Equipment Installers and Repairers, Except Line Installers**: #314 (median wage rank), $53,640 (median wage), $79,500 (90th percentile wage), 228,430 (number of positions), -7.6% (2016--2026 growth), Postsecondary nondegree award (typical education requirement)

767. **Telecommunications Line Installers and Repairers**: #323 (median wage rank), $52,590 (median wage), $83,260 (90th percentile wage),

100,080 (number of positions), 1.6% (2016--2026 growth), High school diploma or equivalent (typical education requirement)

768. **Telemarketers**: #767 (median wage rank), $24,300 (median wage), $39,310 (90th percentile wage), 215,290 (number of positions), 0% (2016--2026 growth), No formal educational credential (typical education requirement)

769. **Telephone Operators**: #550 (median wage rank), $37,000 (median wage), $66,230 (90th percentile wage), 8,860 (number of positions), -22.6% (2016--2026 growth), High school diploma or equivalent (typical education requirement)

770. **Tellers**: #722 (median wage rank), $27,260 (median wage), $37,760 (90th percentile wage), 496,760 (number of positions), -8.3% (2016--2026 growth), High school diploma or equivalent (typical education requirement)

771. **Terrazzo Workers and Finishers**: #476 (median wage rank), $40,930 (median wage), $75,470 (90th percentile wage), 3,420 (number of positions), 12.3% (2016--2026 growth), High school diploma or equivalent (typical education requirement)

772. **Textile Bleaching and Dyeing Machine Operators and Tenders**: #721 (median wage rank), $27,270 (median wage), $38,700 (90th percentile

wage), 10,860 (number of positions), -17% (2016--2026 growth), High school diploma or equivalent (typical education requirement)

773. **Textile Cutting Machine Setters, Operators, and Tenders**: #738 (median wage rank), $26,090 (median wage), $39,880 (90th percentile wage), 15,040 (number of positions), -15.8% (2016--2026 growth), High school diploma or equivalent (typical education requirement)

774. **Textile Knitting and Weaving Machine Setters, Operators, and Tenders**: #719 (median wage rank), $27,470 (median wage), $38,750 (90th percentile wage), 21,550 (number of positions), -18.3% (2016--2026 growth), High school diploma or equivalent (typical education requirement)

775. **Textile Winding, Twisting, and Drawing Out Machine Setters, Operators, and Tenders**: #718 (median wage rank), $27,500 (median wage), $37,880 (90th percentile wage), 30,340 (number of positions), -16.3% (2016--2026 growth), High school diploma or equivalent (typical education requirement)

776. **Textile, Apparel, and Furnishings Workers**, All Other: #742 (median wage rank), $25,890 (median wage), $52,300 (90th percentile wage), 15,650 (number of positions), -3% (2016--2026 growth), High school diploma or equivalent (typical education

requirement)

777. **Therapists**, All Other: #283 (median wage rank), $56,700 (median wage), $95,530 (90th percentile wage), 11,320 (number of positions), 19.7% (2016--2026 growth), Bachelor's degree (typical education requirement)

778. **Tile and Marble Setters**: #480 (median wage rank), $40,460 (median wage), $71,260 (90th percentile wage), 36,830 (number of positions), 10% (2016--2026 growth), No formal educational credential (typical education requirement)

779. **Timing Device Assemblers and Adjusters**: #549 (median wage rank), $37,040 (median wage), $74,740 (90th percentile wage), 790 (number of positions), -19.9% (2016--2026 growth), High school diploma or equivalent (typical education requirement)

780. **Tire Builders**: #463 (median wage rank), $41,680 (median wage), $60,690 (90th percentile wage), 22,280 (number of positions), -12.1% (2016--2026 growth), High school diploma or equivalent (typical education requirement)

781. **Tire Repairers and Changers**: #757 (median wage rank), $25,040 (median wage), $39,040 (90th percentile wage), 109,350 (number of positions), 0.8% (2016--2026 growth), High school diploma or equivalent (typical education requirement)

782. **Title Examiners, Abstractors, and Searchers**: #414 (median wage rank), $45,800 (median wage), $81,800 (90th percentile wage), 54,560 (number of positions), 4% (2016--2026 growth), High school diploma or equivalent (typical education requirement)

783. **Tool and Die Makers**: #343 (median wage rank), $51,060 (median wage), $74,230 (90th percentile wage), 72,210 (number of positions), -7.3% (2016--2026 growth), Postsecondary nondegree award (typical education requirement)

784. **Tool Grinders, Filers, and Sharpeners**: #564 (median wage rank), $36,650 (median wage), $57,590 (90th percentile wage), 9,550 (number of positions), -3.5% (2016--2026 growth), High school diploma or equivalent (typical education requirement)

785. **Tour Guides and Escorts**: #758 (median wage rank), $24,920 (median wage), $43,060 (90th percentile wage), 38,660 (number of positions), 10.9% (2016--2026 growth), High school diploma or equivalent (typical education requirement)

786. **Traffic Technicians**: #426 (median wage rank), $45,150 (median wage), $76,720 (90th percentile wage), 6,410 (number of positions), 9.1% (2016--2026 growth), High school diploma or equivalent (typical education requirement)

787. **Training and Development Managers**: #41

(median wage rank), $105,830 (median wage), $184,990 (90th percentile wage), 32,880 (number of positions), 10.3% (2016--2026 growth), Bachelor's degree (typical education requirement)

788. **Training and Development Specialists**: #253 (median wage rank), $59,020 (median wage), $101,010 (90th percentile wage), 269,710 (number of positions), 11.5% (2016--2026 growth), Bachelor's degree (typical education requirement)

789. **Transit and Railroad Police**: #190 (median wage rank), $66,610 (median wage), $96,670 (90th percentile wage), 4,810 (number of positions), 6.3% (2016--2026 growth), High school diploma or equivalent (typical education requirement)

790. **Transportation Attendants, Except Flight Attendants**: #739 (median wage rank), $26,060 (median wage), $54,450 (90th percentile wage), 18,410 (number of positions), 8.4% (2016--2026 growth), High school diploma or equivalent (typical education requirement)

791. **Transportation Inspectors**: #154 (median wage rank), $72,220 (median wage), $116,990 (90th percentile wage), 27,430 (number of positions), 5.9% (2016--2026 growth), High school diploma or equivalent (typical education requirement)

792. **Transportation Security Screeners**: #489 (median

wage rank), $39,680 (median wage), $47,300 (90th percentile wage), 42,750 (number of positions), 2.6% (2016--2026 growth), High school diploma or equivalent (typical education requirement)

793. **Transportation Workers**, All Other: #585 (median wage rank), $35,660 (median wage), $60,640 (90th percentile wage), 37,660 (number of positions), 8.3% (2016--2026 growth), High school diploma or equivalent (typical education requirement)

794. **Transportation, Storage, and Distribution Managers**: #83 (median wage rank), $89,190 (median wage), $152,730 (90th percentile wage), 113,270 (number of positions), 6.7% (2016--2026 growth), High school diploma or equivalent (typical education requirement)

795. **Travel Agents**: #566 (median wage rank), $36,460 (median wage), $61,890 (90th percentile wage), 68,680 (number of positions), -9.1% (2016--2026 growth), High school diploma or equivalent (typical education requirement)

796. **Travel Guides**: #644 (median wage rank), $32,100 (median wage), $58,400 (90th percentile wage), 3,030 (number of positions), 5.5% (2016--2026 growth), High school diploma or equivalent (typical education requirement)

797. **Tree Trimmers and Pruners**: #595 (median wage

rank), $35,030 (median wage), $56,970 (90th percentile wage), 40,680 (number of positions), 10.7% (2016--2026 growth), High school diploma or equivalent (typical education requirement)

798. **Umpires, Referees, and Other Sports Officials**: #747 (median wage rank), $25,660 (median wage), $58,160 (90th percentile wage), 18,660 (number of positions), 7.4% (2016--2026 growth), High school diploma or equivalent (typical education requirement)

799. **Upholsterers**: #627 (median wage rank), $33,050 (median wage), $51,260 (90th percentile wage), 32,520 (number of positions), 2.5% (2016--2026 growth), High school diploma or equivalent (typical education requirement)

800. **Urban and Regional Planners**: #164 (median wage rank), $70,020 (median wage), $105,310 (90th percentile wage), 34,810 (number of positions), 12.8% (2016--2026 growth), Master's degree (typical education requirement)

801. **Ushers, Lobby Attendants, and Ticket Takers**: #816 (median wage rank), $19,920 (median wage), $29,690 (90th percentile wage), 117,920 (number of positions), 7.5% (2016--2026 growth), No formal educational credential (typical education requirement)

802. **Veterinarians**: #84 (median wage rank), $88,770 (median wage), $161,070 (90th percentile wage), 67,650 (number of positions), 18.1% (2016--2026 growth), Doctoral or professional degree (typical education requirement)

803. **Veterinary Assistants and Laboratory Animal Caretakers**: #753 (median wage rank), $25,250 (median wage), $37,810 (90th percentile wage), 79,990 (number of positions), 19.4% (2016--2026 growth), High school diploma or equivalent (typical education requirement)

804. **Veterinary Technologists and Technicians**: #637 (median wage rank), $32,490 (median wage), $48,330 (90th percentile wage), 99,390 (number of positions), 19.9% (2016--2026 growth), Associate's degree (typical education requirement)

805. **Vocational Education Teachers, Postsecondary**: #347 (median wage rank), $50,660 (median wage), $90,320 (90th percentile wage), 116,430 (number of positions), 1.3% (2016--2026 growth), Bachelor's degree (typical education requirement)

806. **Waiters and Waitresses**: #813 (median wage rank), $19,990 (median wage), $38,460 (90th percentile wage), 2,564,610 (number of positions), 7% (2016--2026 growth), No formal educational credential (typical education requirement)

4 OCCUPATIONS RANKED ALPHABETICALLY

807. **Watch Repairers**: #561 (median wage rank), $36,740 (median wage), $61,880 (90th percentile wage), 1,620 (number of positions), -28.7% (2016--2026 growth), High school diploma or equivalent (typical education requirement)

808. **Water and Wastewater Treatment Plant and System Operators**: #416 (median wage rank), $45,760 (median wage), $73,120 (90th percentile wage), 115,840 (number of positions), -3.2% (2016--2026 growth), High school diploma or equivalent (typical education requirement)

809. **Web Developers**: #193 (median wage rank), $66,130 (median wage), $119,550 (90th percentile wage), 129,540 (number of positions), 13.1% (2016--2026 growth), Associate's degree (typical education requirement)

810. **Weighers, Measurers, Checkers, and Samplers, Recordkeeping**: #689 (median wage rank), $28,790 (median wage), $47,280 (90th percentile wage), 74,460 (number of positions), 1.9% (2016--2026 growth), High school diploma or equivalent (typical education requirement)

811. **Welders, Cutters, Solderers, and Brazers**: #494 (median wage rank), $39,390 (median wage), $62,100 (90th percentile wage), 382,730 (number of positions), 5.5% (2016--2026 growth), High school

diploma or equivalent (typical education requirement)

812. **Welding, Soldering, and Brazing Machine Setters, Operators, and Tenders**: #552 (median wage rank), $36,980 (median wage), $54,300 (90th percentile wage), 46,920 (number of positions), -10.3% (2016--2026 growth), High school diploma or equivalent (typical education requirement)

813. **Wellhead Pumpers**: #366 (median wage rank), $49,610 (median wage), $75,610 (90th percentile wage), 11,610 (number of positions), 21.7% (2016--2026 growth), High school diploma or equivalent (typical education requirement)

814. **Wholesale and Retail Buyers, Except Farm Products**: #318 (median wage rank), $53,340 (median wage), $97,830 (90th percentile wage), 109,440 (number of positions), -1.9% (2016--2026 growth), Bachelor's degree (typical education requirement)

815. **Wind Turbine Service Technicians**: #329 (median wage rank), $52,260 (median wage), $76,250 (90th percentile wage), 4,580 (number of positions), 96.1% (2016--2026 growth), Postsecondary nondegree award (typical education requirement)

816. **Woodworkers**, All Other: #699 (median wage rank), $28,500 (median wage), $50,540 (90th percentile wage), 6,750 (number of positions), 4.1%

(2016--2026 growth), High school diploma or equivalent (typical education requirement)

817. **Woodworking Machine Setters, Operators, and Tenders, Except Sawing**: #698 (median wage rank), $28,510 (median wage), $42,220 (90th percentile wage), 76,130 (number of positions), 0.7% (2016--2026 growth), High school diploma or equivalent (typical education requirement)

818. **Word Processors and Typists**: #509 (median wage rank), $38,740 (median wage), $55,810 (90th percentile wage), 67,230 (number of positions), -33.4% (2016--2026 growth), High school diploma or equivalent (typical education requirement)

819. **Writers and Authors**: #231 (median wage rank), $61,240 (median wage), $118,640 (90th percentile wage), 44,690 (number of positions), 8.3% (2016--2026 growth), Bachelor's degree (typical education requirement)

820. **Zoologists and Wildlife Biologists**: #236 (median wage rank), $60,520 (median wage), $98,540 (90th percentile wage), 17,720 (number of positions), 7.5% (2016--2026 growth), Bachelor's degree (typical education requirement)

ABOUT THE AUTHOR

Jon Macon, Ph.D., author of two books titled America's Best Jobs and The Complete List of American Jobs, has a passion for writing about strategic career choices. Through writing, Jon advocates career planning based on insights distilled from massive employment data now afforded by technological advances. During the waking hours when Jon does not write, he heads up an analytics division at a tier 1 investment bank on Wall Street. Jon can be reached at Jon.Macon@outlook.com.

Made in the USA
Columbia, SC
06 September 2024